Advance Praise for *The Kerala Club*

'In an age in India when "WhatsApp University" has become a byword for disinformation, *The Kerala Club* offers a salutary inversion, emanating as it does from a WhatsApp group of retired civil servants and administrators who are devoted to the state and its model of development and governance. Kerala's saga has long been hailed as the "Malayali miracle", a society that invested in education, social reform, gender equity, local self-governance and democratic accountability long before these became the buzzwords of development discourse, acquiring thereby human development indicators comparable to those of leading Western nations.

Yet these essays remind us that we can never take our triumphs for granted. The achievements we celebrate today were forged through decades of relentless effort, imaginative and collaborative policymaking and execution, and public-spirited leadership. If they are to endure, if they are to be bolstered, we must keep aflame in our hearts the spirit of enterprise and a solution-oriented approach. Only then will we be able to "resolve the mysteries and explain the contradictions of Kerala".

Analytically astute, rigorously researched and incisively argued, *The Kerala Club* is in part a masterclass on policymaking and public administration, and in part a stirring ode to one of India's most exemplary states, which, through its credo of pluralism and progress, brings to life that cherished Idea of India enshrined in the Constitution. For all of us who love Kerala and dream of seeing it scale greater heights still, this is an unmissable book: a blueprint for institutionalising our successes and ensuring their deepest possible permeation. To read *The Kerala Club*, then, is to be galvanised to strive, to seek, to find, and never to yield in the service of God's own country!'

Shashi Tharoor
Author and Member of Parliament

The Kerala Club

THE KERALA CLUB

Keepers of the Flame

Edited by
K.M. Chandrasekhar and
T.P. Sreenivasan

BLOOMSBURY
NEW DELHI • LONDON • OXFORD • NEW YORK • SYDNEY

BLOOMSBURY INDIA
Bloomsbury Publishing India Pvt. Ltd
Second Floor, LSC Building No. 4, DDA Complex, Pocket C – 6 & 7,
Vasant Kunj, New Delhi, 110070

First published in India 2026

ISBN: HB: 978-93-61310-95-9; eBook: 978-93-61314-85-8

2 4 6 8 10 9 7 5 3 1

Typeset in Adobe Garamond by Manipal Technologies Limited
Printed and bound in India by Thomson Press India Private Limited

FSC www.fsc.org MIX Paper | Supporting responsible forestry FSC® C010615

To find out more about our authors and books visit www.bloomsbury.com and sign up for our newsletters

Contents

Foreword

One of India's well-known and undisputed achievements is that it has remained a democracy since Independence, for nearly eighty years. There are few developing countries that can say the same, and none of India's size or diversity. What is lesser-known is the critical role that the non-partisan civil service has played in preserving the democratic constitutional order. Thought experiments will illustrate this: would it have been possible to conduct free and fair elections in India if the returning officers and their staff were political appointees of the incumbent government, who would lose their jobs if the government lost power? Would it have been possible to administer President's Rule in insurgency-affected states if the administration and police consisted of political appointees of the dismissed government?

The civil service has its share of the corrupt, the inefficient and the insensitive. But it also has the scrupulously honest, the extraordinarily efficient and the highly empathetic. Politicians and legislators are often fiercely criticised, but they can counterattack with equal ferocity. Judicial conduct is protected by the law of contempt. Unlike politicians, civil servants are prohibited by their conduct rules from publicly responding to false accusations. 'Contempt' of the civil service is not punishable. Civil servants are duty bound to defend decisions they may not have supported, in the courts of law and the court of public opinion. Unlike in the United Kingdom, in India, it is civil servants who appear before parliamentary committees, explaining decisions their ministers may have taken. The civil service therefore often gets more than its fair share of criticism, but this is a necessary evil which civil servants must bear willingly.

For that reason, it is valuable when the good civil servant writes about his or her experience of administration. Kerala (or Keralam, as it may soon become) is one of India's most developed states. It offers many lessons for other states, both positive and negative.

This book has twenty-nine essays by eminent former civil servants from the Administrative, Foreign, Police, Forest and other services, all of whom were born in Kerala, hail from Kerala or had Kerala thrust upon them (as they were posted there). All of them understand Kerala, India and public administration. The authors include those who have held the offices of National Security Adviser, Cabinet Secretary, Comptroller and Auditor General, Union Minister of State, G20 Sherpa, Chief Secretary, Director-General of Police, Union Home Secretary, Union Finance Secretary, Foreign Secretary and Ambassador. The diversity of perspectives and the depth of experience this collection of essays offers is rare.

The Kerala Club is thus a valuable addition to the literature. It is not only instructive but also interesting. Quite apart from the knowledge that a reader can gain from it, there are many anecdotes that can be savoured for their own sake.

T.V. Somanathan
Cabinet Secretary

Note from the Editors

This book started with the formation of a WhatsApp group of retired officers with links to Kerala – officers who belong to the Kerala cadre, those who originated in Kerala and worked elsewhere, and officers from different civil services who share a common interest in Kerala and an affinity for the state. These individuals have contributed in many ways to the growth and welfare of Kerala, regardless of where they served. They are united by their love for the state of their origin or by the affection they developed for Kerala while working there.

The essays featured in this book cover experiences in public administration and offer different takes on development and local self-governance. Some are personal reflections on Kerala, while others by those who have worked for extended periods for the Government of India bring a national perspective to their knowledge and experiences of Kerala. Many writers have expressed themselves frankly and openly, highlighting both the strengths and weaknesses of the system, in the hope that change can occur within the state and the nation.

When Winston Churchill described the Soviet Union in 1939 as 'a riddle wrapped in a mystery inside an enigma', he could well have been speaking about Kerala today. The state is often characterised as a bundle of contradictions: whatever one may say about Kerala, the opposite may also hold true. For instance, although it is universally recognised as the most literate state in India, illiteracy persists in several segments of society. According to the Census of India, a person is classified as literate if they are seven years or older and can both read and write with understanding in any language. This definition, although technical, has granted the people of Kerala an aura of intelligence. The governments in Kerala have prioritised education, offering free education and various concessions as part of a sustained Total Literacy Campaign and achieved 'fully literate status' in 1991. While this may not mean that every Keralite is literate, it has nonetheless become a label indicative of a high level of competence, even in rural areas.

Similarly, the much-debated 'Kerala model' of development is admired for achieving human development indices close to those of developed nations, yet it is rarely suggested as a universal template. Moreover, newer paradigms, such as the Gujarat model, have emerged to challenge the Kerala model as a viable alternative.

Influenced by Gandhiji and his followers, Keralites at one time viewed alcohol as evil. However, alcohol consumption across the state is high today. A state that considers a certain level of alcohol sales as vital to its economy is indeed an aberration in a land where Sree Narayana Guru preached against the production, consumption and sale of alcohol. While communism has been in decline worldwide, Kerala remains the only state that embraces various forms of communism. Kerala has adjusted to large-scale migration but has not adequately addressed the social challenges it poses. The state has welcomed guest workers from other regions while its own workers migrate abroad to earn a living. The social conflicts arising from this new situation tend to be overlooked. Despite being green, Kerala cannot produce enough vegetables and fruits for its own consumption, leading to the infiltration of poisoned products from outside that ruin lives and livelihoods. Domestic violence is rampant, and the matrilineal system does not guarantee the safety and welfare of women.

Those best positioned to interpret these riddles, resolve the mysteries and explain the contradictions of Kerala are the civil service officers, particularly those belonging to the Indian Administrative Service, the Indian Police Service and the Indian Forest Service (IFS). Kerala's bureaucracy, carefully nurtured by the maharajas and accepted by the British, has become a deep state – sentinels of administration that ensure law, order and stability. It is this bureaucracy that has provided the steel frame for the government. Kerala's bureaucracy has maintained a high standard and is recognised for its honesty and efficiency, sustained by democratic governance.

When the WhatsApp group of senior bureaucrats, most of whom were retired, began sharing their experiences, the idea of making these public emerged in the fertile mind of K.M. Chandrasekhar, a former Cabinet Secretary. He carefully curated this collection of writings from a wide array of officers, resulting in *The Kerala Club* – the first attempt of its kind to analyse the Kerala experience of development diligently, honestly and with great attention to detail.

Each essay captures various aspects of life in Kerala, not just the bare facts of change but also the immense human effort put into transforming the characteristics of our villages. People's participation was ensured at every level to promote transparency. But corruption is often accepted as a way of life, and exposing it is condemned and frequently punished. A tilt of the kaleidoscope usually reveals the darker sides of human behaviour. Nevertheless, numerous civil servants have shone through the darkness, serving as models of integrity. Young district officials, previously viewed as detached ivory tower inhabitants, began to engage actively during crises, embodying a new generation of bureaucracy.

In the section on public administration, the focus is on lessons to be learned and changes to be made. The chapters trace the genesis and evolution of public policies and their limitations in the current context, necessitating drastic changes in the interests of both the state and the nation. Agriculture is prominently identified as a sector that requires significant policy changes to achieve higher productivity and greater prosperity. New challenges posed by a growing economy, such as labour migration across the country, unite the nation while simultaneously revealing glaring gaps in policies to protect these migrants. Chapters are also dedicated to advancing gender equality in governance, evolving project management policies and techniques to expedite infrastructure development, and addressing the paradoxes that exist in the health sector, even though Kerala has made significant progress in health indices. The chapter on gender issues highlights Kerala's experiment with women's collectives called 'Kudumbashree', while the chapter on re-engineering public administration critiques the weaknesses of colonial administrative practices that we cling to, even though many nations, including our former colonial rulers, have discarded them in favour of more flexible, outcome-oriented approaches. One chapter passionately discusses the potential catastrophic consequences of the Mullaperiyar Dam in Idukki breaking, highlighting how its current design could lead to widespread destruction and loss of life in the event of its collapse. Another chapter addresses forestry issues in Kerala, highlighting exciting new projects launched and the political support the author received. This section also contains a chapter that recounts the story of a police officer who pioneered social policing through the Janamaithri Project, engaging the community in policing efforts. The section ends with a hard-hitting chapter that discusses the aggressive nature of trade unions in Kerala, the challenges of regulating them and how political and administrative weakness impedes growth.

The section on perspectives on development includes a chapter offering new thoughts on the evolution of the 'Kerala model', arguing that it is a product of historical change that began even before Independence. Another chapter discusses the cyclical nature of growth in Kerala over thirty-year phases and the urgent need to rethink current policy objectives. Additional chapters focus on the challenges of rapid urbanisation and the recurring failures to effectively address the associated problems, as well as on the collaboration between the bureaucracy and the political system that led to a 'white revolution' in Kerala, transforming the state from milk-deficient to milk-surplus.

The third section explores another unique experiment in Kerala: the mainstreaming of local self-governance. Unlike other states, Kerala took Panchayati Raj seriously and sincerely attempted to devolve real power to local self-government institutions. This approach has been successful, as evidenced by local institutions taking ownership during crises such as the 2018 floods and the Covid-19 pandemic. However, weaknesses persist, including corruption at local levels, inefficiency in scheme implementation and an inability to effectively manage finances year after year. A notable aspect of this section is how the bureaucracy and the political executive worked in tandem to implement decentralisation for the people's benefit, even though such decentralisation diminishes the government's power in Thiruvananthapuram.

The final section contains fascinating personal reflections. There is a narrative of societal inequities that plagued Kerala in the past, alongside accounts from a diplomat who ventured into the education sector and identified urgent issues that require immediate attention. There is a nostalgic piece by a former diplomat, reminiscing about his early days in Kerala and expressing pride in the state's achievements in human development. Chapters by two officers from the north, who learned Malayalam and made substantial contributions to the state, reflect a learning experience they carried back to their work in the Government of India. One chapter focuses on an officer who delved into spiritualism and developed new interests, resulting in significant literary contributions to the study of Vedanta. There is another chapter by an officer who left Kerala early for a post in the International Labour Organization, eventually finding striking similarities between Cambodia and his home state. One gripping piece details the journey of an officer who has worked extensively in both state and Central capacities, reflecting on the nature of policing. His narrative is a rich tapestry of unexpected turns, professional growth and the unpredictable yet rewarding nature of a career in law enforcement. This section also contains a captivating story about a jungle elephant captured in Assam and brought to Kerala, detailing the hardships it faced as a temple elephant. This tale encapsulates the suffering experienced by wild animals captured and treated harshly by humans.

The underlying theme of the chapters is how civil servants – selected for their individual merit – found distinctive ways to tackle the challenges they faced in their various assignments. These officers frequently changed roles and held multiple responsibilities simultaneously. Political leaders of various affiliations came and went, yet the civil servants remained steadfast in their convictions, even at the risk of dissenting from their superiors. Generally, both parties worked harmoniously and adhered to established norms. There have been rare instances of conflict arising from differing values and interests, as well as some cases in which politicians and bureaucrats colluded for personal benefit.

These essays narrate stories of triumph and tribulation, challenge and opportunity, resulting in a complex but beautiful tapestry – much like a kasavu handloom fabric, meticulously woven with a delicate gold border. The hierarchy was largely respected, and differences were amicably resolved with a strong sense of commitment. Some individuals who relocated to Kerala from other states excelled beyond their local counterparts by leveraging their expertise, leaving lasting contributions. Several have even made Kerala their home following retirement.

An interesting feature of the Kerala bureaucracy is that many have developed their own areas of expertise, becoming entrenched in the specific projects and areas of work they have pursued passionately. Fields such as tourism, education, agriculture and land development have greatly benefited from the individual talents and interests of bureaucrats. Those who served in the Central government made their mark at the national level before returning to serve the state. Among the contributors are several IFS officers from Kerala who maintained their connection with developments in the state and offered their expertise.

The Kerala Club stands as a testament to the dedication and hard work of the civil services in Kerala, showcasing their contributions. It is a treasure trove of experiences that aims to bring joy to its writers and readers alike, both now and in the future. In an era when public discourse often questions institutional integrity, *The Kerala Club* will provide a platform for honest dialogue. Keralites, both within India and abroad, who are keenly interested in developments in the state will enjoy reading the book. This collection is intended for administrators and politicians seeking to earnestly evaluate the state's strengths and weaknesses. Furthermore, it holds value for anyone interested in public administration, both in Kerala and beyond. It is particularly significant for those contemplating a career in the civil services, as it contains insights from officers who have distinguished themselves in Kerala and at the national level, and even gained international recognition for their valuable contributions.

The authors, given total freedom to select their themes, have honoured the spirit of this volume. Working closely with our publisher and editors, we believe that we have enriched the texts and their relevance without altering their style or substance. The authors are solely responsible for the quality and content of their contributions.

Part 1

Public Administration

Lessons from Public Policy: From Amsterdam to Palakkad

T. Nandakumar

Windows, Wisdom and Ingenuity: A Tax Tale from Amsterdam

In the heart of Amsterdam, where canals curve like ribbons through the city, the iconic canal houses stand as elegant reminders of Dutch creativity. Their tall, narrow facades – often adorned with ornate gables – are more than just picturesque architecture. They tell a story of civic cleverness and tax smart design.

During a visit in 1983, I found myself enchanted by these homes. One moment, however, stood out: I watched as heavy furniture was hoisted out of a large first-floor window. The front door, it turned out, was too narrow to accommodate it. My curiosity led me down a historical rabbit hole – and what I discovered was as fascinating as it was revealing.

In the early nineteenth century, Dutch authorities introduced a building tax based on the number of windows and the size of front doors. It was a practical solution: easy to assess from the street, sparing officials the trouble of entering the houses for inspection. But the citizens of Amsterdam, ever resourceful, responded with architectural wit. They built homes with fewer windows – each as large as possible – and with narrow doors that minimised the taxable surface area.

This tax-saving strategy shaped the city's skyline. Even after the policy was abolished later that century, its legacy remained etched in brick and beam. Today, older buildings still bear the marks of this fiscal finesse: generous windows for light and ventilation, and slender doors that challenge movers.

What began as a bureaucratic convenience became a canvas for civic creativity. In Amsterdam, even the architecture tells a story – of taxes, tenacity and the timeless Dutch knack for turning constraint into charm.

The Legacy of the Lowest Tender: A British Hangover in Indian Procurement

India's public procurement system – how the government buys goods, services and infrastructure – has long been guided by a principle that seems simple and fair: choose the lowest bidder. But what if this very principle, inherited from colonial rule, is quietly undermining the quality of our public goods? As we strive for better infrastructure, services and value for public money, it's time to examine whether our procurement methods are fit for purpose or relics of a bygone era.

The Colonial Legacy of the Lowest Bid

Let us turn our attention to the British. During their long rule over India, they established elaborate administrative systems – many of which independent India inherited almost unchanged. Among these was a procurement practice that continues to shape how we award government tenders: the least cost method (LCM).

Faced with the need to procure a vast range of goods and services for colonial projects, the British introduced the concept of purchasing based on the lowest bid – commonly known as the 'lowest tender' or 'L1'. Whether it was for construction contracts, material supplies or service provision, this method became the standard. It was seen as transparent, straightforward and, above all, economical.

Even today, our procurement manuals, financial regulations and vigilance guidelines uphold the LCM as the gold standard. But some policy analysts argue that the British emphasis on cost over quality stemmed from a deeper indifference to the long-term outcomes of projects in India. Those of us who have worked within government systems have seen firsthand how this cost-centric approach has often compromised the quality of public infrastructure and services.

Yet, despite its flaws, the LCM persists. Why? Because it is the easiest – and in bureaucratic terms, the 'safest' – option available. Changing it would require not just new rules but a shift in mindset.

Global Lessons, Local Inertia

In the early 1980s, the World Bank introduced a more nuanced approach to procurement: the two-envelope system. Under this method, bidders submitted two separate proposals: one technical, one financial. The first envelope contained details about capabilities, engineering specifications and other technical aspects. Only after these were evaluated and deemed satisfactory would the second envelope – the financial bid – be opened. This ensured that only technically qualified bids were considered, filtering out those that failed to meet predefined standards.

Over time, this system evolved into more sophisticated processes: pre-qualification requirements, two-stage bidding and long-term maintenance contracts. The World Bank's procurement manuals now offer exhaustive guidelines to support these reforms.

Yet, despite these advancements, many procurement processes in India still turn to the familiar L1 method. As discussed earlier, this approach often compromises quality. So where does the problem lie? Is it in the way technical criteria are designed, allowing subpar bids to slip through? Or is it the lack of rigorous testing and monitoring? The answer may be both. These weaknesses continue to undermine project outcomes.

Public money deserves better outcomes. Citizens deserve infrastructure and services that last, and our institutions deserve procurement systems that reflect the aspirations of a modern, confident India.

It is time to move beyond the lowest bid – and aim for the highest standards.

'Revdi' Culture and the Cost of Free Power

Let us turn the lens inward to some of our own policies. Free or subsidised electricity for agricultural wells and tube wells is a popular – and populist – programme across many Indian states. The stated objective is to reduce the cost of cultivation, thereby helping the government to keep food prices under control. But once a benefit is made free, it tends to remain free. No government dares to withdraw a freebie; instead, it keeps adding to the list, deepening fiscal stress.

Pre-election giveaways, colloquially referred to as 'revdis',[1] have become routine.

A Peep into Punjab's Agricultural Landscape

Punjab bears the highest cost burden for free electricity among Indian states. It also ranks among those with the highest debt-to-GSDP (gross state domestic product) ratios.[2]

My association with Punjab's agricultural policy spans nearly two decades, beginning as Secretary, Government of India (Food, Agriculture and Animal Husbandry departments), between 2006 and 2010. This was followed by my tenure as the chairman of the National Dairy Development Board, and later as a member of the Punjab Governance Advisory Committee, the Punjab Economic Advisory Council and as an advisor to the Punjab State Farmers' Commission. These roles gave me a front-row seat to observe policy shifts and their long-term consequences.

Punjab's canal irrigation system, one of the earliest and most sophisticated in the country, is far superior to Kerala's. Yet the landscape is dotted with tube wells. Continuous availability of reliable power during the developmental phase of the state encouraged farmers to install pump sets and embrace power-intensive agriculture. This shift aligned with the Green Revolution, which saw Punjab pivot to intensive irrigation and large-scale paddy cultivation – though rice is not a staple food in the region.

I recall Parkash Singh Badal, then chief minister, telling me with his characteristic wit: '*Hum aap logon ke liye hi chaaval paida karate hain*' (We grow rice for you guys only [the South and East Indian states]). His remark, though light-hearted, reflected a deeper truth. Punjab sells nearly 90 per cent of its rice, amounting to 120–130 lakh tonnes, to the Food Corporation of India.[3] This is roughly 20–25 per cent of the country's total rice procurement. In contrast, Kerala's total rice production hovers around 5 lakh tonnes.

The Hidden Costs of Free Power

This success story, however, has a darker underside. Extensive paddy cultivation has left Punjab severely water-stressed.[4] Groundwater levels are plummeting, water quality is deteriorating and soil degradation has led to increased fertiliser use. The unintended consequence of free power has been the 'privatisation' and overexploitation of groundwater – an ecological and economic challenge that continues to unfold.

Despite mounting evidence, political parties in Punjab remain reluctant to reverse the trend. Farmers fear losing their 'assured' income if rice cultivation declines. Even modest reforms – such as reimbursing power bills instead of offering free electricity – have failed to gain traction.

Revdi culture may win votes, but it exacts a heavy toll on sustainability, fiscal health and long-term agricultural resilience. Punjab's experience is a cautionary tale: well-intentioned policies, if left unchecked, can morph into structural traps. The challenge lies not just in designing better policies but in building institutional courage to implement them.

The Kerala Story: When Good Intentions Go Astray

The story of well-meaning but ill-conceived policies defeating their original purpose is not unique to Punjab. Kerala too offers sobering examples of how political decisions – driven by populism, ideology or misplaced priorities – can distort realities.

Cashew: From Local Strength to Imports

Consider the cashew industry. Once a thriving network of profitable private factories providing employment to a large number of women, it was reshaped by government intervention under the guise of farmer welfare. Monopoly procurement was introduced, private units were taken over and two state-run entities – the Kerala State Cashew Development Corporation and the Kerala State Cashew Workers Apex Industrial Co-operative Society – were set up and expanded to process Kerala's home-grown cashews.[5]

In reality, this restructuring catered more to labour union demands than to farmers. Several efficient private factories were closed; some relocated to neighbouring states. Over time, the government's narrative shifted: instead of supporting local cashew growers, the focus turned to keeping factory labour happy by importing raw cashew – despite the enormous losses the factories incur annually. The local farmer became peripheral, even irrelevant.

In a telling episode, a Kerala minister reportedly requested Andhra Pradesh and Telangana farmers to grow cashews for Kerala's processors.[6] Kerala has also, with pomp, entertained collaboration with African countries[7] to obtain from them raw cashews (for processing) and to keep the factories running while adding to their losses every year. So much for the original intent!

The Rice Story: A Remedy Worse than the Disease

The years 2008 and 2009 are etched in memory for the global food crisis. India had already faced a severe wheat shortage in 2006–2007, triggered by unusually high temperatures in northwest India, forcing the country to import wheat from international markets. A similar crisis in rice was narrowly averted in 2008–2009, thanks to an unprecedented decision to restrict rice exports – excluding basmati. Though this move drew criticism from the international community and some prominent economists, it proved prescient. In the drought year of 2009, it ensured uninterrupted food supplies, particularly for the poor.

Kerala, heavily reliant on food grain supplies from other states, came under pressure during this period. Despite adequate rice availability in the national market, the state struggled to source adequate quantities for its open market. Its hesitation to engage with a volatile commodity market – through the Kerala Civil Supplies Corporation – only compounded the problem. Nor did it take meaningful steps to facilitate private trade, which could have eased the supply crunch.

Some policymakers in Kerala misdiagnosed the issue, attributing the crisis to declining paddy acreage within the state. They believed, mistakenly, that halting the conversion of paddy lands would resolve the problem. To put this in context, consider the numbers: Kerala consumes approximately 40 lakh tonnes of rice annually but produces only 5–6 lakh tonnes. The remainder comes from the central pool – via the Public Distribution System – and from surplus states through open market channels. (We'll return to the acreage and productivity debate shortly.)

The state's ill-advised response was the enactment of the Kerala Conservation of Paddy Land and Wetland Act, 2008 (henceforth the 2008 Act).

This legislation included the following provisions:

1. All designated paddy lands must be cultivated with paddy.
2. Authorities – from the panchayat to the state level – could mandate farmers to grow paddy.
3. If a farmer failed to do so, the authorities could direct another agency to cultivate paddy on their land.

The 2008 Act was highly restrictive – and, in my view, oppressive. It created a labyrinth of committees to approve any deviation or exemption, opening the door to rent-seeking and bureaucratic overreach. Unsurprisingly, paddy farmers were left disillusioned and disempowered.

What did the legislation achieve? In 2008–2009, Kerala had 2,34,265 hectares under paddy cultivation, producing 5,90,241 tonnes of rice (at 2,520 kilos per hectare). By 2019–2020, the area had shrunk to 1,91,051 hectares, yielding 5,87,078 tonnes (at 3,073 kilos per hectare). In 2022–2023, the area remained nearly unchanged at 1,90,170 hectares, with a marginal productivity increase to 3,117 kilos per hectare. Meanwhile, the state's overall net cropped area declined by 62,000 hectares. Cropping intensity fell from 140 per cent (in 2005–2006) to 127.60 (in 2019–2020) and further to 126.46 (in 2022–2023) – a trend that went largely unnoticed.[8] In contrast, most other Indian states increased their cropping intensity during this period.

A Policy Misfire

In essence, Kerala enacted a law to prevent the conversion of paddy land and yet continues to lose net cropped area. The area under paddy has also declined; the law remains rigid and productivity has risen by a mere 14 per cent over 11 years – compared to a 28 per cent increase at the national level. The state finds itself in a policy trap: vested interests have grown around the 2008 Act, making repeal politically risky. Kerala continues to remain dependent on other states for rice and has yet to confront the real barriers to self-reliance – whether through improved yields or enabling private trade. Meanwhile, the focus has shifted away from boosting productivity and farmer incomes.

Adding to the distress, the Kerala government collected upwards of ₹1,500 crore as a conversion fee from farmers and diverted it to other expenditure in spite of a specific provision to use it for agricultural development in the 2008 Act. A public interest litigation in the High Court of Kerala (WP-C Nos. 26592 and 35561) exposed this, and the government has been asked to deposit the amount in the appropriate fund.

This is a textbook case of a well-intentioned policy gone awry: it has burdened farmers without delivering public benefit.

The Farmers' Pension Scheme: A Case of Misguided Design

Another much-touted initiative of the Kerala government is its pension scheme for farmers. In 2019, the Government of India launched a contributory pension scheme offering ₹3,000 per month to farmers who enrol between the ages of eighteen and twenty-four and contribute until they turn sixty. The scheme is subsidised through the Union Budget.

Kerala, determined to offer its farmers a better deal, promised a higher pension of ₹5,000 per month. A more pragmatic approach might have been to simply top up the Central scheme by adding ₹2,000. Odisha adopted this strategy smartly, using PM-Kisan funds to supplement its Krushak Assistance for Livelihood and Income Augmentation, popularly known as the KALIA scheme, which provides income support to farmers.

Kerala, however, enacted the Kerala Farmers' Welfare Fund Act, 2019 (henceforth the 2019 Act), establishing a Farmers' Welfare Fund Board. One might choose to overlook the state's penchant for high-profile boards and their attendant paraphernalia, but the real issue lies deeper. The government was well aware that it lacked the financial resources to deliver the promised pension. Raising farmers' premiums was not a viable option. So it devised an ingenious – and problematic – mechanism: a mandatory contribution of 1 per cent of annual profit from those engaged in value addition of agricultural commodities was framed as a 'right of profit sharing' for farmers (Section 9 of the 2019 Act).

While this sounds equitable in theory, it has serious implications for the economics of agricultural processing. The 2019 Act stipulates that any person who trades in farm products by converting them into value-added goods must contribute 1 per cent of their profit

– specifically profit earned in Kerala – to the fund.[9] However, Central laws such as the Companies Act and the Income Tax Act do not distinguish profits earned in each state; they consider only the total income of a legal entity.

To determine the profit earned in Kerala, the Act requires 'every dealer'[10] (a term left undefined and confusing) to submit a return detailing their annual sales and profits to an assistant chief executive officer of the board, who is 'authorised to make appropriate enquiries and pass necessary orders', as per section 9 of the 2019 Act. How this official will accurately assess state-specific profits is anyone's guess.

Three years into the scheme, farmer enthusiasm remains tepid. Meanwhile, Kerala's vibrant food processing sector is apprehensive – concerned about future financial burdens and potential harassment by officials ill-equipped to evaluate profits. If the board begins issuing notices demanding the 1 per cent share of industry profits, the sector may respond predictably: relocating units to neighbouring states of Tamil Nadu and Karnataka.

This would be a textbook case of policy failure – where the original objective remains unmet and high-potential sectors are driven out of the state.

Intentions and Outcomes: The Fragile Bridge of Public Policy

Public policy often begins with noble intentions. The desire to solve problems, uplift communities or correct systemic imbalances drives many reform efforts. Yet, as experience repeatedly shows, good intentions alone are not enough. The journey from aspiration to impact is fraught with complexity – and the fault lines often lie hidden in the architecture of policy itself.

Design flaws, institutional misalignments and weak implementation mechanisms can derail even the most well-meaning initiatives. Unintended consequences – blind spots in conceptualisation – have a way of surfacing only after a policy is set in motion. And once vested interests take hold, reversing course becomes a formidable challenge. A flawed policy, even when its shortcomings are widely acknowledged, can persist for years, protected by inertia, political expediency or entrenched beneficiaries.

There is no universal template for good policy. Context matters. History matters. So does humility. Policymakers must cultivate the discipline to learn from past missteps, the courage to course-correct when needed and the clarity to prioritise outcomes over optics. In the end, it is not the elegance of a policy's intent but the integrity of its impact that defines its worth.

Notes

1 A. Kabra, 'Decoding India's "Revdi Culture"', *Times of India*, 8 February 2023. Available online: https://timesofindia.indiatimes.com/blogs/voices/decoding-indias-revdi-culture/ (accessed 18 November 2025).

2 This is the author's calculation.

3 These are the author's calculations based on published data from the Ministry of Agriculture and the Ministry of Food, Government of India; the Food Corporation of India; the Department of Agriculture, Government of Punjab; and the *Economic Reviews*, Government of Kerala.

4 The Gravity Recovery and Climate Experiment (GRACE) was a joint mission between NASA and the German Aerospace Centre (DLR) that measured the Earth's gravity field and water reservoirs from 2002 to 2017.

5 Kerala Essential Articles Control (Temporary Powers) Act, 1961; Kerala Raw Cashewnuts (Procurement and Distribution) Order, 1977 (made under that Act); Kerala Raw Cashewnuts (Procurement and Distribution) Act, 1981; Kerala Cashew Factories (Acquisition) Act, 1974.

6 V. Raghavendra, 'Kerala Proposes to Grow Cashew in 50,000 Hectares in Andhra Pradesh', *The Hindu*, 12 February 2017. Available online: https://www.thehindu.com/news/national/andhra-pradesh/Kerala-proposes-to-grow-cashew-in-50000-hectares-in-Andhra-Pradesh/article17289784.ece (accessed 18 November 2025).

7 'Kerala to Procure Raw Cashew from African Nations', *Times of India*, 29 June 2017. Available online: https://timesofindia.indiatimes.com/city/thiruvananthapuram/state-to-procure-raw-cashew-from-african-nations/articleshow/59360000.cms (accessed 18 November 2025).

8 Statistics taken from *Economic Reviews* published by the Government of Kerala and *Agricultural Statistics* published by the Ministry of Agriculture and Farmers Welfare, Government of India, between 2008 and 2024.

9 Section 9 of the Kerala Farmers' Welfare Fund Act, 2019. Available online: https://indiankanoon.org/doc/92459950/ (accessed 18 November 2025).

10 Ibid.

A View from Kerala

N. Ramachandran

In school, we learn about India's rich cultural tapestry and the hallowed ideal of unity in diversity. Yet, as adults, many of us practise our share of exclusionary politics based on religion, caste, ethnicity, parochialism and personal preferences like our dressing and eating habits. We don't feel very comfortable in the company of 'others'. Many of our politicians fuel and cultivate these divisions and happily extract their pound of flesh from different sides of the divide. However, even as we, the self-righteous people, continue to forward hate messages, false information and fake videos in the 'national interest', there is another silent transformation that is underway: the strong winds of integration being quietly fostered by India's humble migrant labourers.

Vulnerable migrant workers are among those who face the brunt of our exclusionary politics. They often become the targets of hate and discrimination based solely on their origins and backgrounds. Our infinite capacity to other 'others' helped us abandon them when tens of thousands of them – including the elderly, the infirm and the toddlers in tow – had to walk to the homes they had left in search of livelihood, thousands of miles away.

Travel to any state in India and you will encounter workers from different regions who have either integrated or are trying to integrate with the local language, food and culture. In many ways, these migrant workers, in their pursuit of a better life, are also informal cultural ambassadors, bridging the gaps between communities and fostering a sense of unity.

Unifying Culture and a Tantalising Menu

India's migrant workers are quietly taking the country through a unique but fascinating maze of cultural crossroads, blending and sharing. They bring with them their traditions, languages and customs, which blend with the local culture. Food, for example, has always been a unifying factor, transcending regional boundaries and bringing people together. Migrant workers bring along their diverse culinary traditions and regional delicacies, introducing new flavours and cooking techniques to the local communities. This exchange of eating practices not only tantalises taste buds but also creates a sense of shared experiences and appreciation for different cultures.

Don't be surprised if you find a Naga bamboo-shoot delicacy on the menu of a restaurant in Pathanamthitta or a combination of Kerala parotta and meen moilee at a roadside dhaba near Kaziranga. There is hardly any restaurant across Kerala that does not employ migrant workers, either as cooks or servers. So if you ask one of them to prepare a machher jhol (Bengali fish curry) or a muri ghonto (fish head and lentil stew), they will gladly oblige.

Cultural performances also exemplify this fusion. Today one can witness a Thiruvathira folk dance performance by local schoolgirls at Srimanta Sankaradeva Kalakshetra in Guwahati or a bunch of migrant men and women spontaneously breaking into a Bihu dance in the midst of construction work in Kochi's Vallarpadam Island. You pass through a village road in Karnataka's Devanahalli and you are treated to an Assamese signature bamboo flute tune wafting from a nearby migrant settlement. The other day, accompanying an Onam pulikali procession near Angamali was a Ghumura dance group of Odia workers. Without our realising it, slow cultural integration is happening.

... And Harmony in Babel Tower

Language serves as another crucial bridge. Despite initial linguistic hurdles, migrants often make an earnest effort to learn and adapt to the languages of their new homes. From picking up basic phrases to engaging in fluent conversations, they dismantle the barriers of communication, fostering a strong sense of belonging. Today, it is not uncommon to hear Assamese, Bihari or Bengali workers conversing in Tamil, Kannada or Malayalam. This language integration not only helps them in their daily interactions but also strengthens the bond between visitors and the locals.

Migrant workers embrace local customs, traditions and ways of life while still holding on to their own identities. This blending of cultures creates a unique fusion where migrant workers contribute to the local culture while keeping their roots alive. It is this sense of balance and respect for diversity that fosters proper cultural integration.

Unknown to many of us, this silent cultural exchange is gradually but significantly enriching India's diverse fabric. From the bustling streets of Mumbai to the serene tea plantations of Upper Assam, this subtle integration is a testament to the transformative power of this silent amalgamation and the promise of true unity in diversity.

Migrant workers crisscross the country in search of a livelihood. At the national level, every year millions of rural poor, driven by a combination of economic, social and environmental factors, leave their homes in search of better job prospects and improved living conditions. This phenomenon speaks to the complex dynamics of rural life, where a myriad of challenges and opportunities compel people to seek livelihoods beyond their native villages.

Kerala's Reverse Migration

Migration patterns within India, driven by economic aspirations, continue to shape the nation's demographic, cultural and economic fabric. The journey in pursuit of livelihood and prosperity transcends state boundaries, showcasing people's resilience and determination to secure their futures and support their families. The movement of people from different states, whether historical or contemporary, emphasises the fluid nature of livelihood-seeking and the role of opportunities in influencing such movements.

As India progresses, understanding and addressing the complexities of migration patterns will be crucial in our quest for inclusive growth and equitable opportunities for all.

Historically, Malayalees have spread across the globe, seeking better opportunities. Paradoxically, there is now a migration of workers from elsewhere into Kerala. Despite a high literacy rate and educational achievements, Kerala has fewer white-collar jobs. The stigma attached to manual labour drives young Malayalees to migrate to other states or countries, where some of them end up happily doing manual work. The salaries they receive in these countries are also significantly higher. This situation has led to a massive scarcity of local workers willing to take on low-paying or manual roles.

Today, in a discernible shift in migration patterns, the Assamese, Bengali and Odia workers who have filled the gap have become the backbone of the labour force in Kerala, particularly in industries such as construction, plantations, healthcare, agriculture, hospitality and services. In turn, Kerala has become heavily reliant on migrant labour. The state's dependency on this workforce has reached a level where it is difficult to overlook these workers' pivotal contribution.

According to a report submitted to the Kerala State Planning Board, recent years have witnessed increasing migration from West Bengal, Assam, Odisha and Bihar.[1]

Migrant Vulnerabilities

The crucial economic role that migrants play is widely recognised. They contribute directly to the gross domestic product, drive local economies and send remittances that help reduce poverty in their native regions. And yet, many migrants are subjected to exploitative work conditions, with long working hours, unsafe environments and a lack of proper accommodation. They often lack legal protections and access to social security measures.

In the absence of legal recognition, they are vulnerable to the vagaries of the employment market. They often face discrimination based on their ethnicity, language or origin, which can limit their social mobility and further isolate them from the local community. Being far from their families and communities leads to social isolation, a lack of support systems, loneliness and other mental health challenges. Some of these mental health conditions lead to criminal and aberrant behaviour. Moreover, access to education, healthcare and other basic services is severely limited for migrant labourers. They often remain excluded from government schemes and welfare programmes due to a lack of documentation or proof of residency.

The devastating impact of the Covid-19 crisis exposed the precarious existence of migrants in different parts of India.[2] As businesses closed and transportation came to a halt, many migrants found themselves stranded far from home, without jobs, money or access to proper food and shelter. With no income and uncertainty about the future, millions of migrant workers embarked on foot journeys, covering hundreds of kilometres to reach their villages. The images of their mass exodus and the humanitarian crisis that followed, with reports of hunger, exhaustion and deaths along the way, resonated across the nation.

In Kerala, the situation was a tad better. Despite the pandemic-related crisis, stories of resilience emerged from different places in the state as communities, NGOs and individuals stepped up to provide relief in the form of food, shelter and transportation. In fact, in Kerala, substantial chunks of the migrant population stayed back instead of leaving for their homes. And the plight of migrant workers during the pandemic sparked discussions on labour reforms, social safety nets and the need to provide them with better living and working conditions. The state implemented some basic schemes and policies for migrant worker welfare, offering support and aiming to safeguard rights and integration.

The bureaucracy should be more empathetic towards the plight of these migrant workers. Sardar Vallabhbhai Patel envisioned the All-India Services (AIS) as a key player in fostering national integration. He perceived it as an instrument that binds the nation into a unified entity. By ensuring that officers from these services are posted across different states, often outside their own linguistic and cultural regions, Patel intended to promote cross-cultural appreciation and administrative uniformity. In the context of migrant workers, AIS officers are in a better position to empathise, as they can also see themselves as migrants.

I have a personal story to narrate here. Upon joining the Indian Police Service, I received news that I had been assigned to the Assam-Meghalaya cadre, and my initial reaction was that of sheer devastation. The prospect of relocating over 3,000 kilometres away, adapting to an unfamiliar culture and confronting the daunting uncertainties that lay ahead was overwhelming. My perceived grief of having been wronged by the system knew no bounds. Yet, when I finally landed in Assam after completing my training, my apprehensions were quickly dispelled, and I realised how unfounded my fears were. The resemblance between Assam and my homeland, Kerala, was striking. The landscape, lush with greenery, rivers, lakes, mountains, paddy fields and tea gardens, was remarkably reminiscent of my native home. Very soon, Assam's warm and affectionate people and my colleagues and seniors made me feel entirely at home. I quickly integrated myself with the state, the language and its people.

Years later, as I observed the migration of thousands of labourers from eastern and northeastern states, heading to the north and south of India, a poignant realisation struck me. The arduous journey that a migrant worker from Assam might undertake to reach the shores of Kerala in search of employment became a subject of contemplation. During my tenure as chairman of the Cochin Port, I discovered that thousands of these migrants, primarily from Assam, Odisha and West Bengal, were contributing to major construction work within the port, mostly on the Vallarpadam International Container Transshipment Terminal, the Cochin liquefied natural gas projects and the connectivity constructions. During occasional breaks, speaking in their native language, Assamese, I would engage in conversations with them. They would recount to me their experiences and the uncertainty that haunted them while travelling such vast distances, leaving behind their families, familiar landscapes and cultural bonds. Surely, the situation of a migrant embarking on such an adventure with an uncertain future was very different from that of an AIS officer who had all the resources, privileges and protection that a young man could dream of. My interactions with the migrants led me to a humbling realisation. It made me recognise how I was carried away by vanity and the false sense of entitlement and how my initial dissatisfaction with being posted to a far-off land was totally unjustified.

A Fairer Deal Called For

If we deal with migrants more fairly, they will remain an integral part of the nation's growth story, despite the precarious conditions in which they live and work. Addressing their plight and tribulations requires a comprehensive policy approach, covering legal protections, access to basic services, improved working conditions and efforts to reduce social isolation.

Recognising their invaluable role and safeguarding their rights are essential for India's aspirations of building a more just and equitable society. The Covid-19 pandemic exposed the fragility of their lives and the sheer lack of preparedness on the part of many state governments, revealing gaps in multiple aspects of labour governance. It is time for nationwide efforts to initiate reforms to provide them with better social protection, working conditions and legal safeguards. As India moves forward, it is crucial to prioritise the welfare and rights of this significant section of our workforce, building an inclusive environment where their contributions are acknowledged, respected and adequately rewarded.

Kerala has taken some small steps in this direction. However, as a pioneer in labour reforms among Indian states, it is time for the state to do more to bring about comprehensive reforms in the sector and show the way to the rest of the country.

Notes

1 J.K. Parida and K.R. Raman, 'A Study on In-Migration, Information Employment and Urbanisation in Kerala', report submitted to the State Planning Board (Evaluation Division), Government of Kerala, March 2021. Available online: https://spb.kerala.gov.in/sites/default/files/inline-files/In-migrationEmploymnt.pdf

2 A.C. Choolayil and L. Putran, 'The COVID-19 Pandemic and Human Dignity: The Case of Migrant Labourers in India', *Journal of Human Rights and Social Work,* 6 (3): 225–236. Available online: https://doi.org/10.1007/s41134-021-00185-x

Engendering Governance: The Kudumbashree Experience

K.B. Valsala Kumari

Gender Governance Expanded

Governance is decision-making that encompasses a broad spectrum of institutional levels and processes in both the public and private domains. Ideally, decision-making – whether at the micro level of the family or the macro level of the state, market or civil society – entails complex interactions among different stakeholders with differing interests and needs. Decision-making is critical as it determines how men and women, boys and girls live, how and where they work, what kind of lives they lead, and how, when and in what quantities resources are allocated.

For thousands of years, decision-making has been a male prerogative due to historical reasons. Brute strength was a significant attribute for human survival. By nature, men, being physically stronger, were more likely to lead and make decisions. However, today we live in a vastly transformed world where human physical strength has been replaced by technological strength. Today, what decision-makers need is intelligence, creativity and innovation.

Gender, which reflects the power dynamics between men and women and boys and girls in a specific time and space, exerts a strong influence on decision-making. As a little girl, I heard about my unseen grandmother who resisted her proposed marriage to a much older man, fought against it, threatened to kill herself and consumed poison to marry a man of her choice. However, in her brother's case, there was no forceful imposition of patriarchal authority in the selection of his life partner. My grandmother had not even heard of the term 'gender', although she was a strong woman who fought for her rights.

In fact, in many Indian and foreign languages, there is no equivalent term for 'gender'.

Gender assigns stereotypical roles to men and women. Thus, girls are expected to cook and perform domestic chores, while boys, exempt from such responsibilities, can freely play outside. These assignments of gender roles are not natural but socially constructed.

Engendering governance implies foregrounding gender equality and social justice in all decision-making processes. It entails critically examining deeply entrenched gender inequalities in decision-making, both at home and in the larger society. In the private sphere of the home, engendering governance means that women have an equal voice in deciding all matters, including family budgets and children's education, providing the same nourishment to sons and daughters, ensuring equal space for their creative expressions, granting both the same freedom to choose their livelihoods and life partners, sharing labour within the household, and determining how to utilise savings and spend leisure time. In the public sphere, engendering governance involves including women meaningfully in all decision-making processes, policy formulations and the distribution of public resources while addressing public problems across all institutions and organisations in society.

Thin at the Top

Engendering the public sphere has two dimensions. First, the establishment of gender representation in all institutions and organisations, and second, the development of inclusive policies. In the higher echelons of governance, progress is extremely slow. For instance, in the Kerala Legislative Assembly, out of a total of 140 members, only 12 seats are occupied by women.[1] At the national level, only 78 members (14.4 per cent) out of a total of 542 members are women.[2] In several international organisations too, the situation is not much better. Whether in Fortune 500 companies or institutions of governance like the legislature, executive, judiciary, military, media or trade unions, the narrative is consistent globally. Women's representation in these bodies often exhibits a pyramidal structure, with a preponderance of women in lower decision-making roles such as secretarial and clerical positions.

As one ascends, women's representation frequently diminishes to mere tokenism. Although certain employment sectors, particularly in the informal economy, may be overcrowded with women, they are usually low-paid and lack a social security network.

Engendering policies that include land distribution in women's names, employment generation schemes, microcredit and poverty alleviation programmes, among others, is perceived as a transformative outcome for women's lives.

Why Should Governance Be Engendered?

For centuries, unpaid reproductive labour by women – through birthing, nurturing and caregiving – has consumed their time, denied them access to knowledge, excluded them from public decision-making and kept them out of politics. Justice demands that this be rectified through engendering governance. In their paper titled 'Women, Work, and the Economy: Macroeconomic Gains from Gender Equity', the International Monetary Fund states: 'Women's ability to participate in the labour market is constrained by their higher allocation of time to unpaid work. On average, women spend twice as much time on household work as men and four times as much time on childcare, thereby freeing up time for male household members to participate in the formal labour force.'[3]

Engendering governance entails understanding the differential experiences of women and men and valuing them equally. Certain bodily functions are unique to women due to biological differences. With the loss of the support system provided by traditional joint family structures, which included many aunts, uncles, cousins and grandparents, women are burdened by the chores associated with multiple gender roles. While female representatives in the government prioritise issues such as the availability of drinking water, agricultural inputs, caregiving and violence against women, male representatives often focus more on infrastructural development. Decision-makers cannot assume that men effectively represent women in expressing their specific needs and priorities. In the face of competing demands for scarce resources, women's needs are often overlooked. These often-silenced experiences must be integrated into decision-making for development to be holistic, equitable and truly democratic, as they relate to 50 per cent of the population.

Engendering governance interrogates deeply entrenched gender inequalities in society. Women are often denied the right to participate in decision-making on matters that vitally affect them. They are paid less than men for the same work, especially in the informal sector, and the care work that women perform remains unpaid. To add insult to injury, many women are subjected to gender-based violence at home and in the workplace. According to UN Women, 'One in three women worldwide experiences physical or sexual violence, mostly by an intimate partner. Violence against women and girls is a human rights violation, and the immediate and long-term physical, sexual, and mental consequences can be devastating, including death. Violence negatively affects women's general well-being and prevents them from fully participating in society. It impacts their families, their communities, and the country at large; it has tremendous costs, from greater strains on healthcare systems to legal expenses and losses in productivity.'[4]

Women constitute a vast reservoir of resources, skills and perspectives. If their potential remains unutilised or underutilised, the nation stands to lose. We must engender governance to bring about a qualitative change by integrating more care and concern for the underprivileged and marginalised, creating a happier world for men, women, boys and girls.

The ultimate objective of engendering governance is to effect cultural change in decision-making processes and within institutions, as well as in human relationships both within and between organisations at all levels – from families to global governance, including schools and media. This entails the equal involvement of women and men in all phases of planning, implementation and monitoring of decision-making processes while ensuring gender justice.

The Kudumbashree Model of Engendering Governance

A stellar example of engendering governance is Kerala's widely acclaimed initiative, Kudumbashree (translated as 'prosperity of families'). Initially started as a state-sponsored poverty eradication programme focusing on women's empowerment, Kudumbashree has spread across the entire state and is now a leader in poverty eradication efforts in twenty other Indian states, guiding women to exit poverty and achieve empowerment. Kudumbashree has also assisted other countries in their endeavours to eradicate poverty and empower women. The community network of Kudumbashree, with nearly 4.1 million women, is the largest and most robust women's network in the world. The foundational units of the Kudumbashree community network are the neighbourhood groups (NHGs), consisting of twenty women from twenty adjacent low-income families. These NHGs are federated into area development societies (ADSs) at the ward level and into community development societies (CDSs) at the local self-government (LSG) level. Initially, Kudumbashree units began as microcredit and savings groups, but their activities now span a vast array of sectors, including microenterprises, education, agriculture, human resource development, health (including palliative and geriatric care), culture and IT. Kudumbashree uses a rights-based approach in the training provided to its members, empowering them to claim the rights due to them.

Engendering Governance at the Family Level

Economic Decision-makers

Most Kudumbashree members earn their income through microenterprises, agriculture, the service sector or other activities. Many are the primary breadwinners or sole income-earners of their families. Notably, many have savings accounts in their names. This capital, however small, is often used at their discretion. They determine whether to invest it in productive assets or use it for consumption or the needs of their children and other family members.

Elevation to the Status of Bankers of the Family

A Kudumbashree member who takes a loan from the network may use it to start small enterprises employing other women or for her children's education and health or sometimes to revive a struggling microenterprise of her husband. She primarily uses the loan to meet her family's needs, thus making her an indispensable banker. Her husband begins to recognise her contribution to the family budget, which often leads to a significant reduction or cessation of gender-based domestic violence. The gender dynamic between the husband and the wife thus becomes less hierarchical and more democratic.

Improved Status Within the Family

This newfound status as an income earner gives Kudumbashree members a voice that their family members respect. Today, many Kudumbashree members watch the news on TV with their husbands and children, and their analyses of daily news receive attention from their families.

Human Resource Development

Enhanced knowledge levels through continuous training programmes organised by Kudumbashree and its district mission coordinators aid in skill acquisition. Keeping abreast of world events, reading newspapers, watching the news and engaging in social networking through the massive Kudumbashree network make these women well-informed and sought-after in domestic decision-making.

Engendering Governance at the Community Level

Society has dichotomised the roles of men and women, boys and girls into discrete boundaries. Contesting these boundaries is often frowned upon. Men are typically privileged over women who are considered deficient or inferior and thus assigned subordinate roles. The traditional categorisation of the 'public sphere' (reserved for men) and the 'private sphere' (allocated to women) discourages boundary-crossing. It is this fortified barrier that the women of Kudumbashree have blurred and broken through sheer hard work and unwavering support from the state.

The NHGs are the first point of contact with the community for Kudumbashree members. Women from similar socioeconomic backgrounds living in close proximity form these NHGs. Their weekly meetings serve as an excellent platform for decision-making. Although these are all-women groups, they provide valuable training for women aspiring to take on leadership roles in higher bodies where decisions that profoundly affect them, their families and communities are made. They start with seemingly minor decisions, such as establishing the weekly savings that need to be remitted to the NHG's account (which requires a good understanding of family budgets), the amount of loans to be taken and the corresponding repayment schedules. They then progress to discussing and finding solutions to local issues in their neighbourhoods. The weekly welcome speeches, votes of thanks and discussions on various topics, including local problems and savings scrutiny, foster confidence that escalates as they engage with higher decision-making bodies like the ADSs and CDSs.

Banking Experiences

The women's collectives, in other words the NHGs, are introduced to banking soon after they start saving. Traditionally, bankers considered poor women non-bankable due to perceived questionable repayment capacity, leading to complications and delays in sanctioning even small loans. Initially, these women, unfamiliar with banking processes, felt hesitant about approaching banks. However, with the knowledge gained through Kudumbashree meetings, they now approach banks with the same confidence they display in their speeches. The NHGs' prompt repayment of loans has bolstered women's credibility with bankers.

Women, many of whom have been victims or witnesses of verbal abuse and violence due to their husbands' alcoholism, have united under Kudumbashree NHGs to advocate for the removal of arrack shops from their neighbourhoods. Their interactions with bureaucrats from various development departments, such as LSGs and Agriculture, have empowered them to engage assertively with officials from regulatory departments like Excise and Police.

Political Representation

The 73rd and 74th Amendments to the Constitution of India in 1992 guaranteed a one-third reservation of seats for women in LSGs. In 2009, the Kerala Panchayati Raj (Amendment) Bill and the Municipality (Amendment) Bill were passed to increase this quota to 50 per cent. This set the stage for genuine grassroots leaders to emerge from within the Kudumbashree network, capable of taking on successful developmental roles within LSGs.

In the December 2020 elections for LSGs, 16,965 Kudumbashree members contested, out of which 7,071 (41.67 per cent) won.[5] One-third of all panchayat members and councillors of urban local bodies are affiliated with the Kudumbashree network. This is a significant achievement, especially considering that just a few years ago these ordinary women would have shied away from public interaction. Now they have become leaders with oratorical skills that rival seasoned politicians. These women leaders have distinguished themselves through hard work, dedication and in-depth knowledge of their constituencies. Many now occupy powerful positions as panchayat presidents, standing committee chairpersons and district panchayat members, with one former Cabinet member, P.K. Jayalakshmi, having been a Kudumbashree member.

Kudumbashree exemplifies the power of networking. Given the substantial social capital generated, one hopes this will translate into political capital. While its women have contested elections and many have outperformed their counterparts without a Kudumbashree background, most of them are still fielded by patriarchal political parties with a few women in their upper decision-making bodies. Unfortunately, when it comes to seeking justice for women, if the perpetrator of violence is a male member of a particular political party, he is often shielded despite incriminating evidence. Even when women representatives from that political party are aware of his wrongdoings, they are often silenced by their party from speaking out against the offender or demanding justice for the victim.

Criticism has also been directed at women in executive and administrative roles, suggesting they are elites detached from the concerns of poor women. It is now widely recognised that women are not a monolithic entity – they are stratified by class, caste, ethnicity, age, ability and more. Elected women representatives face significant dilemmas. Those occupying women's reservation seats have specific mandates to protect women's interests. However, because elections occur along party lines, male-dominated political parties' interests often overshadow the need for women's justice.

Thus, the question arises: why advocate for women's quotas in legislative bodies? The Women's Reservation Bill has languished for decades, occasionally resurfacing for discussions only to be set aside again. Merely achieving numerical preponderance is insufficient to revitalise democracy. What is required is a gender-sensitive pool of both women and men committed to advancing gender justice, equity in opportunities and fair distribution of resources for all. Above all, a strong, autonomous women's movement is necessary to support women representatives who refuse to be co-opted by political parties and facilitate their connection to their constituencies. Only then can we foster a more authentic participatory democracy where women are no longer mere spectator-politicians.

Notes

1 'Women Members: 15th KLA', Kerala Legislative Assembly. Available online: https://www.niyamasabha.nic.in/index.php/content/womanMembers (accessed 8 September 2025).

2 'Information Regarding Global Gender Gap Index (GGGI) and Gender Inequality Index (GII)', Ministry of Parliamentary Affairs. Available online: https://www.mpa.gov.in/sites/default/files/Women%20in%20 Parliament_1.pdf (accessed 8 September 2025).

3 K. Elborgh-Woytek, M. Newiak, K. Kochhar, S. Fabrizio, K. Kpodar, P. Wingender, B. Clements and G. Schwart. 'Women, Work, and the Economy', International Monetary Fund, September 2013. Available online: https://www.imf.org/external/pubs/ft/sdn/2013/sdn1310.pdf (accessed 8 September 2025).

4 'Ending Violence Against Women', UN Women. Available online: https://www.unwomen.org/en/what-we-do/ending-violence-against-women (accessed 8 September 2025).

5 '7071 People's Representatives to Local Bodies from Kudumbashree!', Government of Kerala, Local Self Government Department, 6 January 2021. Available online: https://lsgkerala.gov.in/en/kudumbashree/featured-topics/it-great-achievement-kudumbashree-out-entire-set-peoples (accessed 8 September 2025).

Kerala's Health Paradox

Dr K. Ellangovan

A CATASTROPHIC CLINICAL OUTCOME often triggers emotional turmoil, sometimes erupting into violence against doctors and hospital property. Though rare, such incidents spark doctor protests and the suspension of outpatient services. Doctors are no longer seen as 'demigods'; the era of accepting poor medical outcomes as a fait accompli is over. The trusting patient has become a suspicious litigant. The credibility of the healthcare system is visibly eroding. Still, violence in any form is unacceptable in a civilised society.

Kerala is no exception to the circumstances delineated above, though violence is less frequent. But why does it occur in a state lauded by the NITI Aayog as a healthcare leader? Despite spending 1.1 per cent of its gross state domestic product on healthcare and having a strong public and private network, Kerala faces unique challenges: a greying population with a heavy disease burden, unregulated private hospitals that push people into poverty and unreported medical errors.

This paradox of high rankings amid rising health concerns calls for deeper scrutiny. The shift from Millennium Development Goals to Sustainable Development Goals in 2016 demanded reimagined healthcare systems. Has Kerala adapted? What policy changes are needed to meet new challenges? Should all public health resources be unified under one system to optimise outcomes?

This chapter explores the emerging issues and suggests reforms at both policy and service delivery levels.

Is Kerala the Real Topper?

Kerala has long been a pioneer in healthcare. Contributions from erstwhile rulers and missionaries boosted female literacy, a key factor in reducing maternal and infant mortality and improving immunisation rates. Successive governments built on this foundation, making Kerala a leader in reproductive and child health.

However, Kerala's frequent health awards are often based on broad indices, not core measures like access, quality and cost. Critics such as Sundararaman and Indranil Mukhopadhyay argue that NITI Aayog's health index is flawed and reflects past successes while ignoring present challenges and their economic fallout.

In contrast, global frameworks take a broader view. Bloomberg's health index, for example, includes life expectancy, environmental risks and lifestyle factors. The Global Health Security Index assesses emergency preparedness across six dimensions, from prevention to system strength. Adopting such comprehensive tools could better guide Kerala's future healthcare strategies.

Can Kerala adopt these broader frameworks to assess its performance in the health sector? Owing to the lack of data availability and integrity, it may not be possible to switch over to these frameworks. Over time, as health data for the population becomes available, Kerala could transition to one of these methodologies. However, as of now, fundamental issues that determine the functioning of the healthcare delivery system could be examined closely to find out where Kerala stands today. The following five core domains are worthy determinants:

1. Appropriateness and quality of care
2. Affordable healthcare services
3. Equity issues
4. Environmental protection
5. Promotional and preventive aspects of healthcare

I explore the first three domains below.

Appropriateness and Quality of Care

Quality of care in healthcare refers to how well health services improve outcomes and align with professional standards. It includes safety, effectiveness, patient-centredness, timeliness, equity and efficiency – essentially, it means delivering the right care at the right time in the right way.

Globally, quality varies between hospitals and physicians, depending on factors like clinical support, staff skill, technology and patient cooperation. Medical errors, a serious quality issue, are often underreported and poorly investigated.

India lacks a national index of clinical and medical errors. Dr Girdhar J. Gyani, director general of the Association of Healthcare Providers (India), points out that healthcare staff are not trained to assess such errors. Professor Jha of Harvard Medical School estimates that 5.2 million medical errors occur annually in India.[1]

A 2013 study by Nilay D. Solanki and Chaital Shah analysing 300 cases in a hospital in western India found that 117 cases (39 per cent) involved errors:

1. 62 cases due to prescription errors
2. 28 cases due to transcription errors
3. 16 cases due to administrative errors
4. 11 cases due to dispensation errors

Kerala has no studies documenting medical errors. Often, such errors are buried in records, with no disciplinary action by regulatory bodies like the Medical Council of India. This failure led to medical services being brought under the Consumer Protection Act in the 1990s.

Currently, there are no standard benchmarks to assess doctors or hospitals. Outcomes are often attributed to patient-specific factors, not systemic failures. Without objective metrics, even excellent clinical recoveries may be undervalued if care lacks perceived quality.

Medical errors often occur at the point of care, especially when doctors face complex, multisystem issues without access to updated clinical evidence. Kerala publishes few scientific papers and medical colleges seldom contribute, forcing clinicians to rely on Western data, sometimes misclassifying normal findings as unhealthy. This results in unnecessary medication – a major source of errors. Patient education, a critical component of quality care, remains largely neglected, with no strong policy direction in place.

Affordable Care

According to the 2018–2019 National Health Accounts, Kerala's per capita health expenditure is ₹9,871, nearly four times the national average of ₹2,700. Yet out-of-pocket spending remains high, at ₹7,206 per person (73 per cent), revealing a paradox: despite high public spending, individuals still bear the brunt of healthcare costs.

This mismatch stems from limited insurance coverage, an unregulated private sector and costly branded medicines, which are often prescribed even in government hospitals due to a lack of trust in generics. Most public funds go towards salaries, with minimal allocation for medicines or supplies. Efforts to enforce generic prescriptions have faced strong resistance from doctors.

For Kerala to achieve universal healthcare, the focus must shift to true financial protection through better regulation, increased spending on consumables and a strong safety net. As of now, the state may not be fully prepared.

Kerala merged several health insurance schemes, such as the Rashtriya Swasthya Bima Yojana, Comprehensive Health Insurance Scheme, Senior Citizen Health Insurance Scheme, Karunya Benevolent Fund and Ayushman Bharat Pradhan Mantri Jan Arogya Yojana, into the Karunya Arogya Suraksha Padhathi. This unified scheme provides annual coverage of ₹5 lakh per family, applicable to all families regardless of income. However, the coverage is limited to secondary and tertiary care, meaning hospitalisation expenses. Most healthcare spending in Kerala, however, is on medicines for chronic illnesses. This mismatch continues to strain household budgets and pushes many into poverty year after year.

Equity Issues

Equity in healthcare is an important determinant of the performance of the healthcare delivery system. Kerala's inequity is among the least across other Indian states because of the large number of publicly funded institutions delivering a host of healthcare services to every individual in Kerala free of cost. However, the poor are forced to approach private hospitals that lack a complete range of healthcare services for a variety of reasons, including perceived quality issues and geographical factors. This creates financial hardship, and 4–5 per cent of the poor fall into even greater poverty as a result of one major illness in the family. The only way to ensure that the problem of equity is effectively redressed is by improving services in public hospitals and bringing the poor under health insurance, enabling them to seek services in private hospitals without financial hardship. Services in public hospitals should be standardised, and the public should know what to expect from hospitals in their place of residence. While the Kerala government offers better health insurance compared to other states, it is not adequate, considering the high health-seeking behaviour of the people.

Changing Profile of Morbidity in the Population

Kerala's healthcare model presents several paradoxes. The state is rapidly becoming a hotspot for metabolic diseases like diabetes, hypertension, cardiovascular conditions, obesity and infertility. Yet there are no credible studies quantifying the incidence of non-communicable diseases (NCDs). The high consumption of NCD medications alone signals an alarming disease burden.

Contributing factors include rising disposable incomes, smaller family sizes, access to calorie-dense foods and sedentary lifestyles. Despite rising childhood obesity, there are no obesity clinics proportionate to the need. Digital addiction and substance abuse among children are also rising. While policies exist, they are fragmented. A comprehensive plan to address metabolic diseases is urgently needed.

Despite Kerala's high disease load, there is no mandated preventive or screening policy. Although occasional awareness drives occur, a systematic screening plan for at-risk populations is missing. Of the 886 primary health centres (PHCs) in the state, 630 have been upgraded to family health centres. If primary care centres focus on prevention and secondary/tertiary centres on curative and rehabilitative care, the system's efficiency would improve and resources would be better used.

It is through these very primary care institutions that Kerala achieved its strong health indicators. A clear policy direction is now essential to maintain and build upon that success.

Regular Epidemics: Public Health Engineering Initiatives?

Thick vegetation, high humidity and a dense population make Kerala prone to frequent zoonotic and viral outbreaks. Despite having strong local self-governments (LSGs), diseases like dengue, chikungunya, leptospirosis, H1N1 and H5N1 recur regularly, leaving the population vulnerable. Almost every monsoon is followed by an epidemic, yet the government's response remains reactive, with little effort to implement long-term preventive measures.

Solid waste disposal remains a major challenge for the Kerala government, with midnight dumping of septage emerging as a serious health hazard. According to Suseel Samuel, a water and sanitation expert at the World Bank, open defecation is less harmful than dumping septage in an open space.[2] While open defecation spreads faecal matter around in small quantities, septage dumping means the discharge of highly concentrated pathogens, with a huge potential to cause health and environmental damage. According to one estimate, only 4 per cent of Kerala's population is provided with sewage drainage.[3] The World Bank's Second Kerala Rural Water Supply and Sanitation Project (Jalanidhi-II) aimed to set up a regional septage treatment facility in each district, but progress has been slow. As a result, septage continues to be dumped in open spaces and water bodies, causing Escherichia coli contamination and raising concerns over underreported waterborne diseases like typhoid, hepatitis A and seasonal diarrhoea.

Only 15 per cent of Kerala's population has access to piped water. Despite these public health risks, responsibilities are fragmented across departments like Health, Water Resources, LSGs and Science and Technology, which are working in silos. A unified apex body with representatives from all these sectors is urgently needed for coordinated and effective disease control.

Higher Disposable Income May Lead to a Higher Incidence of Lifestyle Diseases

A scan of Kerala's population for metabolic syndrome, defined by the presence of three of five clinical risk parameters, would likely reveal high numbers of hormonally altered individuals at risk of metabolic diseases. A key predictor is an elevated body mass index (BMI), with childhood obesity indicating early onset. Some European countries assess the BMI of their youth to predict future disease burden. An unverified report suggests that Kerala has the highest density of bakeries and confectioneries per square kilometre. The use of trans fats and inflammatory oils in these foods contributes to poor health and may partly explain Kerala's high cancer rates.

Does the government have supporting evidence, and has it mandated nutritional labelling on food products? Can it issue such regulations under existing laws?

While governments can't fully dictate food choices, Kerala has made no attempt to use incentives or disincentives to influence them. Why not introduce a 'sugar and fat tax' – as has been done for alcohol and tobacco – given sugar's comparable health risks? Political will is required, but the first step is credible data. It is now up to the scientific community to conduct statewide studies and provide the needed evidence.

Changing the Face of Service Delivery Models

As healthcare evolves, a shift towards evidence-based delivery has increased diagnostic investigations, burdening patients. Historically, three care models have emerged. Until the 1980s, India followed a 'trust model', where patient faith guided care and doctors weren't blamed for outcomes. In the 1990s, with the inclusion of healthcare under the Consumer Protection Act, the system moved to 'evidence-based medicine', prompting defensive practices and higher costs. Recently, Western countries have embraced 'value-based care', placing patients at the centre of decisions. At Cincinnati Children's Hospital in the US, for example, parents join grand rounds and help make treatment decisions, improving trust and acceptance of outcomes.

The term 'politics of healthcare', first used by David Walsh in 2010,[4] highlights the role of political parties in healthcare delivery in Western democracies with high public spending. In India, healthcare is rarely prioritised in political manifestos. The value-based model, gaining popularity in the West, redefines patients and families as partners in care decisions. At Cincinnati Children's Hospital, involving parents in clinical discussions has led to greater acceptance of outcomes and reduced conflicts. Despite Kerala's progress and strong health indicators, its system still oscillates between trust- and evidence-based models. Single-doctor clinics often follow trust-based care, while hospitals lean towards evidence-based care. Given the high health spending, Kerala deserves value-based, patient-centric care. The government must create guidelines for patient engagement.

Other Policy Prescriptions

In Kerala, there is a significant gap between policy and practice in the healthcare sector. Some policy prescriptions that could fill the critical gaps are:

1. Redesigning public healthcare institutions and realigning available resources as per people's needs
2. Creating a public health observatory (PHO)
3. Creating a cancer registry
4. Developing a standard treatment protocol
5. Constituting a health quality assurance council
6. Designing and implementing affordable healthcare services
7. Introducing nurse practitioners in care services
8. Encouraging research and the addition of new knowledge
9. Making periodic validation of medical licences to update knowledge and skills
10. Restricting unethical practices

I explore a few of these pointers below.

Redesigning Public Healthcare Institutions

According to Vikas Bajpai and Anoop Saraya, India's current three-tier public healthcare system stems from the Bhore Committee's recommendations.[5] Amid the Second World War and following the Quit India Movement, the Government of India appointed the Health Survey and Development Committee on 18 October 1943, chaired by Sir Joseph Bhore. Its mandate was to assess existing health conditions and propose future developments. Citing unsanitary conditions, poor nutrition, inadequate health infrastructure and a lack of health education, the committee recommended a three-tier system: a primary unit for every 10,000–20,000 people with 75 beds, a secondary unit with 650 beds looking over every 30 primary units (with departments like Surgery and Obstetrics) and a district hospital with 2,500 beds offering specialised care.

Eighty years later, the structure remains largely unchanged despite shifts in disease patterns. The government has made minor adjustments such as adding sub-centres and introducing community health centres. However, the design needs rethinking. The three layers could be merged into two: distal units should expand beyond population-based interventions to include treatment for common and chronic diseases, integrating primary and secondary care to ease the load on higher facilities. The secondary level can be upgraded to deliver multispecialty tertiary care. A detailed study of disease burden and health-seeking behaviour is essential, but what is clear is that integrating services will optimise resources.

Creating a Public Health Observatory

Kerala faces recurring viral and zoonotic epidemics, disrupting public life and tourism. The absence of credible media updates and vague statements by the Health Department leaves the public uninformed. Despite frequent outbreaks, no follow-up studies identify the root causes. Existing virology institutes aid diagnosis but not strategy or treatment planning. Kerala urgently needs expert-led data collection, analysis and interpretation – tasks that lie beyond the Health Department's routine scope. A dedicated PHO is now essential.

Though relatively new in the UK and Ireland, similar institutions have long existed elsewhere. According to John Wilkinson and Eddie Coyle, PHOs in England, Wales, Scotland and Ireland support the growing public health movement. The French term 'observatoire', used since 1976, refers to institutions that compile and interpret data to guide local and regional policy. In Europe, PHOs have existed since the 1980s and are crucial in managing both epidemics and non-communicable diseases. Despite Kerala's high burden of lifestyle diseases, credible data is lacking and medical colleges have not conducted reliable studies.

Only a specialised institution like an observatory can offer objective assessments. It could serve as the government's official voice on health matters, allowing the Health Department to focus on service delivery. Setting one up is not expensive, requiring only the redeployment of experts and the establishment of task-specific roles. This structure could foster collaborations with global observatories, enabling knowledge and skill exchange.

Creating a Cancer Registry

Cancer incidence is rising at alarming rates, yet data on its occurrence and progression remain confined to treatment institutions and rarely support research. In contrast, countries like Taiwan have long-established cancer registries. The Taiwan Cancer Registry, active for forty-five years, collects extensive data including death certificates, insurance claims, screening records, biobank entries and health surveys. In 2011, Taiwan launched the Health and Welfare Data Science Centre (HWDC) to improve public health decisions and support academic research. The HWDC integrates all health databases, laying the groundwork for personalised (P4) medicine using AI-based machine learning and advanced statistical tools.

Given Kerala's high cancer rates, a similar registry would be invaluable. As Taiwan has shown, AI-powered personalised medicine for cancer patients becomes possible when comprehensive data is available. Statewide cancer data is essential to identify causes and tailor treatments. Disaggregated demographic data can uncover new insights and guide targeted therapies.

India lacks clinical cancer trials, partly due to insufficient data. A cancer registry, possibly housed under a health observatory, can change this. Doctors could report cases in a standard format, with patient anonymity protected. Initially voluntary, this reporting can become mandatory once public trust is built.

Developing a Standard Treatment Protocol

It is well known that a few common diseases account for a large portion of the population's disease burden. Using the Pareto principle, a strategy can be developed to address these conditions effectively and affordably, reducing both disease load and disease-specific mortality. For example, identifying the top twenty clinical conditions contributing to 80 per cent of the burden and developing evidence-based treatment protocols can improve care outcomes while optimising limited expert resources.

Despite the availability of medical knowledge, many physicians still rely on personal beliefs rather than evidence. This physician-centric model needs to shift towards a patient-centric approach. Developing standard treatment protocols for major diseases – crafted by expert physicians from both the public and the private sectors – would provide a reliable, flexible guide for clinicians. These protocols would not be mandatory but would support clinical decision-making while allowing customisation for individual patient needs. Regular updates based on emerging research would ensure these protocols remain relevant and scientific.

Such protocols would help even primary care physicians treat conditions typically tackled by higher specialised centres. For instance, standard care templates could address mental depression, now a leading reason for PHC visits, or less-discussed issues like erectile dysfunction, a growing cause of marital discord. Even without constant clinical updates, standard protocols would reduce medical errors and enhance treatment quality. Implementing them would mark a crucial step towards better clinical outcomes in Kerala.

Constituting a Health Quality Assurance Council

Healthcare remains largely unregulated, with existing controls focused more on pharmaceuticals than on clinical care. As a result, medical errors often go uninvestigated and are hidden in institutional records, eroding public trust. There is no proper system to probe negligence, and peer reviews rarely hold doctors accountable, often due to poor record-keeping.

Digitising medical records is key to tackling this issue. With real-time updates, tampering becomes impossible, enabling accountability. Western systems mandate electronic records largely due to insurance oversight. India should follow suit.

Once digitisation is in place, an independent quality council comprising respected clinicians can review negligence cases and conduct hospital audits. Like hotel or Ayurvedic resort ratings, hospitals could be ranked based on clinical quality, initially as a voluntary system and eventually mandatory. This will help patients make informed choices.

Designing and Implementing Affordable Healthcare Services

Rising healthcare costs often overshadow patient recovery, especially for middle- and lower-income groups. Despite the presence of public hospitals, around 66 per cent of Keralites seek inpatient care in private facilities due to incomplete services, low-tech infrastructure and poorly stocked pharmacies in government hospitals. Karunya Medical stores and other free drug outlets also lack essential medicines, forcing patients to buy them from outside. Medicine costs alone can account for up to 60 per cent of total treatment expenses.

In 2013, Kerala mandated doctors to prescribe only generics, but many resisted, citing poor drug quality and a lack of accountability for adverse outcomes. At the time, Kerala had just one drug-testing lab that was capable of testing only 4,000 batches, far below over 2 lakh batches sold annually. While this gap has narrowed over time, quality concerns remain. To address this, the government could boost Kerala's drug-testing capacity and offer incentives such as buy-back schemes to generic manufacturers. Increased testing and local production would promote wider generic use and lower costs, especially for the poor. Alternatively, the state could supply branded (patented) drugs to vulnerable groups.

Introducing Nurse Practitioners in Care Services

Nurse practitioners are highly skilled nurses who can play a vital role in healthcare delivery, especially in countries like India, where nurses currently have limited responsibilities. In the West, nurses handle many care-related tasks, easing the burden on physicians. Empowering nurses to perform minor procedures and manage emergencies, especially in rural areas, can greatly improve patient outcomes.

In India, this shift requires revamping nursing education, extending the course to four years and revising pay scales, with government support. Top hospitals in the US already rely on nurse practitioners in emergency rooms, ICUs and operating theatres. With proper training, nurse practitioners could save countless lives and transform care delivery in India.

Conclusion

Kerala has consistently outperformed most Indian states in healthcare, owing to a strong foundation laid by both historical and ongoing government efforts. The state's health-aware population has also driven greater accountability and expectations from the system.

However, Kerala is now at a crossroads. The rising burden of lifestyle and non-communicable diseases calls for a serious rethink of how healthcare is structured and delivered. This shift demands not just policy tweaks but systemic changes, more trained physicians for chronic care, standardised treatment protocols based on local research and greater investment in disease prevention.

To make real progress, Kerala must bring together fragmented efforts across departments like Health, LSGs and the Kerala Water Authority. A unified forum for collaboration is essential to optimise resources and deliver meaningful outcomes.

The government must take the lead in modernising the system and promoting healthier living. Kerala has met past challenges with determination and now must rise again to meet the demands of a changing health landscape.

Notes

1 S. Akhter, '5.2 Million Medical Errors Are Happening in India Annually: Dr Girdhar J. Gyani', ETHealthworld.com, 2 August 2016. Available online: https://health.economictimes.indiatimes.com/news/industry/5-2-million-medical-errors-are-happening-in-india-annually-dr-girdhar-j-gyani/53497049 (accessed 18 September 2025).

2 S. Samuel, 'Septage: Kerala's Looming Sanitation Challenge', The Water Blog, World Bank, 3 April 2013. Available online: https://blogs.worldbank.org/en/water/septage-kerala-s-looming-sanitation-challenge (accessed 16 December 2025).

3 'Sewerage', Kerala Water Authority. Available online: https://kwa.kerala.gov.in/en/sewerage/ (accessed 16 December 2025).

4 D. Walsh et al., 'It's Not "Just Deprivation": Why Do Equally Deprived UK Cities Experience Different Health Outcomes?', *Public Health*, 124(9): 487–495. Available online: https://pubmed.ncbi.nlm.nih.gov/20223487/ (accessed 16 December 2025).

5 V. Bajpai and A. Saraya, 'For a Realistic Assessment: A Social, Political and Public Health Analysis of Bhore Committee', *Social Change*, 41(2): 215–231. https://doi.org/10.1177/004908571104100202 (accessed 16 December 2025).

Re-Engineering Public Administration: A Concept

S. Subbiah

THE BRITISH COLONIAL ADMINISTRATION in India was based in Calcutta (now Kolkata), Madras (now Chennai) and Bombay (now Mumbai), with many Indians participating in the Indian Civil Service (ICS). Post-Independence, the government made limited administrative changes, mainly in land revenue administration. Public administration in India is thus a continuum of the colonial model, with administrative, executive and district administration functions that require re-engineering.

The District Development Committee, chaired by the collector, has a centralised planning model that neglects location-specific issues and state-level schemes. This committee lacks an official coordinator responsible for the success or failure of development schemes, and the planning process is not based on natural resource management or location-specific needs. This lack of focus on the population's needs has been realised by committee members.

The Existing Functional Structure

Administrative departments draw strength from policies approved by the legislature. They finalise plans and programmes, and then, after due process, inform the executive department to get them implemented, along with handling budget allocation. At the district level, various department units implement development programmes according to the directions of the respective departments.

The district administration coordinates programme implementation. The core departments – the Revenue Department and the Local Self-Government (LSG) Department – have their field offices only up to the taluk level. Beyond that, development administration is managed by the LSG Department through the panchayat system. Only the Revenue Department runs administration up to the village level. The LSG Department has functional units for the panchayats. Development administration, which was earlier the function of development blocks, is now weakened. In Kerala, development blocks are responsible only for implementing Central government-sponsored programmes.

In the present system, there is an almost four-way administration seen across the state: government departments handling programme implementation; the panchayats; the block development office handling development programmes; and non-governmental organisations (NGOs) that get funding under government programmes and from other funding agencies. All these agencies run programmes that employ public money but without the participation of the target groups. A semblance of participation or inclusivity may be present when NGOs plan for programme implementation. In some cases, this is achieved through photo opportunities.

The Government – Not by the People

The government decides policy, and the administrative departments are free to make programmes accordingly. As a follow-up, the administrative departments issue directions to executive departments for sending plan proposals. Once the proposals are received and after due discussions at the Secretariat level, the plan proposals are forwarded to the planning board. The planning board then invites the concerned Secretary for discussion and finalises various programmes for the department. The public has no role in the process.

As part of the decentralised administration, the government allocates about 25 per cent of the budgeted funds to the three-tier system. Of this, 75–85 per cent goes to the gram panchayat, 10–25 per cent to the block panchayat and 5–15 per cent to the district panchayat. However, at the panchayat level, public involvement is not seen in Gram Sabha meetings. Only those who stand to benefit from the funds attend. I have witnessed this in the Chembukavu Panchayat in the Kottayam district. The allegedly inclusive and participatory principles are not clear.

Block panchayats allocate money to local development programmes (in addition to the Central government programmes). Otherwise, the block development office generally implements the Indian government's programmes. This is the outcome of a badly designed functional structure at this level, as no one is held accountable. Moreover, there is no need to allocate separate funds for block panchayats and district panchayats as they do not have a direct connection with other panchayats. I realised this only when I was preparing a report on panchayat-level human resource requirements for the Agriculture Department.

Issues

Kerala is considered one of India's advanced states and is known for its higher human development indicators. However, the ground reality is alarming: while the poverty index intensity in Kerala declined from 36.9 per cent in 2004–2005 to 31 per cent in 2011–2012 and continued to decline to 23.23 per cent in 2017–2018, from 2019 to 2021 only 0.55 per cent of the population suffered from multidimensional poverty. Income from the farming sector constitutes only 8 per cent of Kerala's gross domestic state product (GDSP), against the national average of 14 per cent, but a huge extent of cultivable land is left fallow. Kerala's GDSP is dominated by the service sector; however, the concern is *how much* of the service sector is truly benefiting Kerala. Although we are pleased with the development of many self-help groups, the rate of self-employment is significantly lower than the national average. The female labour force participation rate is higher than the national average; however, in absolute terms, it declined from 32 per cent in 1983 to 24 per cent in 2011–2012. Though Kerala is home to about 15 lakh migrant workers, Keralites are experiencing both unemployment and underemployment – a paradoxical situation.

Challenges to the administration can be addressed by framing budgeted programmes, which can be implemented through a system that can be held accountable and has empathy for the common person. The major causes of concern are:

1. Unemployment and underemployment
2. Shortage of skilled workers as per market demand
3. Short-term migration and labour exploitation

4. Education quality and skill mismatch
5. The agrarian crisis
6. Ageing population

In addition to addressing these challenges, the other goals are:

1. Elimination of poverty existing in a few pockets of Kerala
2. Sustainable consumption through the reduction of waste
3. Responsible use of resources
4. Employing environment-friendly production techniques

Government Efforts

The Government of India strengthened local self-governance through the 73rd and 74th Constitutional Amendments. The responsibilities of twenty-nine development departments were devolved to the LSGs, as per the 73rd Amendment. The 74th Amendment devolved eighteen functions to urban local bodies. Unfortunately, socioeconomic development is at the mercy of the panchayat president and the ruling party's dictates.

Kerala is considered much better at structuring the panchayat system than other Indian states. However, it appears that the state government is reluctant to strengthen LSGs. The top-heavy Secretariat and perfunctory executive departments are the real burden on the exchequer because they ignore the need-based demands of the local population. Given the situation, the administrative challenges on account of centralised planning and administration include corruption, inefficient bureaucracy, lack of transparency, inefficient services, political imbalance, lack of investment, lack of coordination and climate change.

Alternative Options

Kerala is a pioneer in restructuring LSGs. About 25 per cent of the state budget is devolved to LSGs. Among other prominent South Indian states, Karnataka established a district panchayat with a chief executive officer who was given all the required powers. This panchayat, however, has no financial autonomy. In Tamil Nadu, a single-man army executes the Indian government's programmes. Although development blocks were helpful, they are no longer beneficial to the common person's socioeconomic growth.

Therefore, the entire administrative apparatus, from the Secretariat down to the panchayat, warrants restructuring to meet the current plans for socioeconomic development. I realised this while examining the proposal for restructuring the Department of Agriculture and Farmers' Welfare. Keeping in mind the above requirement, I propose the following re-engineering of the administrative framework:

The Secretariat

The Secretariat is a vital body with functions such as development, welfare, regulation, legislation and liaison with the Government of India. Additionally, the administrative department within the Secretariat handles petitions from the public across the state. In light of the 73rd Amendment, which mandates the devolution of at least twenty-nine functions to LSGs, and the 74th Amendment, which devolves eighteen functions to municipal administration, the relevant administrative departments in the Secretariat may need to be resized accordingly. Staff from these departments can be transferred to the district or LSG levels. Staff from the administrative departments, possibly all of them, could be placed at the level of local self-government.

Instead of maintaining a top-heavy administrative structure, development departments could operate through an operational unit led by a government secretary, which could advise the Council of Ministers and handle other administrative tasks. With the support of technology, this operational unit should be capable of managing planning, monitoring and evaluation. I have managed development departments as well as regulatory departments such as Electricity and Excise. Given the strength of digitalisation, managing these functional units should be easy.

The main concerns of the staff of the administrative and executive departments are regular and timely promotion, working in rural areas and the posting of spouses. Continuing the promotion process for existing staff is not difficult. Working in rural areas need not be an issue, as the opportunity to get posted nearer to home would outweigh the cost. As for the posting of spouses, usually they are posted to the same place as there are more placement opportunities.

Executive Departments

Currently, the executive departments issue orders to execute the budgeted socioeconomic and development programmes at the field office level, as the responsibilities have already been transferred to LSGs (as provided in the Constitution). Thus the government is left with the responsibility of directly managing only regulatory departments, supporting other important policy-related issues and completing court-related work.

Today, the army of all executive departments prepares planning documents, processes them in the administrative department and refers them to the planning board for approval. The documents are then transferred to the Finance Department for acceptance and finally referred to the legislature for approval. Kerala follows the five-year plan model and, once the budget is passed, the overall allocation remains within the plan period. So why is there such a waste of time in the processing?

Local Self-Governments

The three layers of LSGs are the district panchayat, the block panchayat and the village panchayat. On paper, LSGs have been implemented in all states except Nagaland, Mizoram and Meghalaya. However, because the implementation of constitutional provisions is left to state governments, the decentralisation of administration and the subsequent establishment of LSGs are not uniform across the country. This creates a developmental vacuum at the panchayat level for need-based socioeconomic schemes.

I once visited a drinking water scheme site in the Pathanamthitta district. The taluk development officer in the Scheduled Caste Development Department was unable to show me the completed work, so I had to inquire and verify the work done there. In many development departments, there are no officers below the levels of the block development office or taluk office. This hinders field inspections, which are necessary to ensure ground-level work is successfully completed. After realising this difficulty, the Scheduled Tribe Development Department and the Scheduled Caste Development Department have created volunteer positions on an honorarium basis.

Functions and Responsibilities of Local Self-Governments

Once the earlier-mentioned processes are completed, staff from the Secretariat and executive departments are made available for deployment to LSGs to ensure the effective use of their services. This is a crucial step because these staff member's services are essential for village development and they will be closely involved in planning and administration.

Kerala is the only state where the government has established agriculture offices (Krishi Bhavans) at the panchayat level. Unfortunately, agriculture officers are not responsible for farm production in their respective village panchayats. Similarly, in the Animal Husbandry, Fisheries and Forest departments, industry extension officers exist, but promoting village industries is not a part of their role.

Therefore, the surplus staff identified in the government Secretariat and the abolished executive departments should be transferred to LSGs to utilise their services effectively and for resource management at the panchayat level. Their promotion prospects should be considered based on the existing seniority list. They must be trained in development administration, human resources and natural resource management for effective farm production, processing and distribution among stakeholders. The marketing of surplus produce and products should be arranged separately.

Manpower Procurement

Staff members for LSGs are initially selected from the local pool, but in earlier times, they may have been chosen based on political considerations and biases. Nowadays, there is an improved system of recruitment through a common entrance system. Those recruited at the grassroots level should be properly promoted and posted to block panchayat offices.

In this model, the Secretariat will have a limited, appropriate number of staff for regulatory departments, while the planning and monitoring divisions will have enough remaining personnel to send to block panchayat offices. Staff for LSGs should be selected through promotion to the district level, where they should undergo training and then be transferred to the Secretariat. This process ensures all government staff gain exposure to ground-level socioeconomic conditions.

Processing Plan Proposals

The village panchayat will need to organise resource mapping and conduct a socioeconomic survey. Based on this data, it should proceed with local planning. To facilitate this, a village-level planning committee comprising farmers, government officials, civil society members or elected panchayat representatives should be established. Officials from development departments should be responsible for achieving target production and managing follow-up activities, including value addition, distribution and marketing. Local farm support from the village should be arranged for all farm operations. Labour management will have to be supported by officials from the concerned department. These developed plan proposals must then be processed, structured and submitted for approval to the district panchayat via the block development office. The district panchayat should then review the plan before forwarding it to the district administration.

In principle, no changes are needed to the proposals. The block-level review should mainly aim to improve them and prioritise market data. The district panchayat should review them, allocate resources and monitor the production programmes. Staffing needs for the district panchayats should be assessed considering all elements: planning, execution, evaluation and revision.

The proposed restructuring of public administration should be used as an opportunity to revamp the village production system so that the benefits of this structural change can be truly appreciated. The system should include resource mapping of all biotic and abiotic resources. Additionally, mapping local human resources and their available skill sets using an inclusive and participatory approach is necessary. A comprehensive report on consumption patterns should also be prepared. This will complete the preliminary work for planning the panchayat. The process will involve all relevant departments and coordinating these departments at the micro level should be manageable. In this re-engineered model, manpower allocation for production will be supported through the collected data on the available workforce and its skills. This will help identify skill requirements. Based on the village's needs for various farm products, the planning committee can develop a production plan.

This plan will address local concerns regarding food security and manpower needs.

Outcome

This exercise will bring a change to the face of public administration. LSGs get their manpower from the panchayats – a part and parcel of the community – for all skilled and semi-skilled work. In this exercise, the responsibilities of the administrative and executive departments are transferred to all the panchayats. The government saves a lot of space, energy and funds for other expenditures. Employers get a seasoned workforce as these workers are exposed to local socioeconomic conditions and are also empowered to handle higher responsibilities when they are hired for secretarial services. Through this process, the Secretariat is rightsized to undertake planning and policymaking for socioeconomic development. It gains access to competent staff members who can handle any development issues because of their training and the knowledge they have acquired through grassroots functioning. Also, the petitions received by the Secretariat are considerably reduced over time. The common person knows their issues and also knows how to resolve them, as they enjoy inclusive and participatory resource management at the panchayat level. Through this exercise, the transfers and postings of government employees are also made easier and streamlined. In this way, the government saves a lot of time and energy in budgeting and resource management.

Conclusion

This is a simple process of redefining the administrative structure based on location-specific needs – a structure defined by the strength of socioeconomic surveys and resource mapping. Human manpower requirements can be assessed and strengthened according to local needs. In this model, staff members are recruited at the panchayat level and promoted to higher levels based on service rules. For positions at the Secretariat level, candidates are selected internally, if necessary, by conducting examinations and interviews. This reduces the burden of providing training at a higher level and also saves space, energy and manpower in the Secretariat. Government officials are held accountable for the productive management of natural resources. This creates more employment opportunities at the grassroots level. Productive management of natural resources, climate rejuvenation through captive forests, planned production, accountable official support, food security and employment for all are the main takeaways from this system. We need to move away from obsolete colonial processes and customise our processes as per local needs and nuances so we can achieve true development through re-engineering.

India Must Move from Process to Performance

K.M. Chandrasekhar

When I first came to Kerala for training in 1971, I was posted for field training to the Calicut district. Calicut was the seat of British power in Kerala. There was a collector of Malabar reporting to the Madras Presidency. There were some famous collectors in the Malabar district: William Logan, whose *Malabar Manual* (1887), a meticulous description of every aspect of the district, is still mandatory reading for young officers posted in the district; H.V. Connolly, who got the Connolly Canal constructed between 1848 and 1850 (still known by his name); and several others who left an imprint on the district. There was also Sir Richard Tottenham, an Indian Civil Service (ICS) officer who devised a system of office management for his district, North Arcot. This system, called the Tottenham System of Office Procedure, was eventually adopted throughout the Presidency and later, when the state of Kerala came into being in 1956, across all its offices.

I found the Tottenham System interesting and valuable. It enabled me to supervise the work of all assistants reporting to me through a periodic inspection of personal registers and to record my observations in a 'running note file'. Through this running note file I could also access my predecessors' remarks, and a continuity in work was thus maintained in all offices. However, as work and the range of government activities expanded, the Tottenham System gradually fell into disuse.

The Tottenham System was my early introduction to the management of work in government. Over the years, I was exposed to administrative reforms of different types. There were two Administrative Reforms Commissions (ARCs) which produced hundreds of recommendations on a wide range of sectors. Some individual commissions and committees even produced multiple reports. We were exposed to training programmes galore as well as numerous helpful systems and practised zero-based budgeting (which prepares the budget from scratch, re-evaluating every cash flow item and justifying all expenditure), performance-based budgeting (where funding decisions are linked to achieving specific performance goals) and outcome-based budgeting (which focuses on creating a budget based on set outcomes). We experimented with bringing in officers from the public and corporate sectors, assuming that the fault lay with us officers rather than with the system; we would try new experiments and then gaily abandon them without giving them the time to mature.

Lingering Coloniality: Issues with India's Administrative System

In hindsight, I realise that there was, indeed, much that was wrong with the system. Discussing the ICS in his autobiography *Toward Freedom* (1936), Nehru wrote:

> Whenever India becomes free, and in a position to build her new life as she wants to, she will necessarily require the best of her sons and daughters for this purpose. Good human material is always rare, and in India, it is rarer still because of our lack of opportunities under British rule. We shall want the help of many foreign experts in many departments of public activity, particularly in those which require special technical and scientific knowledge ... But of one thing I am quite sure, that no new order can be built up in India so long as the spirit of the ICS pervades our administration and our public services. That spirit of authoritarianism is the ally of imperialism, and it cannot co-exist with freedom ... Therefore, it seems to me quite essential that the ICS and similar services must disappear completely, as such, before we can start real work on a new order.

However, nothing materially changed during or after the Nehruvian years. That the civil service system remains essentially the same as the one we inherited from the British is vividly brought out by S.K. Das in his book, *Building a World-Class Civil Service for Twenty-First Century India* (2010). He writes:

> David Potter, Professor of Political Science at the Open University, United Kingdom, wrote an interesting book called *India's Political Administrator: From ICS to IAS* in 1998. Potter came to the conclusion that the central features of the ICS tradition of administration continued in independent India. According to him, 'The content of the ICS tradition was not only the concern of the IAS men and women within it, for it has influenced the behaviour of the other administrators and affected the general character of the Indian state structure as a whole.' Potter found that 'although much had changed by the early 1980s, this basic framework of administration (the colonial administration) was still in place'.

In the British regime, goals were clear – maximising revenue collection in India for Britain's financial enrichment; creating an extensive railway network which would further enrich Britain (as it supported the flow of resources out of India and the penetration of British manufactured goods into the Indian market); developing markets for British products and discouraging competition from India; maintaining law and order, even creating division and discord within society if necessary; and dispensing justice with a firm hand in a manner that best promotes British interests. The British system was also based on rigid control of expenditure and a focus on promoting processes that prevented any kind of financial leakages. The goals were clear and implementation was more straightforward. Thus, when the Indian Administrative Service (IAS) is compared with the ICS and denigrated, we fail to recognise that it is like comparing apples with oranges.

Das goes on to say that the civil service in independent India

> has not merely continued the process-driven, hierarchical, rigid, centralised nineteenth-century bureaucratic model created by the British but also deepened it in all the key aspects. If at all, the Indian Civil Service has become even more bureaucratic. The outdated, rigid and cumbersome rules and regulations continued to operate, and new ones have been added over the years. The overall result is a regulatory environment and an emphasis on process, which is inconsistent with

> contemporary management philosophy and acts as a major inhibitor to innovations and best practice.

By keeping the overall system intact and not making any fundamental changes, we fail to recognise the truth that is staring us in the face. We have to understand that the governmental system is a conglomeration of subsystems. Within these subsystems, with support and flexibility, individual officers have achieved marvellous results – some that continue for long, while most others are short-lived and survive only as long as the officer continues in that position. We have had commissions and committees making recommendations on specific areas. These may or may not have been implemented and, even if implemented, have fallen into disuse in due course. Even the ARC has directed its attention to bits-and-pieces sectoral reforms rather than to reinventing government.

Merely changing personnel while retaining an old system will not deliver desired results. Arun Maira, who distinguished himself at different periods in his life as a corporate manager, consultant, public administrator and eventually as a member of the Planning Commission, writes in his book *An Upstart in Government* (2015):

> I must admit that it is much harder to get tangible results in the government ... I have to also explain that the scope of the government's responsibilities is much larger than that of any private sector company. To produce outcomes that are equitable, and not only efficient, in providing health services to all citizens, for example, is more difficult than selling medicines to only those who can pay the price that covers their costs of discovery and production. The government's job is not to make a profit, it is to improve the world for everyone.

The corporate model is therefore not applicable to government. Present-day civil servants themselves are as good as any in the land, with a few exceptions (as can be found in any profession). But when the system is antediluvian, suspicion overrides performance and mistakes made in good faith are punished with severity, how can they deliver results? They have to be judged not by conformity to procedures but by the achievement of outcomes that are beneficial to the people they serve.

The outcomes themselves should be SMART – specific, measurable, achievable, relevant and time-bound.

The Rise of New Public Management

Unless the administration reinvents itself and becomes outcome-oriented, the civil servant cannot deliver. The United Kingdom initiated such a reinvention under the Thatcher regime. Tired of the existing system which was based on hierarchies and procedures (parodied so vividly in the BBC serials *Yes, Minister* and *Yes, Prime Minister*), Margaret Thatcher decided to start remodelling the administration along the SMART model, turning to what came to be known as new public management (NPM).

The Margaret Thatcher government started an aggressive programme of civil service reform in the United Kingdom, which even led to a civil service strike in 1981. The financial management initiative was introduced, which created departmental cost centres and efficiency scrutiny of departments. In a departure from the past, Thatcher also took a direct interest in the appointment of permanent secretaries instead of leaving it to the civil service structure.[1]

In the second phase of reform in the 1980s, a number of public utility privatisations took place, including British Rail, the British Airports Authority, British Gas, electricity, water and sewerage services. About eight hundred thousand employees were transferred to the private sector, and the share of the public sector in gross domestic product declined from 11 per cent in 1979 to 5 per cent in 1990.

The entire structure of administration changed, with a clear split between the government's provider organisations and purchaser organisations. A significant development that led to the evolution of NPM in the United Kingdom – and subsequently in many other countries – was the use of contracts or quasi-contracts to govern relationships between the government and various public authorities. The executive head who signed the contract agreed to the achievement of specified results within a given time frame, which was reviewed from time to time by the government.

The Next Steps report of 1988[2] led to further change, with traditional departments delegating their executive work to more than ninety new executive agencies. These agencies concluded negotiated contracts called 'framework agreements' with their parent departments. These contracts defined the agencies' purposes, objectives and operating parameters. Prime Minister John Major's Citizens' Charter programme was a subsequent development. The membership of the United Kingdom in the European Union also had a cultural effect on public officials, developing a consensual, negotiating style of administration.[3]

Australia and New Zealand took NPM forward, imbuing it with new reforms. In Australia, merit promotion and efficiency scrutiny were introduced. Australia and New Zealand also reformed NPM by making the budget performance-based and linking it to people's needs. The following public finance reforms were introduced: running costs for departments, three-year forward estimates, portfolio budgeting, allowing for the reallocation of resources and the devolution of financial management. These and other measures were taken after wide consultation and open debate. The Financial Management Improvement Programme and Programme Management and Budget were introduced by the Government of Australia to complement changes in the public service.

NPM, in its most complete form, was introduced in New Zealand. The State Sector Act and the Public Finance Act were the two pillars on which administrative reform was carried out. Permanent heads of the civil service were appointed on limited-term contracts and were given greater autonomy, including the power to hire and fire staff and determine their remuneration. Chief executives were held accountable and were required to sign performance agreements with the ministers, specifying the quantities of outputs they promised to deliver. These agreements became the basis of departmental operation plans, integrated into the budgetary and appropriation process, and a system of parliamentary accountability was thus established.[4]

A committee headed by IBM Chief Executive Basil Logan reported that many public servants felt that the Cabinet had not developed or articulated an integrated view of ultimate policy goals. This led to a strategy of drawing up budget policy statements, prepared by ministers (both individually and collectively), and linking strategic result areas (SRAs) to key result areas (KRAs) in performance agreements between chief executives of departments and ministers. The SRAs defined the objective to be achieved, while KRAs indicated the manner in which the SRAs would be achieved.

In parallel with administrative reform, financial reform took place. Accrual accounting was introduced in 1991. The Fiscal Responsibility Act enjoined the preparation of a set of accrual-based financial reports, including the budget policy statement, economic and fiscal updates for the current year and the next two years, and a fiscal strategy report for the next ten years. Financial statements included a statement of financial position (that is, a balance sheet), information about actual and potential liabilities in a statement of borrowings and a statement of contingent liabilities (both quantifiable and non-quantifiable).[5]

While the NPM system created new integrated structures, it also came under attack for failing to build in people-friendly measures. There was a feeling that outsourcing and privatisation led to public services becoming more profit-oriented than welfare-oriented. The concept of new public governance (NPG) then came into the discourse on public administration. NPG was not limited to the government and the public sector but also included social public institutions and other entities. It emphasised the dispersion of power; the government taking on a more coordinative role rather than a hands-off, autocratic one; a complex network involving the government, market, society, civil society organisations and prominent public persons; efficient resource exchange; trustworthy and stable contracts; and a focus on serving citizens and pursuing public interest.[6]

The re-emergence of New Zealand's Public Service Commission as well as the Australian Public Service Commission, along with a stronger role for the Treasury, meant greater central control. In Australia, the prime minister monitors programme delivery and progress in the Cabinet against milestones using a 'traffic light' format, which involves setting specific sub-goals over time to review progress. Australia is also making efforts to integrate outputs (direct, measurable results of smaller activities) with outcomes (broader, longer-term effects of outputs).[7]

The advent of digitalisation has resulted in quick and significant changes in the systems of governance across the world. In its early stages, NPM stressed disaggregation; however, the advent of new technology has once again led us to administrative consolidation. With the growth of the internet, email and the web, new ways of handling and presenting information have developed and paperwork has declined. Holistic reforms have also changed relationships between agencies and their clients, with traditional lines of communication no longer necessary.

In many cases, agency functions are carried out through websites that clients can directly access. One-stop clearances, end-to-end service re-engineering and procurement through electronic means have become common; transparency has improved as citizens can now monitor governmental action being taken on their requests.[8]

India's Need for Systemic Change

When I became the Cabinet Secretary of India in 2007, bringing a holistic change to the administrative system was high on my agenda. I brought into the Cabinet Secretariat Dr Prajapati Trivedi, who had done excellent work in the Central public sector. He had introduced an outcome-oriented performance system where the government and chief executives could mutually set goals, and the chief executives were given autonomy to perform their tasks. I strongly agreed with this measure because I believed that clearly set goals and the involved parties having autonomy lead to guaranteed growth. The Indian Space Research Organisation and the Bhabha Atomic Research Centre were standing monuments of success in the public space. I had a long session with the Second ARC, where I stressed the need to introduce outcome-based governance. The commissions made strong recommendations accordingly.

The results framework document system was thus introduced. It included each ministry and organisation under the Government of India, defining the annual results each ministry was to achieve, the weightage given to each result and the annual and half-yearly evaluation of these results. However, this system was never allowed to mature; it floundered and collapsed for want of political ownership by both the Manmohan Singh government and the Modi government. It was never integrated into the budget, and an incentive-based remuneration system was never introduced. Instead, technology was thought to be the answer. Now technology can be effective if a process overhaul accompanies it, but what happened here was mere translation, that is, putting existing processes on websites without any simplification. PowerPoint presentations were given too much importance as a mode of governance; training meant only online speeches addressed to bureaucrats – an experiment that Rajiv Gandhi had tried in the distant past through his 'one-week training' programme, which didn't lead to any positive results. The lateral entry of officers from the private sector was seen as another desperate solution. Still, the fact is that whoever enters the administrative system, the results will be the same unless the system itself is redesigned as an outcome-oriented one.

Having reflected for a long time on the shortcomings of our administrative system, I am inclined to believe that we will muddle along and hinder our growth unless we seriously consider the following measures:

1. Political ownership at the Central and state levels. Empowered authorities headed by the prime minister and the chief minister – lasting results are possible only if political leadership accepts and promotes outcome-based governance, as done in Australia and New Zealand.
2. Creating a Cabinet committee on administrative reform which will review progress every month.
3. Gaining all Indian states' approval to implement large-scale administrative change. For instance, even the goods and services tax (GST) became a reality through interaction between various Indian states. The NITI Aayog, which has all the chief ministers as its members, could well be turned into a vehicle for bringing about this change.
4. Studying the systems adopted by Australia and New Zealand and adapting them to India's specific requirements. The Department of Administrative Reforms and Public Grievances (DARPG) and the Commonwealth Secretariat (which has been working on this measure) could well achieve this. The objective should be clear: the creation of outcome-oriented administrative systems both at the Centre and across the states, with accompanying changes being made to the recruitment, training, performance assessment, budgeting and incentive systems.
5. Using technology to meaningfully simplify administrative processes.

6. The Cabinet Secretary and the Secretary of DARPG holding periodic meetings with state Chief Secretaries and Government of India Secretaries. This will enhance coordination between all the states.

Notes

1 R.C. Mascarenhas, 'Building an Enterprise Culture in the Public Sector: Reform of the Public Sector in Australia, Britain, and New Zealand', *Public Administration Review*, 53 (4): 319–328. Available online: https://doi.org/10.2307/977144

2 R.A. Chapman, '"The Next Steps": A Review', *Public Policy and Administration*, 3 (3): 3–10. Available online: https://doi.org/10.1177/095207678800300303

3 C. Pollit, 'Antistatist Reforms and New Administrative Directions: Public Administration in the United Kingdom', *Public Administration Review*, 56 (1): 81–87. Available online: https://doi.org/10.2307/3110058

4 R.C. Mascarenhas, 'Building an Enterprise Culture in the Public Sector: Reform of the Public Sector in Australia, Britain, and New Zealand', *Public Administration Review*, 53 (4): 319–328. Available online: https://doi.org/10.2307/977144

5 J. Pallot, 'New Public Management Reform in New Zealand: The Collective Strategy Phase', *International Public Management Journal*, 1 (1): 1–18. Available online: https://doi.org/10.1016/S1096-7494(99)80083-X

6 X. Runya et al, 'The Third Wave of Public Administration: The New Public Governance', *Canadian Social Science*, 11 (7): 11–21. Available online: http://www.cscanada.net/index.php/css/article/view/7354

7 J. Halligan, 'Reintegrating Government in Third Generation Reforms of Australia and New Zealand', *Public Policy and Administration*, 22 (2): 217–238. Available online: 10.1177/0952076707075899

8 P. Dunleavy et al., 'New Public Management Is Dead: Long Live Digital-Era Governance', *Journal of Public Administration Research and Theory*, 16 (3). Available online: 10.1093/jopart/mui057

Attitude Training: The Heart of Good Policing

Dr B. Sandhya

Introduction

A police officer who served as the convener of the new Kerala Police Act and as the first nodal officer of the Community Policing Project of Kerala (Janamaithri), I focus here on a little-discussed topic: the police attitude to social issues.

In a democracy, the police facilitate social change, earning public cooperation to enforce laws and ensuring that everyone feels the presence of democracy.

How can the police arouse such confidence among the public? How can we inculcate the democratic spirit in the members of the police force so that they will always be firm in action but polite in behaviour?

Background

Historically, the militaristic model of policing prevailed in the world. British India based its first police act (1861) on the Royal Irish Constabulary model, though Britain's Metropolitan Police Act (1829), a democratic model, was available. The police under British India had the mandate to help with revenue collection and suppress uprisings against the British regime at a low cost. Post-Independence, police organisations faced structural challenges like insufficient legal provisions. They also faced functional challenges that dehumanised their personnel, leading them to resort to third-degree methods.

Despite the recommendations of various police reform commissions, the Police Act was not modified until the Supreme Court, in the *Prakash Singh v. Union of India* case (2006), gave specific directions to carry out structural changes in the police to make it accountable to the people.

Following this, the Police Complaints Authority was set up by state governments to address complaints against the police.

In the past few decades we witnessed the increasing capacity of police leaders to appropriate and engineer reforms that were originally powered by external pressure. Community policing, problem-oriented policing, broken windows policing and pulling levers policing were driven by external sources, whereas CompStat and the newly emerged predictive policing are the brainchildren of the police themselves.[1]

Citizens' accessibility to the criminal justice system would depend upon the attitude of the police personnel towards the public. In such circumstances, inculcating the right attitudes in the police personnel is one of the most importantly mandates of any police service in a modern democratic state.

Literature Review

According to Mariena E. Henderson et al., attitude is a tool that serves to see order and consistency in what people think and do, so that given certain behaviours, predictions can be made about future behaviours.

According to Henderson et al., attitudes cannot be directly measured but must be inferred from behaviours, beliefs and other manifestations which may provide evaluators with insight into how people think and behave in consistent patterns.

Personnel with a positive attitude will be more empathetic towards customers. In 'Human Resource Development in Maharashtra Police', B.D. More recommends that refresher workshops should be arranged for all members of the force. Each participant is to complete an attitude measurement inventory at the beginning and at the end of the workshop and the data should be analysed to evaluate the modified attitudes of the participants.

Mike Cummings[2] reports that brief, friendly door-to-door visits by uniformed police officers substantially improve people's attitudes towards the police and increase their trust in law enforcement. The positive effect of the unannounced door-to-door visits was durable, as residents continued to report improved attitudes towards the police.

Engel and Worden[3] suggest that insofar as officers make discretionary choices, based on their judgements, we might expect that their decision-making behaviour would be shaped by and bear strong relationships to their occupational attitudes and values.

What we may have witnessed in the last few decades of the twentieth century was an increasing capacity of police leaders to appropriate and engineer reforms that were originally powered by external pressure. Community policing, problem-oriented policing, broken-windows policing and pulling levers policing (Weisburd and Braga 2006) can all be understood in that way, whereas CompStat and newly emerged predictive policing are the progeny of the police themselves.[4]

Alok Kumar Gupta and Geetanjali Sharma[5] recommend exhaustive, rigorous and consistent periodic training of the line and staff of all the organs and institutions of the government. The training should precede the annual increment of the personnel. Enough thought should be given to the means and mechanisms of comprehensive training so that it addresses the body, spirit and mind. The focus must be on human engineering, which will contribute to citizen-building, the key to a civilised society.

Major Hindrances in Inculcating Right Attitudes

Role of Police Perception

The historical background of the police itself is a major burden leading to an identity crisis about the role and functions of the police force. Changes in law, the establishment of various agencies like human rights commissions, police complaints authorities, women's commissions and child rights commissions are seen as a threat to police authority and as a hindrance to core police work by police personnel belonging to the school of traditional policing.

An Overburdened Police Force

Crime per lakh of population increased by 28 per cent over the last decade (2005–2015) in India. However, the state police forces had 24 per cent vacancies (about 5.5 lakh) in 2016. This means that there are only 137 police per lakh of population in India whereas the United Nations' recommended standard is 222 police per lakh of population.[6]

Occupational stressors in police work increase the risk of officer mental health morbidities. Officers' poor mental well-being is harmful to the individual and can affect professionalism, organisational effectiveness and public safety.[7]

Inadequacies of the Criminal Justice System

Trust begets trust. The nature of their job isolates the police from the public. The diabolical nature of crimes has increased. But even now, the statement recorded by the police (161 CrPC)[8] is not trustworthy for the court. Thus, the criminal justice system, of which the police is itself a part, doesn't trust the Indian police. This greatly affects the attitude of the police towards their professional duties and towards the public. The Eighth Report of the National Police Commission emphasised that the police should be sensitised about accountability to the people. Adequate mechanisms for this are unavailable.

Insufficient HRD Mechanisms

Police organisations need to be supported by robust human resources development (HRD) mechanisms. Organisational development mechanisms based on a long-term perspective plan are lacking. Career development plans for individual police personnel, job rotation and job specialisation are to be in place. There is no mechanism to identify key performance areas in individual and team development.

Insufficient Welfare Measures

A happy force with high morale would deliver more. The availability of sufficient welfare measures for police personnel and their families is important for developing the right attitude.

A sufficient number of family quarters, police housing schemes, insurance schemes, flexible timing for feeding mothers, availability of crèches, education scholarships and subsidised canteen facilities are welfare facilities generally available for most police forces. There is scope for many more welfare measures. We should have police welfare bureaus that undertake periodical studies and surveys and implement schemes as needed.

Police Subculture

The standard of expected demeanour of the police is rude and brute due to the police subculture in the traditional school of policing. The travails of ignominious servitude to those in power and apathy towards the poor continue.

Attitude Towards Marginalised Sections

Police personnel show a lack of empathy towards disadvantaged communities such as women, children, transgender individuals and senior citizens. There are several studies pointing out the discrimination and unwelcome treatment faced by women and the underprivileged at the hands of the police. The prevailing attitudes need drastic changes.

How to Develop the Right Attitudes in the Police

Qualitative Recruitment

Recruitment of educated personnel with specialised qualifications for specialised jobs has to be practised. Psychological tests (suggested by the Fifth Report of the National Police Commission) to measure attitudes would go a long way in selecting personnel with the right attitudes. The organisation itself can be transformed into a lifelong learning organisation if the right personnel of the right age are recruited and retained.

Police Training: Inculcation of Right Attitude at the Outset

As attitude is found to be the most importantly factor in determining police performance and accountability, the seeds of an appropriate attitude need to be sown in the minds of police personnel during basic training. Blended training methodologies need to be adopted so that trainees enjoy their training and imbibe the learning with an open mind. Team-building exercises and communication skills help trainees to retain the right kind of attitude until the end of their careers. State-of-the-art training equipment and modern methodologies make adult learning a cherished experience. Such a professional approach to training has been used in the Kerala Police Academy. A mentoring system helps each trainee to integrate into the system. After reaching the police station, the academy mentors continue to counsel the trainees in professional and personal dilemmas.[9]

Experience During the Covid-19 Lockdown Period: A Kerala Police Academy Study

During the period of the Covid-19 lockdown, the Kerala Police Academy became a confidant of the young trainees. Mentors reached out to trainees to ensure that each trainee fully understood the online lessons. Any deficiencies were taken care of. Online physical fitness lessons and mindfulness meditation audio sessions were administered in a structured manner to give them a positive environment amid all the chaos.

A project named 'Operation Protect the Protectors' was put in place to ensure personal hygiene, safety and health of the police personnel and their families during the Covid-19 threat period. The trainees felt that they were part of a community-oriented service organisation.[10]

In-Service Training

The Kerala Police trained all 60,000 personnel in basic hands-on cyber skills. Through the Gender Sensitisation Programme conducted by the Women's Development Corporation, the Kerala Police aims to give gender training to all its personnel.

Pre-Promotional Training

Pre-promotional training at every level prepares the police personnel to be professional and equipped to handle the new role. Hands-on training and practical experiences shared by officers and structured training materials like interactive videos, notes and role-play equip police personnel well. Technological interventions have made the pre-promotional and other in-service training courses appealing and accessible to everyone.

Specialisation and Certified Trainers

Specialisation in various police subjects is necessary. Tie-ups with Cochin University, University of Calicut and Mahatma Gandhi University are in place and police personnel have graduated in cybercrimes, forensic science, etc. Entry to the courses is made through rank-agnostic online entrance tests and paid study leave is granted for certain courses. These specialists undergo a certification process. As personnel get the opportunity to work in their area of interest, their attitude towards work improves tremendously.

Opportunity to Attend Training in Specialised Institutions

According to the needs of the department, personnel are sent to specialised institutions such as the National Security Guard and Greyhounds to pursue advanced courses. State police organisations can upgrade the skills of their officers through such courses. Training imparted by top-class specialised organisations provides great motivation and upgrades the skills of police personnel.

Upgrading the Training Infrastructure

Every police training institution needs to upgrade its infrastructure and logistics to suit changing times. E-learning capabilities, cyber forensic labs, artificial intelligence centres and other facilities give police officers opportunities to learn subjects through short courses. Training needs analysis should be ongoing and all the needed specialised skills can be imparted through structured, periodical training courses. The Bureau of Police Research and Development (BPR&D) is taking a lead role in this in India.

National-Level Systems

National-level projects like the Crime and Criminal Tracking Network System give personnel access to any police station in the country. The Dial 112 Pan-India helpline has made police response to distress calls faster and more transparent. Large states like Uttar Pradesh and Madhya Pradesh have achieved pioneering success with this system. The National Cyber Crime number, 1932, is a great resource for victims of cybercrime.

Career Planning in an Evolving Organisation

Police organisations need a perspective plan to evolve into a professional force with great organisational goals side by side with scope for personal growth. Proactivity, communication skills, etc., need to be encouraged. Individual and team growth need to complement each other. Police personnel who pass out from universities through special tie-up programmes get posted to jobs which are suitable to their newly acquired skills.

Evidence-Based Research

Evidence-based research on various aspects of policing can be undertaken by the National Police Academy and the BPR&D. Various premier universities and academic institutions, in collaboration with the state police, can also do such research. Rajasthan and Kerala have undertaken such research studies. The Kerala Police documented their experiences during the great floods of 2018 and this resulted in a book, *Mahapralayam*, published by Mathruboomi Books.

Performance Measures, Rewards and Punishments

HRD mechanisms for periodic, objective performance appraisal with feedback should be in place. A Rand Corporation study[11] provides a framework for measuring the performance of police.

Officer Conduct Measures

Evaluating the conduct of police officers is essential for understanding and improving the quality of policing. Several key indicators are commonly used to assess officer behaviour and ethical standards in the field.

Handling of Routine Incidents

A key measure of professionalism is how officers manage routine interactions such as assisting the public or conducting stops. These engagements offer insights into the officer's demeanour, communication and respectfulness. Brief, targeted surveys administered to individuals who have interacted with the police can provide valuable consumer feedback on the quality of service delivered.

Citizen Complaints

The volume and nature of citizen complaints are also important indicators. This includes the total number of complaints received, the proportion deemed valid (that is, sustained) and the percentage of cases resulting in officer discipline. These statistics, often found in annual reports of oversight or complaints agencies, reflect the department's accountability mechanisms and responsiveness to public concerns.

Officer Morale and Ethics

Internally, the level of job satisfaction and perceived ethical climate among officers is another essential dimension. Surveys conducted within the police force can give insights into leadership, integrity and workplace culture. Higher morale and a strong ethical environment often correlate with reduced misconduct and improved public-facing behaviour.

Together, these indicators present a comprehensive view of officer conduct – combining external evaluations with internal perspectives – to support evidence-based reforms, performance management and improved community trust.

Rewards and punishments need to be linked to police attitudes. Even informal appreciations are important. Judicial and media persecutions need to be dealt with professionally. Legal assistance to face profession-related legal matters needs to be institutionalised.

Community-Oriented Policing Strategy: Empowering Constabulary

The National Micro Mission for Community Policing has made an overarching model of community policing, collating good practices of various states. The Saanjh Model of Punjab Police is a successful example.

The Police Accountability Commission, appointed by the Government of Kerala and headed by Justice K.T. Thomas, recommended in 2006 that the Kerala Police should venture into community policing. The

Kerala Police started its fully government-sponsored community policing project, namely the Janamaithri Suraksha Project, in 2008. Now the project is fully functional in all police stations in Kerala.

During the great floods in Kerala in 2018, police personnel became instant heroes, reaching out quickly and saving lives as they had intimate knowledge of the local terrain and the people. 'Nowadays God appears before us in uniforms!' said a seventy-year-old woman as she was rescued from her half-submerged house.[12]

During the Covid-19 pandemic too, the police were in the forefront, serving the community and came to be seen as a friend, philosopher and guide by the people throughout India. They enforced lockdowns with minimum use of force (the Kasargod Model).[13] The uniformed personnel were often seen radiating compassion towards all of nature's creatures by helping those in distress. This was highly appreciated by the people and portrayed a police force that is positive, benevolent, humanitarian and all-embracing.

Janamaithri: The Kerala Model of Community Policing

I worked as the nodal officer for the Community Policing Project funded by the Government of Kerala for twelve years since its conceptualisation in 2007. It became evident that the attitude of beat officers who got an opportunity to work responsibly among the community they policed changed tremendously.

This project was adopted with firm conviction and clarity about the philosophy of community policing. To achieve the basic objectives of policing in a democratic society, the law-abiding public and the law enforcement agency must cooperate. In a democracy, by definition, laws are created by the people, for the people. It follows that there is no logical justification for conflict between the public and the police, the chief law enforcement agency. On the other hand, there is every justification, if not compulsion, for active cooperation and collaboration between the police and the public by promoting police–public partnerships in achieving the most fundamental objectives of policing. Society as a whole stands to gain by this. Perhaps the only possible losers are the individuals who break the law and the police who have mala fide motives.

Methodology of Implementation

An important step towards the introduction and implementation of community policing in the jurisdiction of a police station is the formation of a people's committee which represents all major social segments and stakeholders. This committee is constituted after careful scrutiny and selection. Special care is taken to ensure that the local administration, such as municipalities or panchayats, residents' associations, non-governmental organisations, senior citizens, weaker sections, educationists and sociocultural organisations are represented. The main consideration in the selection is that the person should be known for responsible citizenship and social commitment and can devote adequate time to this work. Obviously, nobody with any taint of involvement in a criminal offence is inducted. Nobody is either included or excluded merely on the basis of political affiliation. The selection is approved by the district police chief based on recommendations by the station house officer and scrutiny by supervisory officers. The committee will ordinarily have about twenty-five members.

Beat Patrolling

Beat patrolling is the most crucial activity in the implementation of the community policing project in Kerala. If beat patrolling fails, every other activity for implementing the project is bound to fail. Most other activities are either directly or indirectly connected with the activities of the beat officer. The professional competence, dedication and commitment of the beat officer have to be very high.

Beat officers are imparted intensive training on various aspects of community policing, including professional skills and behavioural competencies.

The uniqueness of the Kerala model of community policing lies in the house-to-house visits of beat officers. This empowers the beat officers with the information and trust of the citizens of the community. In many instances, the mere visit of the beat officers has prevented violence against bedridden women and children, domestic violence against housewives and ill-treatment of children leading to delinquency later on. Some school dropouts resumed education after the intervention of beat officers. Timely information from housewives led to the prevention of crimes like robberies and theft. These are all living examples of how crime prevention happens through Janamaithri. The traditional concept that crime can be prevented only by running after and shooting criminals is being broken.

In the Kasaragod district, women's self-help groups were formed under the auspices of Janamaithri. The members belong to various communities, some of whom had suffered severely during communal riots. The women learned jewellery making, bridal make-up, painting, embroidery, etc., and they make a living out of the trade they have learned. Above all, the opportunity to work together fostered communal harmony. They work in groups of two or three and in each group there are members of different communities. In 2021 Hosdurg Beach witnessed a communal flare-up with massive loss of property. Following that, the Janamaithri Police, the district administration, the local MLA and the local municipal chairperson worked together, and they started using only the white 'Janamaithri flags' for all types of functions and processions in the locality. Communal harmony was re-established.

The community policing strategy was included in the new Kerala Police Act, 2011, with sections 64 and 65 outlining key features of community policing functioning, the role of each person, the beat system, responsibilities of each committee, etc.

Empowering Police Stations and Modernising Systems

The Ministry of Home Affairs initiates police modernisation projects from time to time. Financial awards for such projects may be linked to police station improvements, constabulary empowerment and gender equity.

Systems like a Digital Control Room and GPS-fitted patrol vehicles duly supported by robust technology help the police to reach out in time. This gives a sense of pride and thus the right attitude is created.

Periodic Job Evaluation, Social Auditing

Policing is risky and all-encompassing. Commensurate salaries and allowances need to be recommended by pay commissions. Once such mechanisms ensure adequate pay and compensation, their performance needs to be subjected to periodical social auditing. This would motivate personnel to maintain the right attitude.[14]

Improving Attitude Towards Weaker Sections

Gender budgeting, special legal provisions to protect the Scheduled Castes and Scheduled Tribes, juvenile police units, etc., have improved the attitude of the police towards disadvantaged groups.

Women have received attention as victims of crime. As Karmen[15] indicates, this has resulted from the move from crime prevention towards victimisation prevention within the criminal justice policy.

Gender sensitisation training needs to be given to all police personnel. A gender policy covering all genders, including transgender individuals, needs to be in place.

According to Nancy Foy[16] the presence of women is needed in organisations trying to shift from power and control towards networks, cooperation and empowered employees. Women are good at sharing information as well as power. It has frequently been suggested that only when women make up at least 25 per cent of an organisation's total workforce will men's conceptions of what policing is about, why they became police officers, etc., change. The Government of India's policy that at least 33 per cent of the police force shall consist of women will go a long way in achieving the right attitude of the police force towards women.

Future Challenges

Recruiting educated and skilled personnel with the right attitudes through modern methods is crucial for police organisations.

The nature of cybercrimes, economic crimes involving cryptocurrencies and darknet drug sales is making a vast difference in policing. Crimes are becoming complex and hydra-headed. The nature of police duties is changing and diversifying. To cope with ever-increasing burdens, the police need to decentralise and function efficiently. They also need to network with sister organisations nationally and globally. The work which could be delegated to artificial intelligence, algorithm-based predictions and private agencies needs to be identified and delegated. Force-multiplying equipment like CCTVs or digital applications needs to be employed so that core work can be done by police personnel who are emotionally stable and technologically empowered.

Conclusion

The future of the police force as an organisation lies in the police personnel learning to be amicable and being as close to the people as possible, for which an attitudinal change of both the police personnel and the public is necessary. The police must modify their appearance from a 'low emotional quotient' and apathetic organisation to a people-centric, empathetic, innovative organisation that delivers quality service.

For this, it is important to inculcate the right attitudes from the time of basic training and to continue with periodic pre-promotional and in-service training. The mental and physical fitness of personnel must be maintained throughout their careers so that the spirit of policing is maintained.

Empowerment of the constabulary and the rank-agnostic specialisation of police officers are critical in developing the right attitudes and enabling effective policing. Modernisation of police forces should aim at making the job of police personnel in police stations more interesting and smoother, which in turn makes the police easily accessible to the public. Women need to be a critical mass in the police forces to ensure gender justice. Representation of all sections of society in the force is also needed for inclusiveness in policing.

Adequate welfare measures covering police personnel and their family members are required to maintain a police force with high morale. Police leadership needs to focus on timely recruitment and development of infrastructure and tap the advantages of advancements in technology. A sensitised police force can be developed only by mentoring the right attitudes by a sensitised police leadership.

A police force which can think globally and act locally to the satisfaction and confidence of the citizens and which can protect all sections of society from serious crimes would be an effective police force with the right attitude towards the needs of lawful citizens.

Notes

1 David Weisburd and Anthony A. Braga (eds), *Police Innovation: Contrasting Perspectives* (Cambridge: Cambridge University Press, 2006) and S.D. Mastrofski and J.J. Willis, 'Police Organization Continuity and Change: Into the Twenty-First Century', *Crime and Justice*, 39 (1): 55–144. Available online: https://www.jstor.org/stable/10.1086/653046?seq=1

2 M. Cummings, 'Study Finds Community-Oriented Policing Improves Attitudes Toward Police', *YaleNews*, 16 September 2019. Available online: https://news.yale.edu/2019/09/16/study-finds-community-oriented-policing-improves-attitudes-toward-police

3 Robin S. Engel and Robert E. Worden, 'Police Officers' Attitudes, Behavior, and Supervisory Influences: An Analysis of Problem Solving', *Criminology*, 41 (1): 131–136. Available online: https://www.researchgate.net/publication/227663546_Police_officers'_attitudes_behavior_and_supervisory_influences_An_analysis_of_problem_solving

4 Lucy Mason, review of *Police Innovation: Contrasting Perspectives* by David Weisburd and Anthony A. Braga (eds), in *Policing: A Journal of Policy and Practice*, 1 (2): 245–247. Available online: https://academic.oup.com/policing/article-abstract/1/2/245/1567082

5 Alok Kumar Gupta and Geetanjali Sharma, 'Indian Police: Crisis of Credibility', *The Indian Journal of Political Science*, 73 (2): 299–310. Available online: https://www.jstor.org/stable/41856592

6 A. Chaturvedi, 'Police Reforms in India', PRS India, June 2017. Available online: https://prsindia.org/files/policy/policy_analytical_reports/Police%20Reforms%20in%20India.pdf

7 Amit Purba and Evangelis Demou, 'The Relationship Between Organisational Stressors and Mental Well-being Within Police Officers: A Systematic Review', *BMC Public Health*, 19 (1): 1286. Available online: https://link.springer.com/article/10.1186/s12889-019-7609-0

8 T. Clarke, 'Students Prove Trust Begets Trust', *Nature*, 2003. Available online: https://doi.org/10.1038/news030310-8

9 B. Sandhya, 'Behavioural Health of the Police Personnel: Breaking the Silence', *SVP National Police Academy Journal*, 66 (2): 1–10. Available online: https://www.svpnpa.gov.in/static/gallery/docs/b803b77994b04b57a20621b921a620c3.pdf

10 'Kerala: Paramedic Cops Team Up for Covid-19 Fight', *Times of India*, 28 April 2020. Available online: https://timesofindia.indiatimes.com/city/thiruvananthapuram/paramedic-cops-team-up-for-covid-fight/articleshow/75415061.cms

11 Rand Centre on Quality Policing: https://www.rand.org/search.html?query=title:(quality%20 policing) &is Advanced=true)

12 B. Sandhya, 'Role of Community Policing in Responding to Natural Disaster – A Study Based on Kerala Floods – 2018', *SVP National Police Academy Journal*, LXVIII (2): 1–40. Available online: https://www.svpnpa.gov.in/static/gallery/docs/00424f409dab4e1d8833b654875a0bbc.pdf

13 T.K.V. Kumar, 'Role of Police in Preventing the Spread of COVID-19 Through Social Distancing, Quarantine and Lockdown: An Evidence-based Comparison of Outcomes Across Two Districts', *International Journal of Police Science and Management*, 23 (2): 196–207. Available online: https://doi.org/10.1177/14613557211004624 (original work published 2021) and A. Kyprianides et al., 'Policing the COVID-19 Pandemic: Police Officer Well-Being and Commitment to Democratic Modes of Policing', *Policing and Society*, 32 (4): 504–521. Available online: https://doi.org/10.1080/10439463.2021.1916492

14 *India Today*, 24 April 2020. Available online: https://www.indiatoday.in/india-today-insight/story/the-kasargod-model-1670735-2020-04-24; see also *India Today*, 27 April 2020. Available online: https://www.indiatoday.in/india-today-insight/story/kerala-s-heroes- in- khaki-1671804-2020-04-27

15 A. Karmen, *Crime Victims: An Introduction to Victimology* (Pacific Grove: Brooks/Cole Publishing Company, 2014.

16 Nancy Foy, *Empowering People at Work* (London: Gower Publishing Limited, 1994).

Giving Forests a Voice: Kerala's Initiatives in Making Forestry Responsive, Relevant and Real

Dr Bransdon Corrie

Introduction

Forests are humanity's home. They are nature's lifelines – providers of clean air, fresh water and a host of other ecosystem goods and services. Forests are also reservoirs of biodiversity. They provide stability and sustainability to our world. Without forests, there can be no life on earth. Yet forests are the first casualty in humankind's quest for development. Humankind chops the very branch on which it sits.

B.N. Kirpal, chairman of the National Forestry Commission, 2006, observed that 'Forests have neither voice nor votes and, therefore, one acid test of good governance should be the government's handling of forests and wildlife of doing the right thing for the nation'.[1]

To give forests a voice, foresters and society must alter their perceptions of forests. They should not be viewed as mere resources to exploit, but as a legacy to pass down to our children so that we secure their future. This is possible through sound stewardship and innovative approaches.

Kerala's Forests: A Natural Treasure, the Nation's Pride

Kerala's forests comprise thirteen distinct forest types, ranging from wet evergreen to dry deciduous. These forests are part of the Western Ghats – a global biodiversity hotspot and home to exceptional ecosystems like shola-grasslands, Myristica swamps and mangroves.

The interesting forest types are:

1. Tropical evergreen forests, which have high species diversity and are home to major animal species – the lion-tailed macaque (*Macaca silenus*), the Nilgiri langur (*Semnopithecus johnii*), the giant squirrel (*Ratufa macroura*), the tiger (*Panthera tigris*) and the elephant (*Elephas maximus*).

2. Shola-grassland ecosystems, which are a climatic climax vegetation comprising stunted evergreen tree growth. They are home to the Nilgiri tahr (*Nilgiritragus hylocrius*), and these forests are montane temperate.
3. Mangroves, aptly christened the 'rainforests of the sea', which are highly productive ecosystems, protecting the shoreline and offering a natural nursery for marine species. The mangroves are salt tolerant, and some species exhibiting 'vivipary' have seedlings that grow on the mother plant and then fall off and take root on the ground.
4. Wetlands, which offer a habitat for many bird species.
5. The Myristica swamps.

More than 1,200 endemic plant species thrive in Kerala's forests, alongside the iconic animals mentioned above. Kerala is home to two UNESCO biosphere reserves – Nilgiri and Agasthyamalai – and nineteen World Heritage sites that are located in the Western Ghats. These accolades are not merely symbolic; they reflect a deep, institutionalised commitment to conservation.

A unique cultural contribution to this ecological legacy is the Kerala homestead model, a decentralised and deeply sustainable system where each household cultivates a biodiverse micro-ecosystem. Fruit trees, timber species and medicinal herbs grow alongside crops, supported by on-site water harvesting (ponds or wells) and organic waste composting pits. This ecosystem provides a home to a wide variety of fauna, including reptiles, birds, butterflies and dragonflies. This model creates agro-ecological balance and food security at scale. However, urbanisation and vertical housing threaten this heritage, displacing backyard biodiversity and human–wildlife coexistence.

Kerala has a large population of captive elephants and a long history of elephants associated with culture and religion.

What Makes Kerala a Unique Place for Foresters?

Kerala's uniqueness lies not only in its forests but also in its people, institutions and culture. Literacy levels are among the highest in India. Public awareness of environmental issues is robust. An aware citizen is a conservationist's delight and can vote for forests. Citizen activism – from the Silent Valley Movement to localised actions, be it wildlife rescues or the protection of special habitats and trees on public lands – is Kerala's hallmark.

Forest personnel are intelligent, innovative and willing to go the extra mile. It is easy to explain to them new concepts and programmes and be confident that what has been explained will be correctly understood and implemented. Support for progressive, innovative schemes thus becomes easy.

Importantly, Kerala's democratic ethos allows foresters to innovate, enforce law without fear or favour and engage with civil society. The political leadership is environment-sensitive, the media acts as a watchdog, the judiciary is known to stand tall for environmental justice and the citizen is ever-alert to report any illegal act. For a forest officer, such an enabling environment is a powerful force multiplier.

From Timber to Ecosystems: The Evolution of Forest Management

Indian forestry has transitioned from a colonial, timber-centric model to one that embraces ecosystem services, biodiversity and climate resilience. All forests are managed based on the forest working plans in territorial forests and wildlife management plans in protected (wildlife) areas. The working plans are based on the National Working Plan Code. The National Working Plan Code 2023 has enriched the quality of the working plans tremendously; it integrates, among other things, sustainability indicators and participatory tools. Forest management now includes hydrological restoration, climate adaptation and community-driven planning. Scientific institutions like the Wildlife Institute of India support protected area management with field-based ecological data. The result is a paradigm shift: forests are no longer mere resources – they are dynamic, living systems to be co-managed with people.

Key Inputs That Gave Forests a Voice

My efforts to give forests a voice drew largely from:

1. Experience in human resource management and wildlife conservation

2. Studying appropriate managerial tools in consultation with professors from management schools in India and abroad
3. Advances in forestry sciences
4. Experiential learning through the Fulbright Indo-American Environmental Leadership Fellowship
5. Emerging technologies

Creating an Enabling Environment for Personnel

A motivated workforce is central to sound forest governance. For the first time, motivational courses were conducted in the Kerala Forest Department. The feedback from personnel was that it was the first time they had been valued and appreciated.

To follow up words with action, personnel were provided with a fair work environment where promotions were prompt and their personal grievances were settled in a time-bound manner.

A code of ethics was formulated and circulated to encourage professional pride. Its voluntary adoption and adherence were intended to put an end to groupism, anonymous petition writing, gossiping and other negative activities to reduce workplace toxicity.

An aesthetic work environment boosts productivity and morale. Therefore, Smart Saturday was introduced – a weekly exercise for decluttering files, repairing facilities and sharing learning.

Professionalising the Service

We moved away from transactional routines and promoted systems thinking in forestry through the following measures:

1. A 'service to citizen charter' was introduced to create a mindset focusing on a service culture. Each officer had the charter placed in his line of sight, which carried a photo of Mahatma Gandhi with the words:

    Serving the citizen is my prime duty.
    All I do today must benefit the citizen.
    I shall greet the citizen with a warm smile.
    I shall politely and speedily respond to all requests.

I shall offer the citizen the finest service.
I will do so with Pride, Enthusiasm and Dignity.

2. A Teak standard for mobile phone usage and for interacting with citizens was formulated and shared.
3. To help each staff member align with the department's goals, a vision, mission and individual purpose statement was formulated and shared with all. Kerala forests aim to be a world-class organisation where professional foresters work in a fair, respectful and vibrant environment, exhibiting sensitivity and responsiveness to citizen needs, performing to their full potential and delivering amazing results.
4. To keep track of one's progress and to encourage staff members to perform to their full potential, a personal action plan (PAP) was formulated and introduced at training programmes and at the unit level. The PAP is a self-assessment, goal-setting and monitoring tool maintained by individual officers to track their own progress.
5. A far-reaching mindset change involved encouraging personnel to transcend silos – treating wildlife, territorial and social forestry as part of one interconnected mission.
6. The use of planning tools – annual work plans and monthly and quarterly calendars – was incorporated in the form of a forest planner.
7. Forest management focused on the removal of invasive species, assisting natural regeneration and habitat improvement. Protected areas saw initiatives in wildlife monitoring, human settlement relocation and eco-development programmes. Outside forests, mangrove restoration, urban greening, school planting drives and homestead sapling distribution expanded our footprint.
8. The success of the North American model of conservation – hunting drives conservation – rests on its robust inventory and monitoring protocols. Drawing from this, I introduced beat-level multi-species inventory and monitoring of habitat and species. This is the first of its kind in the country, where personnel are encouraged to look at natality, mortality and population dynamics. All this is essential to address matters related to human–wildlife coexistence.

9. Technology was used to improve performance through:
   i. The development of the forest management information system
   ii. The introduction of video conferencing
   iii. Digital platforms for bookings, grievance redressal, biometric attendance, e-auctions, document tracking, storage of data, field capture of data and service-to-citizen initiatives streamlined governance and service delivery
   iv. The SARPA app, which provides citizens a facility whereby they can report the presence of a snake in their surroundings and have a trained person arrive at the scene and rescue it
   v. A real-time compensation mechanism that ensures rapid payouts for crop and livestock loss
   vi. Beat-level data collection that enabled hotspot mapping and seasonal prediction, aiding mitigation strategies

Building Citizen Awareness

Public awareness is the cornerstone of conservation. Outreach programmes were given top priority through the Forest Information Bureau and the other wings of the department.

The public was provided with facilities to enjoy the wilderness through the protected area network and ecotourism destinations. Sensitisation of citizens was undertaken at these destinations. Students and citizens were provided with the Nature Camp programme, which was quite popular. Ecotourism was expanded with interpretation centres, trails and lodging options across forest divisions. These were platforms to immerse citizens in forest experiences. Joint forest management committees such as van suraksha samitis (VSSs) and eco-development committees (EDCs) were engaged to run these programmes, ensuring income and ecological ownership among locals.

Various international days were celebrated. The Environment Day celebration has evolved as a flagship programme, with full participation by school children. This is a popular programme among the children and has helped instil in them a love for plants. Children take seedlings home and nurture them, with the family getting involved in the activity of nurturing. Two heartwarming incidents reveal that this programme has touched the hearts of not only the children but the entire family. In one case, the planted seedling was destroyed by rats and the little boy wanted the same seedling. The father drove forty kilometres to the forest nursery to get it. It was not available, but an officer arranged for it from another nursery and sent it to the boy's house. In another incident during evaluation, the evaluators found the grandparent watering the plant. The grandparent said that after seeing the child's enthusiasm for watering the plant before going to school and after returning home, he started watering it at noon.

Fillers for the visual media, poster campaigns, photo exhibitions, forestry clubs, exhibitions, films and school outreach programmes were designed to bring many into the fold.

At the heart of the outreach programmes is building an ecological ethic, particularly among children.

Here is a lesson-learning experience at the Eravikulam National Park. A visitor from Ernakulam drove up in his swanky car, pulled out his last cigarette and threw the empty pack to the ground, only to be told by the park's student volunteer, 'Sir, we don't do this here.' The lesson was instantaneous and electrifying. The visitor said, 'Sorry, son, won't do it again,' as he bent down, picked up the empty pack and placed it in the bin. He had learned the lesson of his life, so powerfully delivered that it makes one realise that students are the best teachers. An informed student can reinforce forest values more effectively than enforcement.

Deepening Citizen Collaboration

Kerala institutionalised participatory forestry long before it became a national trend. Village-level VSSs and EDCs received micro-planning training using participatory rural appraisal tools. These were not token consultations; they informed budget allocations and operational targets.

Flagship community collaborations included the following:

1. Sea turtle conservation in coastal villages, where volunteer groups were supported to protect turtle eggs and ensure their hatching and safe release into the sea.

2. Sparrow nesting projects in traditional marketplaces. With the advent of supermarkets, sparrows lost their habitats. In this project, we focused on traditional marketplaces where, along with the help of headload workers of the market or other interested persons, nesting boxes were installed and monitored for nesting.
3. The Kerala Bird Atlas, the first state-level atlas in Asia, involving more than a thousand citizen scientists, was undertaken with support from the Kerala Forest Department.

The Periyar Foundation, India's first government-NGO for forest management, became a reality when I was heading the wildlife wing. It provided the framework for a replicable model. It channelled tourism revenue into conservation and employed tribal communities for park operations, balancing equity and ecology. For the model's continued success, proper monitoring and mature leadership are essential.

Planning for Human–Wildlife Coexistence

We share this planet with a host of other species, each having the right to its share of resources. In nature, a delicate balance exists. However, in the case of humankind, this balance is upset because on the one hand we have conquered disease to a large extent and on the other hand there is this large spectre of greed. In fact, instead of conflict, the better term is coexistence. As habitats shrink, coexistence becomes challenging. Kerala has adopted an evolving approach that combines rapid response with proactive coexistence planning.

Ultimately, the goal is to shift from reactive conflict management to coexistence frameworks rooted in ecological planning and community dialogue.

Legislative and Policy Support

Progressive laws form the scaffolding of Kerala's forestry success. The Ecologically Fragile Lands Act and the Preservation of Trees Act strengthened forest cover outside traditional reserves. Rules on tree felling on private lands and elephant welfare reflect Kerala's nuanced understanding of ecological complexity and human–animal relationships.

Challenges That Continue to Challenge

The first – and the greatest – challenge is to institutionalise initiatives that are steeped in sound science, as they evaporate upon officers' transfers, resulting in the loss of institutional memory. The second challenge is to rein in negative elements. They form vested interest groups and prevent the smooth implementation of reforms which can help address a major issue the department faces: human–wildlife coexistence. Decision-makers must be able to identify these elements, as they are uncanny and will point out the good apples as bad apples so that the bad apples continue to hold sway. If we successfully address these challenges, we can, indeed, have forests forever.

Conclusion: A Call to the Future Generation

Kerala's forestry journey is not just a case study in administration; it is a moral narrative. It tells of men and women who chose difficult paths, who turned down expedient gains for long-term ecological truths and who found joy in service to the land.

We did not merely administer forests; we stood up for them, spoke up for them and fought for them. Now the baton passes to a new generation of foresters. To them, we offer this simple counsel:

1. Let your science be rigorous – but let it be rooted in compassion.
2. Let your policy be pragmatic – but let it be shaped by people's needs.
3. Let your leadership be strategic – but let it be defined by integrity.

Because forests cannot have a voice without you. And it is only through you that forests can be heard.

The Great Hornbill (Buceros bicornis), the state bird of Kerala. Hornbills are monogamous. The female nests in a tree hollow and seals the opening. During the nesting period, the female moults and the male feeds her, as can be seen in the picture.

Notes

1 *Wildlife First v. Union of India*, Writ Petition No. 109, Volume 2, 2008. Available online: https://cjp.org.in/wp-content/uploads/2019/07/Writ-Petition-Vol.2-in-Wildlife-First-vs.-UOI.pdf (accessed 28 November 2025).

The Mullaperiyar Dam: A Ticking Water-Bomb?

K.J. Alphons

As a Kerala bureaucrat turned politician, with experience as an IAS officer in the Kerala cadre, a member of the Legislative Assembly in Kerala, a member of Parliament in the Rajya Sabha and an independent minister in the Central government, I occasionally spend sleepless nights over the fate of the Mullaperiyar Dam.

The Mullaperiyar Dam, which was conceptualised by John Pennycuick, a British Army engineer, was commissioned in 1895. Located in Kerala, it is owned and operated by Tamil Nadu through a lease agreement executed between the Maharaja of Travancore and the British government in 1886. A supplementary agreement was executed in 1970, authorising the production of electricity.

Constructed before the age of steel and concrete, it is made of surkhi, the traditional building material which is a mixture of lime, jaggery and egg white. Not a gram of steel or cement was used, and it cannot be considered secure by any stretch of the imagination. If the dam breaches, it could potentially kill 3.5 million people in Kerala, wash away many towns (including Kochi and Ernakulam) and deprive 10 million people of water in 5 districts of Tamil Nadu, besides also leading to the desertification of 2,50,000 acres of fertile cultivated land in Tamil Nadu.

Kerala has often raised the issue of the dam's stability with the government of Tamil Nadu and the Centre since the dam turned more than a century old, proposing the construction of a new dam.

For close to fifty years, Kerala has been negotiating with Tamil Nadu to construct a new downstream dam below the existing Mullaperiyar Dam. Representatives of Kerala and Tamil Nadu tentatively agreed on the location of the proposed dam during a joint inspection held on 20 December 1979.

Within months, the Government of India also got involved, and a meeting was held on 29 April 1980 between the chairman of the Central Water Commission (CWC) and senior officials from both states. This meeting discussed short-term, medium-term and long-term measures.

I think this is where Kerala was taken for a ride by the CWC and Tamil Nadu. Tamil Nadu and the CWC were talking about the long-term strengthening of the old dam and awarding the work to a contractor. Though Kerala protested, its voice was drowned. From that moment, the entire focus shifted to permanently strengthening the existing dam, and Tamil Nadu ensured that the idea of a new dam remained moribund. After the dam was strengthened in the 1980s, Tamil Nadu torpedoed any effort by Kerala to raise the issue of constructing a new dam, arguing that the strengthened dam was safe enough. The CWC approved the design for strengthening the dam and stated that the reconstructed dam could hold 152 feet full reservoir level (FRL) of water.

Kerala continued to resist raising the FRL beyond 136 feet. Various parties filed petitions before the Kerala High Court and the Madras High Court on the issue. The Mullaperiyar Environmental Protection Forum directly approached the Supreme Court through a writ petition. While considering the petition in 2000, the Supreme Court transferred to itself all petitions pending before the Kerala High Court and the Madras High Court. The principal petitioner's prayer was that the lease agreements of 1886 and 1970 be declared null and void.

After hearing arguments on both sides, the Supreme Court ruled on 27 February 2006: 'Regarding the issue as to the safety of the dam with the water level being raised to 142 ft from the present level of 136 ft, the various reports have examined the safety angle in depth, including the viewpoint of earthquake resistance. The apprehensions have been found to be baseless.'[1] It observed that even if the dam were to break, the downstream Idukki Dam could hold the surging waters. Further, it allowed the FRL to be raised to 142 feet.

Kerala's Irresolute Step

Within three weeks of the Supreme Court judgement, the Kerala State Legislature amended the Kerala Irrigation and Water Conservation

Act, 2003, through the Kerala Irrigation and Water Conservation (Amendment) Act, 2006. Notably, in the Second Schedule appended to the 2006 Amendment Act, the Mullaperiyar Dam, owned and maintained by Tamil Nadu, was included as 'Item No. 1', where the height of the FRL was fixed at 136 feet mean sea level (MSL). As a member of the Kerala Legislative Assembly, I had argued that the legislation was deeply flawed, as the right thing to do was to decommission the dam if it was a threat to life and property.

Immediately thereafter, Tamil Nadu filed Suit No. OS 3/2006 (under Article 131 of the Constitution) against Kerala in the Supreme Court. It contended that the legislation was a 'device to defy, obstruct, and nullify the judgment of this Court'.[2] The case was heard initially by a three-judge bench in 2006 and was then shifted to a five-judge constitutional bench in 2009. An empowered committee (EC) was appointed by the Court in 2010 to look into the safety aspects. The EC examined the dam's hydraulic safety, structural safety and seismic safety and concluded in 2012 that the dam was safe in all three aspects. Kerala strongly challenged the EC's findings.

The Court heard arguments from all sides and concluded in 2014:

> 2006 (Amendment) Act plainly seeks to nullify the judgment of this Court, which is constitutionally impermissible. Moreover, it is not disputed by Kerala that 2006 (Amendment) Act is not a validation enactment. Since the impugned law is not a validating law, it is not required to inquire whether, in making the validation, the legislature has removed the defect that the Court has found in the existing law. The 2006 (Amendment) Act, in its application to and effect on the Mullaperiyar dam, is a legislation other than substantially legislative, as it aimed at nullifying the prior and authoritative decision of this Court. The nub of the infringement consists of Kerala legislators revising the final judgement of this Court in utter disregard of the constitutional principle that the revision of such final judgement must remain exclusively within the discretion of this Court … Where a dispute between two States has already been adjudicated upon by this Court, which is empowered to deal with, any unilateral law enacted by one of the parties that results in overturning the final judgement is bad, not because it is affected by the principle of res judicata, but because

> it infringes the doctrine of separation of powers and rule of law. As by such a law, the legislature has clearly usurped the judicial power.[3]

Regarding the dam's safety, the Court ruled:

> We do not find any merit in the objections of Kerala challenging the findings and conclusions of the EC on hydraulic safety, structural safety, and seismic safety of the dam. The findings of EC with an elaborate analysis of reports of investigation, tests and studies lead to one and only conclusion: that there is no change in the circumstances necessitating a departure from the earlier findings on the safety of Mullaperiyar dam given by this Court in the 2006 judgment.[4]

There seems to be a silver lining for Kerala in the 2014 judgement. It is in the nature of an observation by the Court, akin to an obiter dictum, in paragraph 149:

> It is true that the safety of [a] dam is an aspect which can change from time to time in different circumstances but then the circumstances have to be shown on which it becomes necessary to make departure from the earlier finding[s]. It is always open to any of the parties to approach the Court and apply for re-assessing the safety aspect … If the circumstances have changed which necessitates a re-look on the aspect of safety, the Court itself may exercise its discretion to reopen such [a] case…[5]

However, the Court ruled that there were no substantial changes between the 2006 and 2014 judgements. If any interested party can prove that there are significant changes between 2014 and now, the Court might be open to hearing a fresh round of litigation.

I tend to agree with the findings of the Court except on the issue of the dam's safety. The Supreme Court relied solely on the EC's report. Out of the five members of the committee, three, including the chairman, were former judges of the Supreme Court. In fact, the chairman was a former Chief Justice of India. Even though the other two members were technical experts, they must have looked upon the Supreme Court judges in great awe. Having been in public life for more than forty-five years, I know exactly how the other two members would have felt in the presence of their lordships. It can be scary. Even if the technical members were competent in their fields of specialisation, did either of them have any expertise on surkhi dams? I do not see anything on record to show that they knew anything about surkhi dams. Neither of these members would have been part of a team that built or maintained a surkhi dam. Nothing is on record to show that they visited any major surkhi dams anywhere in the world. India does not have any other surkhi dams with a comparable capacity. Mullaperiyar is the largest surkhi dam in India. The second largest surkhi dam in India, Tungabhadra, was constructed only in 1970. A Google search did not throw up evidence of surkhi dams anywhere else in the world.

The Dam Can't Go On Forever

I do not know if Google is correct, but one thing I know for sure: everything in this world has a life expectancy. Human beings, including Supreme Court judges, die. Similarly, a dam has a limited lifetime. A 130-year-old surkhi dam, without a gram of steel or cement in its core, can never be deemed 100 per cent safe forever. It will break down at some point in time. Nobody can authoritatively say when, but it *will* happen. It certainly will not last for 999 years, which is the tenure of the lease. Article 21 of the Constitution of India guarantees citizens the right to life. Is it a 25 per cent, 50 per cent, 75 per cent, 90 per cent or a 99 per cent guarantee? The EC had no 100 per cent guarantee that the dam was fully safe. The right to life guaranteed by the Constitution to a citizen is unlimited – a 100 per cent right. Imagine when the right to life of not just 1 citizen but of 3.4 million people is at stake! It is possible that vested interests completely misled the EC. There is a strong belief in Kerala that there are things beyond what meets the eye – perhaps in this instance, that is probably true.

The Supreme Court has graciously left one loophole open for further litigation: if circumstances changed, either party could approach the Court. Circumstances have changed dramatically since the 2014 judgement. Due to global warming, rainfall patterns have greatly changed. Some locations in India have received over 500 per cent of excess rain within twenty-four hours, with some places also having received more than 1000 per cent of excess rain within twenty-four hours. This is all documented.[6] What happens if the catchment area of the Mullaperiyar Dam receives 500 per cent excess rain in twenty-four hours? The dam will breach even with a much less excess rain. In 2018, the entire state of Kerala experienced abnormally excessive rains, with many places going underwater. If the Mullaperiyar Dam, with a live storage of 15 TMC (thousand million cubic feet), breaches, the water will inevitably flow into the Idukki Dam, with a capacity of merely 70 TMC. There is no doubt that the Idukki Dam will not be able to hold the overflow from the Mullaperiyar Dam.

The 2014 judgement regarding the Idukki Dam's capacity to hold water, in case the Mullaperiyar Dam breaches, was based on data from the 2006 judgement. This makes the judgement rather fallacious. Global warming has drastically affected the intensity of rainfall during the past decade, and there is plenty of available data to prove this. The Supreme Court might be open to the idea of a fresh litigation based on this data.

Almost 3.5 million people in central Kerala go to bed every day in fear that the Mullaperiyar Dam will break. And if it does breach, most parts of the Idukki, Kottayam, Alappuzha, Pathanamthitta, Ernakulam and Thrissur districts will get washed away. It will be the biggest man-made tragedy in the world, and I will hold the Supreme Court wholly responsible. When there was a simple solution to the problem, which was agreed upon by both parties (Kerala and Tamil Nadu) as early as 1979, why is the Supreme Court so adamant about not constructing a new dam? It is playing around with not just a few lives but those of millions – it is going to be a massacre if the Mullaperiyar Dam breaks.

I do not think that the way forward is through litigation, even though the Supreme Court has kept the route open. I believe that an amicable settlement is favourable and even possible, as the dam breach will be tragic for both states. I made an impassioned plea in Parliament, urging the people of Tamil Nadu to save Kerala. I told them that Kerala had lost the Supreme Court case and that we had no hope of survival unless the people of Tamil Nadu looked at the issue dispassionately. I also reminded them that 3.5 million Malayalees will die if the dam were to break. But it does not end there: over 8 million Tamilians will also die of water starvation in 5 districts of Tamil Nadu.

The New Dam Imperative

The solution is pretty simple: construct a new dam. Who will bear the cost is something that can be decided through dialogue. Among my suggestions in Parliament was that Kerala should unilaterally decide to provide the dam's water to Tamil Nadu for free, since Kerala is getting only ₹2.4 lakh a year as rent anyway. This annual amount is peanuts and should thus be done away with. I also suggested that the levy on electricity produced, that is 0.8 paisa per unit, should also be dispensed with, since Kerala receives only ₹10 lakh or so a year on this account. Kerala could also give up its right to fish in the dam, as they have hardly caught any fish from it since 1970. I am sure that Kerala's government and its people will agree with me, as the right to life is more importantly than any financial benefit. What is the point of getting money, and that too peanuts, if we won't be alive?

Kerala has plenty of water that flows into the sea, not being used by anyone. As India is one and since we all believe in the philosophy of Vasudhaiva Kutumbakam (the world being one family), let us be magnanimous and give Tamil Nadu free water and electricity. It will benefit 8 million people in the state.

Let Kerala and Tamil Nadu start a dialogue. However, there is a hitch here: Tamil Nadu does not believe Kerala when it says that the terms of the 1970 agreement will continue to hold after the new dam is constructed. Perhaps Tamil Nadu would agree if it got a guarantee from the Government of India to this effect. A tripartite agreement could be signed, reiterating all the concessions. After all, the Mullaperiyar Dam's water and electricity are critical to the existence of millions in Tamil Nadu. This calls for urgent action from the Government of India too. I hope the prime minister will personally intervene and solve this long-pending issue in his inimitable manner.

Notes

1 *State of Tamil Nadu v. State of Kerala & Anr* (2014) 12 SCC 696 (Supreme Court of India). Available online: https://indiankanoon.org/doc/41744252/ (accessed 26 September 2025).

2 Ibid.

3 Ibid.

4 Ibid.
5 Ibid.
6 'U'khand Records 369% Excess Rainfall in 24 hrs, Red Alert for 4 Dists', *Times of India*, 30 August 2025, Available online: https://timesofindia.indiatimes.com/city/dehradun/ukhand-records-369-excess-rainfall-in-24-hrs-red-alert-for-4-dists/articleshow/123589032.cms (accessed 22 November 2025).

Kerala's Trade Unions: Some Hard Truths and the Way Forward

E.K. Bharat Bhushan

THE TERM 'TRADE UNION' evokes strong reactions of varying kinds in Kerala. The working class, owing their allegiance to organised trade unions, view them as true champions of labour emancipation and brave soldiers beating back the dark forces of capitalism. People on the other side of the spectrum see them as irresponsible disruptors of production who will not hesitate to resort to violence with little provocation. Both these divergent views may be correct in part. Collective bargaining has ensured that wages in the state are the highest in the country, with government after government taking a benevolent view of their assertive zeal. On the other hand, they have more or less driven all large enterprises out of the state with unviable demands and threats of industrial action, sending educated young men and women looking for employment elsewhere.

The first trade union to be established in Kerala was the Travancore Labour Association in 1922, which mobilised workers of a coir factory in Alleppey (now Alappuzha). It quickly developed into a body that represented the workers in the entire sector. It provided succour to thousands of workers during the Great Depression. Politicisation grew with their numbers, along with a willingness to resort to direct action in pursuit of their demands. The first general strike that crippled the sector took place in 1938. And in the 1940s and 1950s the movement shifted its allegiance entirely to the Communist Party of India. Then onward the communists have been the dominant force in the labour movement in Kerala.

I was a student at one of the city colleges of Trivandrum (now Thiruvananthapuram) in the 1970s and had a ringside view of the tempestuous politics of the time. Combative politics mixed with extremist elements made a combustible combination. Student unions, taking a leaf out of their political cousins, were a restive lot, with strikes called for issues ranging from local disputes to international conflicts. These frequent shutdowns had a profound impact on public life. It was as if every group was waiting for the opportunity to cause maximum distress to the people. Examination time was the chosen time for Electricity Board unions to go on strike. And when we, outstation students, were ready to go home for vacation and the general public also wanted to travel, Kerala State Road Transport Corporation (KSRTC) unions would go on strike. I have horrid memories of waiting in line for train tickets, with queues extending to a mile or more. The only cry heard in those days was of the 'avakasam' (right) of the workers. With the government ever ready to acquiesce in their caprices, the strikes would invariably end in a 'historic victory' for the strikers. The Emergency, grossly misused by the party in power in other spheres, brought a period of lull to this macabre circus but the organised unions were back with increased vigour once it ended.

I entered the civil service in 1979 and was posted to Malappuram in 1981. One of my frequent duties was to chair conciliation meetings to resolve strikes by timber unions in Nilambur, which used to cripple the entire hill region. The unions were directly allied to various political parties and had no difficulty in enlisting support from the faction-ridden polity of those days. They would invariably block the interstate highway and so generous was the government of that time that it was left to my lot to urge upon these hooligans the virtues of good behaviour. To recall, the government had issued strict orders that the police should not interfere in labour disputes, and I managed most of these situations with hope in my heart and a prayer on my lips. Later I came into a head-on collision with the ruling party's trade union when I was assigned the task of saving the State Film Development Corporation. This public sector undertaking (PSU) owned the magnificent and unique Chitranjali Studio, the first composite film production facility in India. But it was in dire straits when K. Karunakaran, then chief minister, sought my services. Not a single film had been fully made there till then as no producer was ready to put their fortune in the hands of the rebellious unions which professed loyalty to various political parties. With the unstinted support of the chief minister, I set about restoring order, and in the succeeding two years thirty-two feature films were made entirely at Chitranjali. These included some classics of the Malayalam film genre. I am told those were the only two years in which the company made profits.

In my next assignment after collectorship, I met with unqualified failure. The Plantation Corporation of Kerala (PCK), which I came to helm as managing director, was saddled with a board of directors consisting entirely of trade union representatives except for the two government nominees. It was a full-fledged battle with the chairman, a senior leader of the ruling coalition, who was constantly interfering in day-to-day administration. He countermanded my orders to transfer managers to take charge of our estates (where they should have been working in the first place). For my part I countermanded his orders and the charade ended with my transfer. The large estates of the PCK lapsed back to the tenuous charge of senior tappers and the managers went back to twiddle their thumbs at the headquarters. I will never forget my meeting with V.V. Raghavan, minister for agriculture, when I took leave of him. A most amiable and splendid individual, he was sorry to see me go but was helpless to remedy matters.

After my return from the US on completing the Mason Program, I was posted as managing director of Kerala Minerals and Metals Ltd (KMML), the largest PSU under the Industries Department. It also accounted for the largest losses and had already been referred to the Board for Industrial and Financial Reconstruction (BIFR) for restructuring. Set up in Chavara, home to some political bigwigs and a multitude of unions, nothing seemed right in the company. Rank indiscipline, subsidies amounting to crores of rupees and outright malfeasance pointed to an imminent end. Innovative marketing efforts targeting units in tier-2 and tier-3 cities that helped sell off unsold stocks, ensuring accountability at all levels and some old-fashioned stubbornness led to the company making its first-ever profits in the two years that followed and getting out of the BIFR dragnet. As a reward, I had to face the anger of the union leaders who found their control slipping away. There were threats aplenty and even an urgent motion in the assembly, which was moved by an MLA who headed a minuscule union, seeking my removal.

An embarrassed minister, P.K. Kunhalikutty, moved me to Travancore Titanium Products (TTP) as chairman and managing director. If

KMML was a slippery slope, TTP was a snake pit. Forty-eight unions prospered in the company, which had a monopoly over TiO2 production through the sulphate route. Naturally the unit was running at a profit, but the moot question was why the profits were not ten times bigger. Some of the best officers of our cadre had to pay the price for asking this question. Personnel claiming to be office-bearers of one union or the other loitered around, making a nuisance of themselves. Discipline was non-existent and any move to enforce it was too dangerous to attempt. Change was impossible through discussion and finally had to be achieved through stealth. An order was obtained from the high court to conduct a referendum and derecognise all unions except those that had support from 20 per cent of their workforce. Only three unions succeeded in retaining recognition. The forty-five others, which included those of my minister's party, were declared illegal and their office-bearers were asked to report for work. The company scaled new heights in production and sales. But life became particularly difficult for me. All kinds of anonymous or pseudonymous petitions against me flooded the Secretariat, alleging misdemeanours of just about every kind. On the positive side I brought to an end a constant conflict between TTP and the people of the locality, thereby getting them to agree to build a wall on the seashore separating our land from theirs, an attempt abandoned more than a decade ago amid mob violence. A rational and cost-friendly proposal was moved as a permanent solution to the ever-festering pollution problem. It is a different matter that later one of my successors burnt his fingers trying to take it forward.

White-collar workers in government offices were so well organised into unions that they were free to indulge in all kinds of work disruptions. The Secretariat itself was no exception. Each time a government came to power after elections, the unions supporting the parties in power did as they pleased. They packed all the chosen departments with their own and chased their rivals away to distant posts. Their leaders took up vantage positions as Private Secretaries to ministers. Neither the Secretary of the concerned department nor the Chief Secretary had any say when it came to promotions and postings. For their favourites, promotions came automatically and often. I have seen instances of Under Secretaries becoming Deputy Secretaries in the morning and going on to become Joint Secretaries in the afternoon, casting technicalities like the completion of probation to the wind. With promotion being delinked from performance and no fear of punishment, getting work out of staff has become a matter of luck for the Administrative Secretary. With multiple staff unions and associations present in every government organisation, they have come to possess veto power almost over every aspect of their organisation's operations. Reforms in the educational sector cannot be considered until they are approved by the teachers' unions. You can forget about health reforms unless they have the stamp of approval of the doctors' union. No improvements in the transport sector will come about unless the KSRTC unions are brought on board. The poor consumer is often the only party who does not have a say in matters that directly impact them.

If the organised unions hold the public in the industrial sector at their mercy, their colleagues in other spheres are no better. Unviable wages and uncertainties of the market have ensured that land under agriculture has come down year after year. Unabashed extortionate behaviour, exemplified by practices like 'nokkukooli' (by which headload workers insist on payment while doing no work), is an aberration one can see only in Kerala. Successive government diktats against such practices have mostly remained on paper.

The gloomy picture that I have given above has been mostly drawn from my own experience as a bureaucrat and a citizen. But that is not how the initial leaders had conceived the development and growth of trade unions. The labour legislation of the earlier part of the twentieth century was indeed trend-setting rule-making of the most progressive kind. Given the oppression and penury faced by the workers, the leaders of the movement were true men and women of destiny who devised solutions for the ills of those days. They were instrumental in society getting over the prejudices of class and caste that were the bane of those times. They also ensured the growth of a democratic system, which ensured that the people who worked at the grassroots had a say over the direction the movement took.

This contributed to several pathbreaking legislative measures, such as the adoption of the Kerala Land Reforms Act. The close link between political parties and trade unions made these possible.

Unfortunately, this useful relationship developed to a pernicious level as time progressed. Trade union captains grew into political leaders, and the latter started treating trade unions as foot soldiers in their political battles. The welfare of the sector or its stakeholders became less and less important to the leaders' scheme of things as they climbed the steps of political power. Trade unions like the Centre of Indian Trade Unions, All India Trade Union Congress and Indian National Trade Union Congress became willing pawns in the hands of their political masters. Even in the same union, regions and units came to be parcelled out to individual leaders who held sway as unopposed satraps. The marriage between trade unions and political parties became complete when some union leaders changed hats and became ministers making policy and, when out of power, went back to the unions which they 'owned'. This had a deleterious effect on all sectors, including industries. Labour Department officials, armed with jurisdictional powers to arbitrate trade disputes, became silent accomplices to the high-handedness of the unions since they knew that the leader sitting opposite was a former or a future labour minister.

Fortunately, the malaise of political trade unions has not infected information technology and other knowledge industries. But they are also prey to hartals and unscheduled shutdowns called by political parties, which are disastrous for units doing business with overseas principals. I have no doubt that the uncertainties about our labour behaviour are the primary reason for large industries ignoring our state when almost every major company in the world is making a beeline to other South Indian states.

Perhaps the solution lies in the people of the state realising the harm the multiplicity of unions and their threatening postures are causing to our state. At last the intelligentsia, other than those enjoying political patronage, and the powerful media have started throwing light on the pernicious cost that the myriad trade unions are forcing us to pay. The state government is also slowly veering towards the view that remedial measures are necessary, although no leader of consequence would dare to publicly call for more responsible behaviour from trade unions. To check the multiplicity of unions in one sector, competing for members with exaggerated demands, legislation like the Kerala Recognition of Trade Unions Act, with accompanying Rules, was adopted. The Act called for periodic referendums in both private and public enterprises.

Realisation is slowly dawning on all that the present structure and outlook of trade unions are those of a bygone era and that sweeping changes are necessary, taking into account the changes in the nature of work and the increasing role of the informal sector. As for the PSUs in the state, one cannot remain oblivious to the fact that most of them are huge drains on the state's perilous finances. The nature of the public sector itself has undergone profound changes in the national sphere and no amount of outdated ideology can resuscitate our state-owned enterprises, many of which subsist only for the workers and their unions.

However, a word of caution is called for here. One can see that nationally labour laws are slowly being modified in favour of capital. This is by no means an entirely desirable outcome. The fragmented trade union movement and the political parties that look on unions as mere vote banks are in no position to challenge this inexorable development. Growing unemployment, the decline faced by traditional industries, loss of investor confidence, worsening wage relativities and even the re-emergence of the moribund contract system are all huge challenges. The time has come for setting up a meeting ground for saving industries in the state and for building trade unions cutting across political and ideological compartments.

Part 2

Perspectives on Development

Kerala's Development Perspectives

Joy Vazhayil

'DEVELOPMENT' IS A TERM subject to mixed interpretations. Looking at it from the angle of traditional welfare economics, it signifies mere economic development represented in terms of economic growth. The Nobel laureate Amartya Sen challenged this traditional approach, advocating and promoting the capability approach towards human development.

Sen's approach brought into focus the human development index (HDI) and the multidimensional poverty index (MPI) in the discourses on development. Even though neoclassical economics continues to be a critical factor in these discourses, it is apparent that the growth of the gross domestic product (GDP) alone is meaningless unless accompanied by social policies for the redistribution of wealth, as reflected in low Gini coefficients.

Now, it is more or less accepted that economic development without corresponding human development is mere empty rhetoric. Therefore, the focus has shifted to the quality of life for all, achieved through inclusive policies and sustainable development, and ensuring intergenerational equity in the use of natural resources. Another important aspect of social development is in terms of the human happiness that a society is able to achieve. This depends on several factors like social support, equality and freedom, which may not appeal to the competitive spirits of market forces.

Surely, all these considerations are important when we examine the strategic development pathways of a state like Kerala, which has been – and remains – a preferred setting for experiments relating to democracy as well as development. Because Kerala has been at the forefront of such experiments, it has generated a lot of interest in the past due to the insights afforded by its experience at the phenomenon of social transformation. This chapter surveys the salient features of Kerala's development to chart the future course of development in similarly placed societies.

The idea of Kerala's model of development was highlighted during the 1990s, when scholars like Amartya Sen lauded Kerala's approach to development as innovative and worthy of emulation by developing economies. This was when the state had achieved HDIs comparable to some of the developed countries, despite having a low per capita income (PCI).

A Unique Leapfrogging

Kerala has a unique development story, as it leapfrogged from a predominantly agrarian economy to a service-based economy without passing through the intermediate stage of industrialisation. In 2022–2023, Kerala's service sector contributed about 64 per cent to its gross state domestic product (GSDP)[1] – a departure from the traditional developmental trajectory, which starts with agricultural growth, progresses towards industrial growth and eventually towards the service sector's growth. Perhaps this has been facilitated by foreign remittances. Despite low industrialisation, today Kerala has reached the fifth and final stage of high mass consumption as per Rostow's take-off model of growth.

Three Aspects of Kerala's Development

If we look at Kerala's experiences since its formation in 1956 from a developmental perspective, we can identify three distinct phases, each lasting for roughly thirty years. (We must also keep in mind that demographically a period of twenty to thirty years represents an entire generation.) Kerala's development narrative during the first tri-decade (from 1956 to 1986) after its formation has been summed up in terms of radical reforms by some analysts, when growth took place despite the PCI remaining low. This phase started with the introduction of substantive land reforms and ended with the advancement and empowerment of local self-governance institutions. Sandwiched between them were reforms for the effective public distribution of food, an inclusive public healthcare system, universal school education and total literacy. These reforms paved the way for laying the foundation of sustainable development in the state. Social reforms for the eradication of the disastrous effects of the caste system and the improvement of gender equality continued simultaneously. During this period, the Gulf region was the key destination for skilled workers from Kerala, and so foreign remittances started contributing substantially to the state's development efforts by the end of this phase.

The early 1990s heralded the era of globalisation and liberalisation in India. Kerala was ready with a literate and skilled population to participate in this transformation. However, the non-availability of a large extent of land and the radical nature of collective bargaining during the first developmental phase acted as deterrents to industrialisation. With high population density and a skilled workforce, Kerala sought and provided manpower to the world across many sectors, including health and education. During this period, the Malayalee diaspora spread to all parts of the world, establishing its presence globally. The state's per capita income increased substantially during this phase, transforming it into one of the five high-income states of the country. Though Kerala's HDI was high even during its first phase of development, it scaled even greater heights in the subsequent phase due to being coupled with higher incomes. The infrastructural development of the state also took on a faster pace, which helped in the development of Kerala's tourism, leading to a virtuous cycle of growth. Kerala's natural endowments, coupled with its rich culture, hospitality and stability, provided an ecosystem in which the tourism sector thrived and became a key sector of Kerala's development.

Environmental concerns during this phase led to public initiatives on biodiversity, afforestation and agricultural land preservation. The state continued its emphasis on sustainable development through the continuous improvement of HDIs. As a result, the live birth rate started declining towards the end of this phase (by 2010). However, Kerala could benefit only partially from the information technology (IT) and higher education revolutions that swept through the South Indian states due to certain ideological prejudices.

Kerala Maintains Its Zigzag Trajectory

The unique nature of Kerala's development journey continues further during the present tri-decade (starting in 2016). During this period, Kerala has been focusing on infrastructural and industrial growth in knowledge industries. For the last four years, it has consecutively occupied the top position among Indian states in sustainable development indicators.[2] This is the result of the development philosophy followed by the state since its inception. As per the National Energy Trilemma Index 2022, Kerala is the top Indian state in terms of managing energy needs to achieve energy security, energy sustainability and energy equity.[3] It also ranks highest among Indian states in terms of several human development and quality of life indicators.[4]

Let us now examine the future course of action the state needs to pursue to achieve a PCI comparable to that of developed countries, with a better quality of life for all citizens, especially its burgeoning elderly population.

During the current third phase of development, the growth strategy being pursued by the state aims to bridge the gap in industrial development by establishing knowledge-based industries. This may help correct the earlier lack of industrial development and make the economy more sustainable. The creation of employment opportunities for the educated youth has assumed utmost importance, for which the policy imperatives need to shift focus from the appeasement of interest groups (political or religious), which breed inefficiency in the system, to the implementation of policy prescriptions dictated by unequivocal public interest at large.

Given the environmental imperatives, the thrust is on advanced technologies like biotechnology, nanotechnology, biomedical devices, computing and IT. The state's focus is on developing a knowledge economy and building a knowledge society. While the former is aimed at increasing the PCI, the latter has the potential to transform society to an advanced level scientifically, socially, culturally and technologically. Sustainable development focusing on employment and livelihood needs to be taken to the next level too.

Brain Drain

The improvement of higher education and skill enhancement should be critical areas of attention for Kerala. The exodus of Malayalee students to foreign countries in search of high-quality education underlines this need. Universities and other centres of excellence in the state would need to gear up to face the challenge of making Kerala a knowledge society. Simultaneously, the industrial sector needs to focus on a quantum leap in knowledge-based industries to provide jobs to the qualified and aspiring youth. If a comprehensive strategy to achieve these objectives is worked out and pursued by Kerala during the current tri-decade, the state will choreograph new histories in its development saga, initiated since its inception, to become a developed egalitarian society with a high happiness index. However, this would require Kerala's organisations – representing various interest groups and ideologies – to arrive at a consensus and follow a common development paradigm. The time has come for an objective focus on policies of wider public interest and for simultaneously reducing the influence of ever-expanding pressure groups with myopic outlooks and perspectives.

Notes

1 'Kerala Budget Analysis 2024-25', PRS Legislative Research, 5 February 2024. Available online: https://prsindia.org/budgets/states/kerala-budget-analysis-2024-25 (accessed 8 September 2025).

2 'Kerala Retains Top Spot in the Latest SDG India Index Rankings', *The Hindu*, 13 July 2024. Available online: https://www.thehindu.com/news/national/kerala/kerala-retains-top-spot-in-the-latest-sdg-india-index-rankings/article68400190.ece (accessed 8 September 2025).

3 'National Energy Trilemma Index 2022', World Energy Council India, 2022. Available online: https://wecindia.in/downloads/WECI-National%20Energy%20Trilemma%20Index%202022.pdf (accessed 8 September 2025).

4 'List of Indian States and Union Territories by Human Development Index', Wikipedia. Available at: https://en.wikipedia.org/wiki/List_of_Indian_states_and_union_territories_by_Human_Development_Index (accessed on 8 September 2025). Kerala ranks at number 2 with an HDI of 0.758.

God's Own Country Goes to Town: The Growing Pains of India's First Urban State

P. Joy Oommen

'It's so green!' is the predominant sentiment of visitors to Kerala. The evergreen tropical forests of the Western Ghats with large plantations of tea, coffee and cardamom on its slopes and valleys, the midlands with dense teak and rubber plantations, endless rows of coconut trees on the long coastal belt, fruit trees interspersed with pepper vines and ornamental plants and shrubs in the homesteads, all leave a green imprint on their minds. Along with Himachal Pradesh, Uttarakhand, Jammu and Kashmir, and some Northeastern states, Kerala is a major tourist destination for its enticing physical features and year-round green appeal. Yet it differs from the other states in that it rapidly moved on from its 'rural' status to become the most urban among the large states of the country. Let us track that story.

Seeking Greener Pastures

Life in Kerala till some years ago was hardly the idyll that it may appear to a visitor to the state today. In the pre-Independence days, with no flood control or irrigation schemes in place, floods and famines regularly ravaged the lives of landless labourers and marginal farmers, who formed the bulk of Kerala's rural population. Central Travancore was particularly vulnerable, as people depended on paddy cultivation, which in turn was influenced by the vagaries of the weather. The net returns available to sharecroppers were, in most years, barely adequate for their survival. Some of them had their own small homesteads but had no land of their own for farming. Famines were frequent and hunger rampant.

Meanwhile, the forward-looking rulers of the princely state of Travancore had not only set up schools and colleges in major towns but also allowed 'Missions' and churches to run schools in interior areas, sparking a yearning for education across classes and castes. Many children walked long distances, crossing streams and rivers, to reach their schools. Education helped a few from rural areas to find jobs in towns and many others to reflect on their lives of poverty, deprivation and caste discrimination. Many of them had also been hearing from traders and, more reliably, from some Christian priests that vast areas of land were available at dirt-cheap prices in the Malabar district of the Madras Presidency and that the families which had reached those areas earlier had become big landowners, with their children studying in colleges in Madras. These tales sparked in them a burning desire to break free from their miserable lives and try their luck in Malabar. Getting some land of their own was an irresistible attraction. They abandoned or left behind their modest homes to the care of relatives and boarded trains and buses to towns in the Malabar region, from where they walked many more miles with their families and household belongings to reach their final destinations. A good part of the land on offer in Malabar was hitherto uncultivated land or forests in the possession of local janmis, or big landlords, who happily parted with the lands, earning them no returns for some ready cash. Life was hard for the new settlers, and many of them succumbed to malaria, snakebites and attacks by wild animals.[1] Yet they fought on, and stories of their hard work, courage and relative prosperity inspired many more families from Travancore's villages to migrate to the Malabar area. In the 1940s and 1950s, over half a million people from Central Travancore districts reached various corners of Malabar.[2]

Red Star Over a New State

The new state of Kerala came into existence in 1956, with the merger of the Madras Presidency's Malabar and Kasaragod districts with the Travancore–Cochin state, bringing all Malayalam-speaking regions together. The rapid spread of education in these areas after India's independence inevitably led to people gaining greater exposure to political and social movements within and outside the country. The world communist movement caught the imagination of not just peasants and workers but also of writers, poets, artists and students. In the first elections to the state assembly in 1957, the Communist Party of India scored a sensational victory. Since then, communist parties have become entrenched in the state and have wielded considerable influence on economic and policy issues. Changes in land tenure laws to give 'land to the tiller' and confer land titles on sharecroppers and homestead occupants throughout the state heralded not just a change in agrarian relations but also a social revolution that empowered thousands of rural families. New regulations on admission procedures and teacher recruitment in private schools and colleges, along with a salary reimbursement facility for the teaching staff, helped increase the enrolment of students from economically weaker sections in educational institutions. The healthcare sector also saw impressive growth, with many hospitals and clinics being set up by charitable/religious trusts or private practitioners. Higher investments by the government in the health sector, with special attention given to community health, sped up the demographic transition that the state was already undergoing.

The outlook for the industrial sector, however, had been bleak since the early 1960s. Traditional industries like coir and cashew processing were among the earliest to face industrial unrest in the state. Handloom and beedi-making units as well as brick kilns and tile-manufacturing units in the northern districts were the next to be affected.

The eventual closure of many of these traditional industries had a traumatic impact on the state's economic and social development.[3] The decline of inland water transport boats for the movement of people and goods to and from these traditional industries adversely affected the prosperity of port towns like Kollam, Alappuzha, Beypore and Kannur. Militant trade union activities, resistance to technological upgrades, supply-chain bottlenecks, government control over the bulk supply of raw materials and the reluctance or inability of farmers and entrepreneurs to invest in their lands/industrial units were factors that contributed to the state's economic decline in the 1970s.[4]

Golden Lights of Distant Shores

For many Keralites, the Malabar migration had normalised adventurous migration to any place within or outside the country as a means of coping with adversity. While their educational attainments kept increasing, employment opportunities in the state were falling steadily. This triggered a new wave of migration by educated and skilled youth to the big cities of the country – Madras (present-day Chennai), Bombay (present-day Mumbai), Calcutta (present-day Kolkata) and Delhi – and to industrial towns like Bhilai, Rourkela and Ranchi. In fact, sensational accounts of youngsters running away from their homes in the middle of the night to board trains to Madras and Bombay were the 'breaking stories' in the tea shops of Kerala's villages during the 1960s and early 1970s.

Meanwhile, stories of rich 'Persia-returned adventurers' or those who had found jobs in countries of the Persian Gulf (later, Arabian Gulf) region had also started trickling down. Trained nurses (all women in those days) were the pioneers. Other experienced and skilled professionals, like accountants, stenographers and technicians, were also able to get visas for countries like Kuwait, Bahrain and Oman. It, however, took a decade more for a breakthrough to happen. Looking back, it is difficult to believe that an 'oil boom' in the Arabian Gulf countries in the 1970s would lead to a dramatic turn in the fortunes of a distant, tiny state of India. Those with some experience in the construction sector, technicians, nurses, stenographers and accountants were among the first to find their way to new destinations like Dubai, Abu Dhabi, Qatar and Saudi Arabia. Indeed, luck favoured many of them, with the new jobs fetching them salaries unimaginable for similar jobs anywhere in India. If the remittances from the Gulf countries were just a trickle until the end of the 1980s, they became a steady stream in the 1990s and a flood in the early years of the new century. These remittances initially led to a high demand for consumer durables and gold, but a good part of the remittances moved to the construction sector as well. A new house, preferably the largest in the village – or at least bigger than those of their neighbours – became the dream of many who had grown up in modest, thatched homes. Other family members back in Kerala were helped financially to set up new business ventures. Liberal spending by these non-resident Indian (NRI) account holders helped existing local businesses and new ventures. Shops selling groceries, readymade garments, gold ornaments, and restaurants, garages and workshops sprang up even in remote corners of the state. Later, hotels, resorts and homestays became popular investment avenues. Indeed, the great escape to the Gulf changed Kerala's spatial, economic and cultural landscape forever.[5] In recent years, the USA, Canada, Australia and Germany have become popular destinations for those with higher educational qualifications like doctors, information technology (IT) professionals, engineers and scientists.

Many Hues of an Urban State

Those who had kept track of the rapid social and economic changes taking place in Kerala would no doubt have sensed a powerful undercurrent of urbanisation sweeping the length and breadth of the state. For others, Census 2011 revealed a surprising reality. The data showed that the urban population of the state had shot up from 25.96 per cent in 2001 to 47.72 per cent in 2011 – an unprecedented growth of 92 per cent over the decade.[6] This catapulted Kerala's position in the list of large, urbanised states of India from 11th to 2nd, marginally behind Tamil Nadu (which had 48.45 per cent of its population classified as urban). Demographers and economists had been waiting to see if Census 2021 would confirm those trends. Though Census 2021 was postponed on account of Covid-19, we have some credible data in the 'Population Projections for India and States 2011–2036' published by the National Population Commission.[7] The projected percentage of the urban population of Kerala for 2025 is 88 per cent, conclusively confirming it as the most urban among the major states of the country. Tamil Nadu is the only other state that has crossed the 50 per cent mark, with 54 per cent of its population projected to be living in urban areas in 2025.

Demographers are hard-pressed to explain the dramatic pace of urbanisation taking place in Kerala. Some believe that the definition of 'urban area' in the Census 2011 was largely responsible for this change.[8] More charitable explanations highlight the relentless growth of Kerala as a state of shopkeepers and food vendors in recent years, fuelled by the continuous flow of remittances from abroad. More significantly, it is now known that the contribution of non-agricultural sectors to Kerala's gross domestic product has crossed the 90 per cent mark.[9] The belated but robust blooming of the IT sector in the state and the steady growth of tourism have stirred growth impulses not only in cities or towns but also in rural areas. Overall, however, it is not so much a case of urbanisation happening in the state because of migration to urban centres. It is rather a case of Kerala's cities' suburbs and larger villages themselves qualifying as 'urban' according to the definition in the Census 2011. In fact, the Census 2011 showed the emergence of 461 new census towns in the state. Many geographers describe Kerala as a rural–urban continuum, with rural areas seamlessly connected to urban areas physically, economically and culturally.

The Skies Are Turning Grey

Connectivity has all along been the magic that enabled Kerala's urban areas to retain their quaint looks and liveable environment compared to other cities in India. Many who work in the cities and towns have continued to stay in their homes in nearby villages or towns and commute to their workplaces. This has helped to moderate congestion, rental rates and pollution from wastewater and solid waste. However, in recent years, the boom in the retail trade, hospitality and construction sectors has thrown up new challenges, and local authorities appear ill-prepared to handle them. Kerala's cities have performed poorly in both centralised and decentralised waste management. A devastating fire in a large landfill near Kochi in 2023, which enveloped the entire city and adjoining areas for many days with black and toxic fumes, forced state and local officials to sit up and consider more scientific options for managing the problem.

Kerala's dispersed but high-density settlements, combined with a large road network, make it an ideal state to have an effective and efficient bus-based public transportation system. However, successive governments have succumbed to populism and pressures from trade unions, which has led to a grossly inadequate number of buses on the roads. In absolute terms, the number of buses on Kerala's roads has dropped significantly over the years.[8] Tired of long travel hours and unreliable and inadequate bus services, Keralites have purchased personal vehicles in large numbers, leading to ever-increasing traffic snarls, air pollution and road accidents. It is time for the state government to make policy changes to revive public transport. A step it can consider is establishing a regulatory authority for public transport with the power to fix fares for both state-owned and private operators.

Green vs Brown: Better Use of Land Resources

The steady rise in land prices in the state, in both urban and rural areas, has become a matter of concern, especially for low- and middle-income families. Since government-owned vacant lands are scarce, it has also become impossible for the government to find land for infrastructural development or large projects.

In this context, we cannot ignore the irony of having large areas of erstwhile paddy farmlands lying idle in the state, yielding no economic returns to their owners but which cannot, under the Kerala Conservation of Paddy Land and Wetland Act, 2008, be converted for any other use, including the cultivation of crops other than paddy. The state government has, in recent years, attempted to give some relief to the landowners but has faced opposition from political parties and environmentalists.

Most farmers in the state have moved away from paddy cultivation, which they consider unviable. Coercing them to restart rice cultivation is unlikely to work. The best bet probably is to incentivise the cultivation of special or traditional rice varieties of the state and support it with a reliable procurement plan. Otherwise, the farmers should be allowed to use the land for horticulture, vegetable cultivation, and dairy and poultry farming. These lands, due to staying fallow for indefinite periods, get filled with weeds and waste and become breeding grounds for mosquitoes and other pests. One model that can be followed for the development of these fallow paddy lands would be the land pooling scheme or town development scheme, effectively used by government agencies in Gujarat and Maharashtra to get the willing cooperation of the landowners in developing physical and social infrastructure. In Kerala, even smaller towns or panchayat areas could adopt such schemes for the construction of stadia, parks, bus stations, parking lots and public offices while also helping the landowners, who could retain a part of the developed land for their use or sell it for approved uses.

Building Blues

Kerala has an enviable record in housing in terms of the total housing stock and the quality of houses. In recent years, there has been an outcry over thousands of these new houses staying vacant and locked when many people in the state are struggling to find land at reasonable prices to build homes.[10] Many others talk about difficulties in getting rented accommodation. Most homeowners, especially NRIs, are not confident about renting their houses as they foresee problems in getting the houses vacated later. A more equitable and easier-to-enforce rental law can make a difference to this 'deadlock' and induce confidence in the homeowners to rent out their properties when they are abroad for lengthy periods.

Another flawed policy followed by successive state governments, which has impeded better utilisation of the built-up properties, is the high rates of stamp duty and registration charges on property transactions in the state. Many houses that are currently vacant or locked may find buyers who would prefer to buy old houses instead of building new ones. Premises of many sick industrial and commercial ventures – in financial distress and unable to generate profits – could also be bought by new entrepreneurs, who will thereby save time and effort in starting their ventures.

Kerala as the New 'Gulf'

The large-scale migration of educated and skilled Keralites to other parts of India and the world has had an impact on the state's labour market. Estimates by official agencies put the total number of migrants from Kerala at 8 million, out of which 5 million are to other countries.

The construction sector was the first to feel the pinch, with large numbers of experienced masons, carpenters and electricians having moved to other states or countries. Wage levels in Kerala, estimated at three to four times those in other states of the country, made it easy to attract skilled and semi-skilled workers from other states of India.[11] Carpenters and masons from the eastern states of the country were the pioneers in reaching Kerala. The good word about the working conditions in Kerala appears to have spread, and many more workers from other states have poured in. The number of migrant workers in Kerala is currently estimated at 2.5 to 3 million.[12] Most of these workers are happily adjusted to life and work in the state and send substantial savings to relatives back home. Kerala has become to these migrant labourers what the Gulf countries were to the migrant workers from

Kerala some years earlier. In the process, they are also contributing to the growth of Kerala's secondary and tertiary sectors.

An Urban Fairytale With a Happy Ending?

What do we make of this story of a strip of land called Kerala, caught between the imposing Western Ghats, with its fragile slopes and large, dark and mystery-filled forests on the east, and a brooding, temperamental Arabian Sea constantly nibbling away at its shores on the west? Or of its restless and intrepid people, who refused to be boxed into their tiny homesteads surrounded by lakes or rivers, rocky cliffs or dense forests, and broke free to reach for the skies? Together, this land and its people have catapulted Kerala to the top of the heap among the states of India. Kerala has emerged as the state with the best human development index, which is the most literate (and e-literate), has the highest road density, the lowest levels of poverty and is the most urbanised too. Kerala is the best in many other development indicators as well.

There are, at the same time, many concerns about the sustainability of these achievements. The rising levels of unemployment, especially among its educated youth, and the falling standards of higher education have put a question mark on the economic future of the state. Rising levels of crime and drug abuse have instilled a sense of insecurity in the minds of the people. The negative impact of climate change in the form of torrential rains, landslides and floods on the one hand and heatwaves in the summer months on the other has been unsettling. The continued dependence of the state's economy on remittances from abroad, rising debt levels of the government and the excessive politicisation of everyday life are all reasons for worry. There is concern too about the steady environmental degradation taking place.

These problems, however, are not insurmountable. Better governance at the municipal and panchayat levels can make a world of difference to the quality of life in existing and new urban settlements in the state. Kerala's civil society has an enviable record in times of natural calamities and disease outbreaks. Many voluntary bodies, charitable trusts and women's groups too have shown their resourcefulness and capabilities in times of crisis. If the state government could ensure better coordination among these organisations and government departments, a breakthrough is possible in areas like waste management, energy conservation, community evaluation of healthcare and educational institutions, and the management of cultural and recreational events. At the state government level, there is an urgent need to cut wasteful expenditure and find resources for strengthening infrastructure and public transport. It is high time to review unproductive and populist schemes and free up resources for more effective programmes that would contribute to public welfare. As India's first urbanised large state, Kerala has the potential to become an economic powerhouse that generates employment opportunities and fosters creativity and innovation. Kerala's civil society and its government cannot afford to let this opportunity slip away if their beautiful state is to stay green and vibrant.

Notes

1 V. Thottekad, *Malabar Kudiyettam* (Thiruvananthapuram: Kerala Bhasha Institute, 2014).

2 P.K. Viswanathan, 'Farmer Migration and Agrarian Transformation in Kerala: Impacts on the Local Economy, Society and the Agrarian Landscape in the Erstwhile Malabar Region', Discussion Paper No. 43, National Research Programme on Plantation Development (NRPPD), Centre for Development Studies, Thiruvananthapuram, 2015. Available online: https://cds.edu/wp-content/uploads/2021/02/NRPPD43_Viswanathan.pdf (accessed 10 September 2025).

3 K.K. George, 'Kerala Economy: Growth, Structure, Strength and Weakness', Working Paper No. 25, Centre for Socio-economic & Environmental Studies (CSES), Ernakulam, April 2011. Available online: https://csesindia.org/wp-content/uploads/2020/08/KERALA-ECONOMY-GROWTH-STRUCTURE-STRENGTH-AND-WEAKNESS-1.pdf (accessed 10 September 2025).

4 B.A. Prakash, *Fifty Years of Kerala's Economy (1956-2006): Development Issues, Economic Policies, and Performance* (Thiruvananthapuram: Economic Studies Society, 2017).

5 K.C. Sachariah, E.T. Mathew and S.I. Rajan, 'Impact of Migration on Kerala's Economy and Society', Working Paper No. 297, Centre for Development Studies, Thiruvananthapuram, 1997. Available online: https://www.researchgate.net/publication/5127033_Impact_of_Migration_On_Kerala's_Economy_and_Society (accessed 10 September 2025).

6 'Census of India 2011: Provisional Population Totals', Paper 2, Volume 1, *Rural-Urban Distribution of Population*, India Series 1, Government of India, 2011. Available online: https://censusindia.gov.in/nada/index.php/catalog/1430 (accessed 10 September 2025).

7 'Census of India 2011: Population Projections for India and States 2011–2036', National Commission on Population, Ministry of Health and Family Welfare, July 2020. Available online: https://ruralindiaonline.org/en/library/resource/population-projections-for-india-and-states-2011-2036/.

8 'Population Projections for India and the States 2011–2036: Report of the Technical Group on Population Projects', National Commission on Population, Ministry of Health & Family Welfare, Nirman Bhawan, New Delhi, November 2019. Available online: https://nhm.gov.in/New_Updates_2018/Report_Population_Projection_2019.pdf (accessed 10 September 2025).

9 D. Jayaram, 'What's Choking Kerala's Roads?', *Times of India*, 17 June 2018. Available online: https://timesofindia.indiatimes.com/city/kochi/whats-choking-keralas-roads/articleshow/63683737.cms (accessed 10 September 2025).

10 M.A. Jacob, 'The Ghost Houses of Kerala', *New Indian Express*, 6 October 2024. Available online: https://www.newindianexpress.com/magazine/2024/Oct/05/the-ghost-houses-of-kerala (accessed 10 September 2025).

11 G.C. Prasad, 'Kerala Top State in Daily Wage Payments', *Mint*, 22 November 2022. Available online: https://www.livemint.com/Object/141EnEHrj3MSsNLtT8BEaK/aboutus.html (accessed 10 September 2025).

12 S.I. Rajan, 'Kerala Migration Survey 2023', *Kerala Economy*, 5 (3): 1–13, Gulati Institute of Finance and Taxation, Thiruvananthapuram, 2024. Available online: https://www.gift.res.in/wp-content/uploads/2024/09/Kerala-Migration-Survey-Report-2023-Irudaya-Raj.pdf (accessed 10 September 2025).

When the Desert Bloomed

T. Balakrishnan

MALAYALEES ARE A PROUD people and have much to be proud of. Surveys have ranked them among the highest – if not at the very top – on social and economic parameters across Indian states. Kerala is at the very top when it comes to literacy, education, health services, poverty reduction, the Physical Quality of Life Index, the environment, per capita income (PCI), number of cars per thousand people, internet connectivity, housing and people's bank balances.[1] Kerala's prosperity is explicitly visible, from its glittering markets to its varied eateries and prosperous-looking houses scattered all over.

It all started in 1957, when the new state of Kerala was formed by merging the erstwhile princely states of Travancore and Cochin with the British-administered district of Malabar in the north – a land for the Malayalees. A communist government, the first to be elected in the world, rolled out a slew of imaginative and bold reforms to transform the state from a poor land to the envy of India that it is today. It was this government that introduced comprehensive land reforms to give land to the poor and wipe out poverty in the state. It also exponentially increased funding for health and education to make Kerala a truly inclusive place for all and to claim the top position among Indian states. The Congress government, coming into power next and socialist at heart, continued the good work, built on the earlier achievements and added its own measures to make the state even better in every aspect. A hardworking, imaginative, non-political and – at least in the initial days – least-corrupt bureaucracy served both the Congress and the communist parties equally and impartially to implement their policies in letter and spirit to turn a dream into reality. This is the story, but what is the reality?

It's quite a journey for the people of Kerala, who till as late as the 1960s belonged to one of the poorest states in India. The state took to English education early on, and educated young men moved out to the vast British Empire in search of jobs, mostly as clerks and typists; women followed as nurses and housewives. Malayalees went abroad, came back rich, bought land, built homes and retired. As a result, pockets of prosperity emerged in several isolated villages across Kerala, in contrast to the widespread poverty around them. These Malayalees were the pioneers who created the foreign dream among the young, and real change came much later due to the Gulf boom between 1977 and 2007. Gulf countries, with their sudden newfound oil wealth, were on a construction spree. They were willing to pay good money to workers who were willing to toil in the 50-degree-Celsius desert heat. Malayalees were willing, attracted by the high wages, and were the first from India to go to the Gulf.

The Gulf boom was slow in the beginning, starting in isolated villages and created mostly by the Malabar Muslim community of workers and small traders. They first started moving to Dubai in dhows, often illegally, and later began settling all over the Gulf legally, using their old trade connections, rudimentary knowledge of Arabic and the friendly welcome of the faith. This migration soon translated into a statewide, secular economic growth, fuelled by remittances of foreign exchange that, in some years, reached as high as one-third of the state's gross domestic product (GDP); the proportion of remittances in Kerala's GDP almost never fell to single digits from the late 1970s through 2023, leaving poverty behind only in some pockets of the state where the Gulf boom's impact did not reach. A large number of people – as many as 3.5–4.5 million (almost 10 to 12 per cent of Kerala's population) – eventually moved to the Gulf states – the United Arab Emirates, Saudi Arabia, Bahrain, Kuwait, Qatar, Oman – and beyond.[2] This lowered population pressure in the state, leaving open opportunities for those who stayed behind to grow and prosper in their own backyard. Unprecedented remittances from these hard-working Malayalee expats also created a huge demand for all consumer goods and building materials, resulting in sky-high prices for the inelastic supply of land (agricultural, residential and commercial), further accelerating the growth.

First-generation unskilled workers and petty traders were quickly followed by qualified professionals and experienced, ambitious businesspeople, transforming Kerala's immigrants from semi-skilled and semi-literate labourers to executives, professionals and businesspeople who started creating new businesses, jobs and wealth both in the Gulf and in Kerala. The governments – the Left Democratic Front government led by the Communist Party of India and the United Democratic Front government led by the Congress – were the greatest beneficiaries of all this. Remittances led to more domestic spending, which in turn filled their coffers as tax revenues ballooned. They did not have to do much, apart from collecting and spending. And spend they did in earnest. They took the opportunity to shift the focus of taxation from direct taxes to indirect taxes. While indirect consumption taxes affected the poor more, these were favourable for the government's image as it was then not seen by the public as increasing taxes that directly bit the citizens. Governments spent as if there was no tomorrow. They had reasons for not worrying, for one thing was sure: successive governments would have only one five-year term each. Until 2021, no political party had ever been re-elected for two consecutive terms – a reflection of their poor performance. And this became an incentive for the current government to spend as much as possible – to empty the treasury and ensure that the successive government didn't have much left. Not to be outdone, the other team would borrow and spend more. Amid all of this, the bureaucrats were the happiest. Their salaries and perks were revised every five years, their numbers kept increasing exponentially, and if they were bored they could take leave for as long as twenty years and go work in the Gulf to earn tax-free dollars.

Tax money did not create infrastructure in the state, nor did it focus on creating economic assets that would further growth. This is because Kerala's successive governments did not focus on using this money for transformative reforms and instead directed it to welfare purposes and for the construction of government offices. They would compete with each other to increase the salaries and perks of organised labour, both in government and in the private sector, leading to wage inflation and pushing the state into a unique situation where labour would soon become unaffordable.

Governments opened more and more unprofitable public sector undertakings (PSUs) ostensibly to create employment and economic growth. They opened more schools and hospitals even though many well-run and better-equipped private-sector institutions were being created across Kerala through Gulf money. People were willing to pay for the better services that these private-sector schools and hospitals offered. Kerala's government moved away from the initial goal of providing services where they were not available to competing with the private sector where it was thriving.

While the economy was moving towards long-term decline, the government naturally took credit for all the success, including the Gulf boom, though many felt that the Malayalees migrated in the first place due to the government's bad policies. The communist government in Kerala attributed the state's topmost position in education and public health to its increased spending on health and education. However, a closer examination revealed that this increased spending only went into higher salaries for government employees in these sectors instead of improving the overall quality of education or health facilities. Kerala was formed in 1957 by merging Travancore, Cochin and Malabar. Even then, these component princely states held the topmost position in health and education in the country, and so the newly formed state of Kerala was ahead of the rest of the country in these two areas in 1957 too. The much-touted land reforms, while greatly benefiting some, harmed quite a few and resulted in reduced agricultural output. Later developments were equally aided by social and religious organisations. If 'earn, save and spend' was the mantra for households, 'borrow, spend and borrow more' became the government's mantra.

Many government policies in fact harmed the private sector more than they helped it. Governments clearly favoured the public sector, cooperative sector and trade unions, neglecting and discriminating against the private sector. Kerala has some of the most restrictive building, land and environmental codes in the country, resulting in valuable land remaining unused and many new (and superior) buildings in the state being seen as 'violations' of the building code.

The government competed unfairly in every sector (including health, education and manufacturing) and in other services to keep away the private sector, while declaring their eternal love for new and more private investments in the state. Land ceiling laws prevented any meaningful investments in agricultural technology or machinery, making the state more dependent on buying most agricultural products from external sources. Kerala introduced comprehensive land reforms in 1970. One of the reforms restricted the ownership of agricultural paddy land to 15 acres per family. This 15-acre ceiling ensured that no commercial farm could introduce technology or mechanisation to its functioning. It also prevented large-scale commercial or industrial developments even though the industry and commerce sectors are technically exempt from land ceiling laws. Severe restrictions on the use of land ensured farmers could not decide what to grow on their own lands. Restrictive practices resulted in the agricultural sector's inability to absorb capital, making it increasingly dependent on debt and resulting in more farmer indebtedness and resultant tragedies. In the past, labour wings of political parties regularly engineered strikes, not only in manufacturing but also in service sectors. Since labour unions are extensions of political parties, they have direct access to ministers who decide on policies and their implementation. The industry and the private sector, on the other hand, are needed and thus paid attention to only during elections, for the funding of campaigns. This has created a fear psychosis among investors – understandably so, many argue. While the state is extremely labour union-friendly, it is not necessarily investor-friendly. The constant – often unreasonable – demands of political parties, their generally unhelpful attitude and continuous harassment of business owners and investors, along with the spread of all-pervading corruption among unionised government employees, have only added to the problems pertaining to growth and development.

May It Not Be a Spanish Silver Curse

Gulf money could not go into manufacturing, agriculture or wholesale trade – where it could substantially add to employment and economic growth – mainly due to the wrong policies. Real estate, the most favoured sector of the non-residents, was severely constrained. As a result, only certain sectors that did not need workers, especially blue-collar workers, thrived in the state, for workers meant strikes in Kerala.

Moneylending, retail trade in gold, textiles, supermarkets, healthcare and education grew despite government policies. Although the government claims huge success in the information technology (IT) sector, Kerala occupies the last position, both in exports and in human resources, among the four South Indian states. Real estate investment made by the government in IT parks gave the initial, much-needed push for IT companies in Kerala. Continuation of this policy without any subsequent review created just the opposite result, discouraging private sector investment in this area due to the unfair advantages enjoyed by the government and unfair competition practices. Since the government used its own land free of charge and used taxpayers' money to construct IT parks, it could afford to charge lower rent. On the other hand, a private-sector real estate developer building a park to let out to IT companies had to buy expensive land at commercial rates and use its own (or borrowed) money to construct buildings. The government's claim of great success in tourism also needs to be taken with a pinch of salt, for it has just managed to scratch the surface. And this success too was mainly due to the investments made by local and non-resident Keralite businesses in the face of stiff, unfair competition from the government (despite its claiming to treat tourism as a priority sector). The state is proud of its citizens' automobile ownership, but what often remains unacknowledged is that this is largely a result of the absence of reliable public transportation.

The Gulf boom certainly lifted the state out of poverty and made it a better place to live. However, it may not be an unmitigated blessing for the state as it has caused wage inflation and made many economic activities unviable. Land prices have become unsustainable for any meaningful economic activity. More and more young people are looking to migrate, leaving behind old parents, probably never to return. Lifestyle diseases and the consumption of medicines in the state are high. Many large buildings dotted around the state lie empty, some falling behind in maintenance and upkeep, without anyone to live in them. In short, the state has missed the demographic dividend and is growing old fast before being able to achieve prosperity. Kerala is one of the most indebted states in India. Official figures may not reveal the whole picture, as much more debt is hidden in PSUs and other organisations that are not directly included in government records.

Kerala is ageing fast; its population is starting to fall and is now fully dependent on migrant labour from outside the state.

Labour relations continue to be a challenge in the state. Young people prefer to get an education outside the state or the country to escape toxic campus politics and prefer to stay away for good if they can. While earlier generations dreamt of seeking better pastures outside so that they could return to their homeland with money, build a house, buy a farm and retire peacefully, the new, young and educated workforce leaving the state has a different dream altogether: to stay away from Kerala forever. Gulf states are providing long-term visas to aid this process, which will lead to less money flowing back to Kerala.

The toxic public sector culture of the state discourages the private sector. It also pushes young people towards government jobs, which involve less work and more pay. Claims by Kerala pundits that the state is a model make it clear that good is the enemy of better. More than four decades of precious foreign exchange continuously flowing into Kerala – averaging 20–25 per cent of its gross state domestic product (GSDP) yearly and often reaching one-third of its GSDP – should have, in normal circumstances, transformed it into a middle-income state, with its PCI exceeding $10,000. However, Kerala's current PCI stands at about ₹2,41,131 (or approximately $3,000), and in 2022, the state was ranked fourth among the five South Indian states in terms of PCI. A fair comparison can be that of China's growth during the same period (late 1970s to early 2020s): the country also received similar investments from Chinese people overseas and used them to generate further wealth instead of splurging them all and therefore had a PCI of over $12,000 in 2022. That the restrictive policies of governments in land, labour and other areas have in fact throttled the growth of the economy, while factually correct, will never be acknowledged by the court pundits.

In short, the Gulf boom catapulted the state from one of the poorest to one of the richest states in India. The credit for this transformation, claimed by the government machinery, is far from tenable. It neither created the boom nor aided it and certainly did not invest the windfall properly. The fear that the Gulf boom could be the Spanish silver curse[3] for the state isn't an alarmist view. The state needs to take a realistic look at the present situation and correct its course now. It needs to change the model from borrowing and spending to generating income and creating long-term wealth.

This is not the end of the story for Kerala. Things are changing. A culture of risk-taking, innovation and entrepreneurship among the young is transforming the state. Investments in infrastructure are growing. The state is much more peaceful on the labour front. Violent student agitations are subsiding. Political parties are showing more restraint and openness. Hopefully, this willingness to talk and listen may convert into a consensus. Kerala will rise again.

Notes

1 'National Family Health Survey (NFHS-5), 2019–21: India Report', International Institute for Population Sciences (IIPS) and ICF, Ministry of Health and Family Welfare, Government of India, Volume 1, March 2022. Available online: https://dhsprogram.com/pubs/pdf/FR375/FR375.pdf (accessed 6 November 2025); S. Mukherjee, 'Physical Quality of Life Index: Analysing State Wise Level of Development in India', *Indian Journal of Applied Research*, 10 (7), July 2020. Available online: https://www.worldwidejournals.com/indian-journal-of-applied-research-(IJAR)/fileview/physical-quality-of-life-index-analysing-state-wise-level-of-development-in-india_July_2020_1593606303_4813705.pdf (accessed 6 November 2025).

2 K.C. Zachariah and S.I. Rajan, 'Dynamics of Emigration and Remittances in Kerala: Results from the Kerala Migration Survey 2014', Working Paper No. 463, Centre for Development Studies, Thiruvananthapuram, 2015. Available online: https://cds.edu/wp-content/uploads/WP463.pdf (accessed 6 November 2025); S.I. Rajan, 'New Evidence from the Kerala Migration Survey 2023', *Migration and Development* 13 (2), 23 December 2024, pp. 139–175. Available online: https://doi.org/10.1177/21632324241306512 (accessed 6 November 2025).

3 Spain discovered silver in its American colonies in the early sixteenth century. This large quantity of silver was poured into Spain and drove up the prices of everything, making life unaffordable for ordinary people. See: M. Drelichman, 'The Curse of Moctezuma', *Explorations in Economic History*, 42 (3), July 2005, pp. 349–380.

Of the White Revolution in Kerala

R. Narayanan

AFTER OVER TWO YEARS of 'collectoring' experiences in Alleppey, I was posted to the Planning and Economic Affairs Department of Kerala when C. Achutha Menon was the chief minister. I joined as Joint Secretary of the Planning and Economic Affairs Department. My Secretary was Dr P.K. Gopalakrishnan (Dr PKG henceforth), an economist who had a close working relationship with the chief minister. Initially, I was at a loose end since nothing specific under the rules of business was allocated to me. I had numerous in-house discussions with Dr PKG and, perhaps realising my predicament, one fine day he took me along to meet the chief minister. My first encounter with the redoubtable Achutha Menon will always stay etched in my memory. He was so gracious and spoke with such an intellectually perceptive mind that I became an instant admirer of his foresight, his incorruptible outlook and his eagerness to get things moving.

To cut things short, I am dedicating this short write-up to the many undertakings achieved by Achutha Menon, in which my part, though minuscule, was a significant phase of my career.

Before coming to these milestones in Kerala's growth, I must narrate something personal.

A Flashback: Baker

We were residing in a rented house on Golf Links Road with our two young children. In those days, Golf Links was almost a deserted part of Trivandrum, with hardly any traffic, particularly on the downhill road beyond the golf club. Most evenings, my wife and I used to take a walk along this road facing the club. My wife was fascinated by a beautifully designed house right opposite the club and, much to my annoyance, she would hang on to its gate, starry-eyed, while I fidgeted and stood by her side, wanting to get away before the owners noticed us. To my horror, one day the front door opened and out marched a handsome, middle-aged man. He was charming and friendly, and we introduced ourselves to him. His name was A.M. Jacob, and he was a civil engineer-turned-architect. He invited us for a tour of his house and told us all about the English architect Laurie Baker, who in collaboration with him had designed and built his home. Hearing him talk about Mr Baker whetted our appetite to meet him and, as it turned out, Jacob invited us to lunch that Sunday to meet Mr and Mrs Baker. That was the beginning of a long and fruitful friendship between Laurie Baker and us.

We were amazed at his humility and sense of humour. Suffice it to say that thereafter Baker constructed a low-cost house for us very close to Jacob's house, incorporating several features to accommodate my wife's hobbies: a lovely, sunny kitchen overlooking the garden and a mini stage for her to perform Bharatanatyam, to name a few. Baker specifically designed the roof of the house to resemble what he called the 'twirl of a dancer'. Gautam Bhatia, in his book on Baker, has devoted a whole chapter to this house. We had several soirées in this house, not only of classical dances but also of music, both vocal and instrumental, and among the many attendees were my Indian Administrative Service (IAS) colleagues Dr Venkatnarayan and Gopalan and his wife, Sarala. Other than the IAS officers, there was Rajeswari Menon, who would play the jal taranga and the veena. Once in a while Baker would bring guests from England, brightening up the evenings. Supper used to be potluck and, by the end of the night, we would be laughing heartily at Baker's wisecracks. But while we were enjoying the benefit of living in a Baker-special house, we had relegated the financial burden to the background.

Before we started the construction of the house, I had had a word with the chief minister, who had heard of Baker and was highly appreciative of his endeavour to promote low-cost buildings suitable to Kerala's environment. After I applied for a housing loan, the chief minister told me that IAS officers should be role models and go for low-cost houses. Although he was happy that I had entrusted the task to Baker, he insisted on sanctioning only ₹20,000 as a government loan. Baker, however, was not deterred and started his work enthusiastically. I borrowed the remaining amount from my brother-in-law and eventually the house was completed for an amount of ₹41,000. When I told the chief minister about it, he had a slight smile on his face.

The Strategic Leader of Modern Kerala

Our friendship with Baker blossomed, and Achutha Menon was aware of his pioneering work in erecting low-cost houses. He wanted the Public Works Department (PWD) to build houses and village offices based on the Baker model. One day he summoned me and asked for my opinion about living in a Baker house. When I gave him positive feedback, he said he was going to organise a seminar with the top brass of the PWD and some eminent architects from both within and outside the state. He desired that I, being the first IAS officer to have built and lived in a Baker house, narrate my experience to the attendees.

Views were expressed freely for and against adopting the Baker method for constructing government buildings. I was only an incidental participant, but I recollect the PWD harping on the long-standing structural safety of such buildings, even though Baker himself gave these a maximum life of only twenty-five years. So, despite the chief minister wanting a sea change in the PWD's approach and Baker being deeply involved in his schemes, using the Baker model for the construction of government buildings in Kerala did not quite materialise.

As the Joint Secretary of the Planning Department, I had the privilege of participating, albeit only marginally, in various visionary projects that were conceived and implemented by Achutha Menon. A few are worth mentioning: the Centre for Development Studies (CDS) at Ulloor is a standing testimony to Achutha Menon's farsightedness and Baker's genius. The Tropical Botanical Gardens and the Centre for Earth Sciences are also his creations.

I would also like to mention a few words about the Kuttanad Development Project. In 1970, while I was the collector of Alleppey, the then Chief Secretary, Gopal Menon, ICS, had come to witness the annual Nehru Trophy boat race along with his wife. During lunch, Menon told me that he had recommended my name to the Government of India to attend a course on development administration at Cambridge University under what was then known as the Colombo Plan. He mentioned that I would have to leave by early September. While I was in Cambridge, I learned about social cost-benefit analysis, where shadow prices were utilised to assess the net worth of a project. On my return from Cambridge, the then Additional Chief Secretary, George Thomas, agreed with my suggestion that I could utilise the method of social costing in the formulation of the Kuttanad Project, in which the main idea was to prevent the ingress of salinity and introduce multiple cropping in select areas. I introduced shadow pricing to justify the expenses and, in those days, it was sent to the Agricultural Refinance and Development Corporation (ARDC), the forerunner of NABARD, for approval. They took up the matter and, to my surprise, loans were sanctioned. I am not sure of the outcome since I was soon deputed to Delhi, but what I want to emphasise is the unstinting support I received from the chief minister to pursue the project right up to a meeting with the Reserve Bank of India (RBI).

I want to conclude this write-up by narrating what is probably an unmentioned phase of Kerala's development efforts.

The White Revolution

One day, Dr PKG told me that there was a directive from the Government of India instructing the states to implement a centrally sponsored scheme, which was euphemistically called the 'Half a Million Jobs Programme'. The Government of India would primarily fund it, but the implementation responsibility would be entirely with the states. The then Union minister who monitored the proposal was Mohan Dharia and Indira Gandhi was the prime minister. As the time given to formulate schemes was minimal, Dr PKG asked me to put on my thinking cap and submit employment-oriented schemes as early as possible, get Cabinet clearance and avail of the Government of India grants. That is what I did. Within a few days, I formulated five different schemes. Two of them did not get Achutha Menon's clearance. One was a scheme for setting up crèches in government workplaces and the other was to form societies of unemployed youth in urban areas to service the needs of householders, helping them in paying corporation dues, electricity bills, etc. The approved schemes were the mass cattle insemination programme, the Encos unit for unemployed engineers and the Kerala Human Resource Workers Society (KHRWS), in which pay wards were constructed and managed by graduates.

Here, I will confine myself to the first programme because it set in motion what is today referred to as the 'white revolution' of Kerala. Although I shaped the contours of the programme, the inputs and logistics were shaped by a zealous and visionary officer who was then the director of the Department of Dairy Development. He was Philipose Thomas, who, by his outstanding abilities, distinguished himself in all his endeavours. He was, quite befittingly, inducted into the IAS, where he made a name for himself as collector of Ernakulam and later as director of public instruction (DPI).

After I got the nod to go ahead with the scheme, I telephoned Philipose and told him that I needed an urgent meeting with him. He turned up the very next day, and I told him what I had in mind. The idea of a mass insemination drive was very much on my mind since my 'sub-collectoring' days in Devicolam. While I was there, I had the occasion to visit and learn about the pioneering work undertaken in the Indo-Swiss Project at Mattupatti. The Swiss director, Dr Quinzi, was an extraordinary person who converted the Mattupatti wilderness into a resplendent farm, housing Brown Swiss cattle and cultivating vegetables like cabbage, cauliflower, Brussels sprouts, carrots, potatoes and more. My wife and I – then newly married – looked forward to these visits with the utmost joy, and we became good friends with the Swiss community as well as the Indian director, Dr Padmanabhan. Quinzi told me that their objective was to improve the local strain of cattle to high milk yielders through artificial insemination of Brown Swiss semen. I am not sure how much he succeeded because my tenure in Devicolam ended soon, and I got absorbed into the bureaucratic mass of the Secretariat. However, even when I was in Cambridge, I had observed Jersey cows in the luxuriant English meadows, and I kept thinking of Mattupatti and the potential Kerala had in improving milk yields.

I told Philipose about my idea – developing a programme to make cows in every nook and corner of Kerala ready for impregnation and to make quality semen easily available to all farmers. This could be done by involving the unemployed youth, who would be remunerated for each insemination. For positive results, the remuneration could be higher.

Philipose's eyes lit up. He took to the idea most enthusiastically, but cautioned that it would require a great deal of coordination between departments like dairy development, animal husbandry, panchayats and so on. I told him that the chief minister would table it in the Cabinet and get all the parties concerned to cooperate. He then asked me how much time *he* would get. I don't recollect my reply, but he tells me that I said 'twenty-four hours'! Anyway, Philipose worked tirelessly and, with the help of his minister, Vakkom Purushottam, he prepared a neatly integrated scheme which involved locating the farms, identifying volunteers who would be given basic training on how to inseminate cows, transporting high-grade semen by refrigerated transport to strategic storage points, procuring semen of Brown Swiss, Jersey and Holstein Friesian cows, and finally monitoring the efforts through weekly reports. Most importantly, he ensured that the payments duly reached the volunteers. The farmers would pay these cattle improvement assistants (CIA) ₹10 for every successful insemination done on their premises. The scheme went on to become a roaring success, thanks to the extraordinary vision, perseverance and leadership given by Philipose and the energetic involvement of the panchayats.

I came to realise much later, after my exit from the Planning Department, that Kerala shortly became a milk-surplus state. Every farmer wanted a cross-bred, high-yielding variant. The scheme, which started in the 1970s, has now firmly established its roots.

Before the mass crossbreeding programme, the Trivandrum dairy was handling only 2,000–3,000 litres of milk per day. The average milk yield of a cow at that time was only 1 litre a day. Due to the successful implementation of this programme, the milk yield of cows has gone up to 15–20 litres per day *without* increasing the population of cows in and around Trivandrum. The Trivandrum dairy is now handling 5–6 lakh litres of milk per day! Apart from increasing milk production, this programme has also created jobs for more than thousand educated youth as CIAs.

A Sense of Fulfilment

Philipose, who became my golfing partner after my retirement, often talks about this little but significant episode in our lives. Full credit goes to him and his band of dedicated workers, without whom the scheme may have fallen by the wayside. Kudos also to the visionary Chief Minister Achutha Menon, whose unstinting support was of crucial importance.

I must conclude by stating that in June 1975 the Emergency was declared in India, and a few days later the chief minister called me to his chamber to tell me that I had been appointed to the Central Cabinet Secretariat as a Deputy Secretary. Being in the midst of the Emergency, I was unable to say no. So I had to leave Kerala and, as fate would have it, I was away for ten years, of which nine were spent in Sikkim. Now in quiet retirement, I would like to relive some of those years in the Planning Department where, apart from myself, I had the company of Varadachary and K.L.N. Rau – who was like a family member in our household. The influence of television and computers was almost non-existent, and so interactions among colleagues and friends were much more intense. I hope that sharing our experiences and thoughts through this medium will revive at least a modicum of the camaraderie we had in our time.

Optimising Infrastructure Development: The Imperative for Effective Project Management

Alkesh Kumar Sharma

THE INFRASTRUCTURE SECTOR IS one of the key drivers of Kerala's economy. This sector is responsible for propelling Kerala's overall development and enjoys priority focus from the government for initiating policies that ensure the timely creation of world-class infrastructure in the state.

However, traditional project management practices need remodelling using modern tools and techniques. They must acclimate to fast-paced changes, disruptive thinking, diversity of experiences, age, gender and geography. They also require real-time communication, real-time data management, the Internet of Things and, above all, a skilled workforce.

Thus, it needs an enabling framework to make the field of programme/project management mainstream and achieve effective project delivery. The framework should consider the best global standards for project/programme management. It should prescribe procedures and guidelines for effective execution of government/public sector and public–private partnership (PPP) projects. A project management course that would help in preparing an industry-ready workforce should be made mandatory in the senior school curriculum.

Project Management in Kerala: The Current Scenario

Kerala has initiated a wide portfolio of infrastructure projects to address mobility constraints, enhance logistics and support industrial growth. Investments are concentrated in roads and highways, railways, ports and waterways, airports, energy, communication, water supply, urban mass transit and industrial corridors. Financing is provided through the Kerala Infrastructure Investment Fund Board (KIIFB) and Central schemes such as the Pradhan Mantri Gram Sadak Yojana, Bharat Mala, Atal Mission for Rejuvenation and Urban Transformation, and Smart Cities Mission. While these projects expand capacity and modernise infrastructure, several of them are affected by time and cost overruns, which increase fiscal burden and delay the intended economic benefits.

The KIIFB has committed over ₹32,000 crore to major projects, including the Thiruvananthapuram–Kasaragod Coastal Highway, the Thiruvananthapuram–Kasaragod Hill Highway and the 62.7-kilometre Outer Ring Road in Thiruvananthapuram, designed to link Vizhinjam Port with hinterland clusters. The Vizhinjam Port rail link is the flagship project – a 10.76-kilometre alignment, including a 9.5-kilometre tunnel, designed to provide direct port connectivity. The project, sanctioned in March 2022 at about ₹1,053 crore, has since been revised upwards to ₹1,482 crore in March 2025, with projections suggesting that the eventual costs will rise above ₹1,800 crore. Its completion has already slipped beyond the forty-two-month schedule.

I have been associated with project implementation for over thirty years in various posts that I held in Kerala and in the Government of India and have handled several infrastructure projects. Through my experience, I have found that the track record of completing projects on time is abysmal due to multiple issues and challenges. Poor project management costs the government in many ways, including:

1. Additional expenditure burden due to increased costs, which crowds out funding that could be used for more deserving projects
2. The creation of a culture of accepting delays and avoidable costs which leads to more such cases
3. Economic burden due to delayed return on investments
4. Increased cost of procurement due to the monetisation of higher risks perceived by contractors (such as delays and scope creep associated with publicly funded projects)

Issues and Challenges in the National Project Implementation Model

A number of issues have been encountered across different sectors with the current methods of project delivery. These include uncertainties in land acquisition and regulatory approvals, a lack of comprehensive, upfront planning and risk management, and, most importantly, low maturity of project management processes to plan for such factors adequately.

Other issues that hamper the timely completion of projects include the non-availability of raw materials and skilled workers (masons, carpenters, etc.), inadequate water and power supply, and the supply of incomplete designs and frequent changes in them. Due to local issues and a lack of proper project planning and control, effective project delivery schedules get delayed, impacting the overall economy. In urban infrastructure projects, issues include a lack of comprehensive planning and management by urban local bodies as well as a lack of adequate skilled workforce and resources in the local self-government institutions.

The quality of the project management team executing and overseeing the projects is another major problem. Lack of timely and effective communication between the implementing agency and the contractors at the work site also leads to delays.

Project Monitoring Systems in Kerala

The Government of Kerala has set up various monitoring mechanisms for its developmental projects. It has set up the Programme Implementation, Evaluation and Monitoring Department, paving the way for speedy project implementation. The KIIFB has come up with a platform for different project management and monitoring activities. Besides, infrastructure departments have their own monitoring mechanisms.

The existence of multiple project monitoring systems and agencies across various departments also facilitates effective project implementation and monitoring.

The Project/Programme Management Approach

While working as the chief executive officer and managing director of the Delhi Mumbai Industrial Corridor Development Corporation (now known as the National Industrial Corridor Development Corporation), I adopted a comprehensive programme management system for effective project delivery, involving advanced technologies and a more global approach.

Effective project management techniques include values such as transparency, accountability, efficiency, effective use of resources, improved implementation of policy and maintenance of public trust and confidence. India's private sector has responded to the increased demand for project management through the establishment of the International Project Management Association (IPMA), which is an international project management, training and education association with members from over sixty countries. IPMA promotes the project management profession while establishing standard guidelines for project management known as the IPMA Competence Baseline. These project management guidelines have brought about definite, positive results in the project delivery systems in some of the leading developed and developing nations.

We first adopted these guidelines in the Shendra Bidkin Industrial Area Project (a part of the National Industrial Corridor Development Programme) and then in three other greenfield industrial township projects. Now they are being adopted in the Palakkad Smart City project (under the Kochi–Bengaluru Industrial Corridor project).

Programme Management

Programme management is the disciplined, systematic orchestration of human resources, time, money and information to plan, design, construct and deliver a collection of projects in a coordinated and profitable manner. If these projects were to be managed separately, such efficient orchestration wouldn't be possible.

Programme management uses well-defined and proven business and project delivery processes and tools to achieve the overall mission objectives within the specified time and budget. It is typically applied when a project involves a significant expenditure of resources, consists of the integration of disparate activities (for instance, nine different disciplines – design, quality, safety, cost, schedule time, operations, maintenance, connectivity and online approvals – had to be integrated in the Shendra Bidkin Industrial Area Project), requires the achievement of extraordinary objectives and demands quality performance, keeping in mind schedules and budgets.

Some essential features adopted in the Shendra Project are given below:

1. Programme management consultants (PMCs) were engaged to ensure day-to-day monitoring and resource planning for effective project delivery so as to avoid inordinate time and cost overruns.
2. The programme managers worked in an integrated manner, entwining all the projects and sub-projects envisaged in the Industrial Corridor Programme.
3. The PMCs constituted a team of technical experts ranging from engineers, schedulers, planners and architects, headed by a project manager.
4. Owing to the highly complex nature of such projects, the hybrid model of project management was followed, combining the traditional approach with more agile and technologically driven management practices.
5. The above measure enabled timely delivery of infrastructural works under the contractual period, without cost overruns. The allotment of land began, and industries also started commercial production with a turnaround time of ten to twelve months.

Some other project management practices that were followed in the Shendra Project are as follows:

1. The project's key stakeholders were identified early, and the vision and end goal were mutually established between the government and private stakeholders, as was the vision implementation plan. This plan was a binding agreement between all parties involved. A hundred-day implementation plan was developed, which set the way forward.
2. Key staff from the PMC team were identified for conducting workshops to explain the project's vision and goal to all those involved in it. Then individual assignments were given to all the workers and contractors.
3. The majority of projects fail due to a lack of project planning and because the schedule, budget and overall vision are not aligned. The PMC team in the Shendra Project spent three months planning and developing an implementation schedule. The planning and preliminary design work took almost eleven months, resulting in the implementation being completed within twenty-four months

(as against the usual time frame of forty months). The project was completed within the budget and with no additional change orders.

4. The main path and critical goals were determined during the planning stage itself, and measures were taken to give the float for utilities and allow the contractor to work on multiple fronts.
5. A document control system, that is a management information system, was implemented for all the projects from day one, and progress was tracked live.
6. Workshops were held with the contractors for design and implementation so that both teams knew each other's expectations and understood how to work together as one team. The usage of advanced software systems like Geographic Information Systems and Building Information Modelling eliminated the need to rework utility connections at the allotment stage.
7. From the day the contractor came onboard, safety was emphasised, and the monitoring and implementation started. Awareness materials on safety were provided to all the workers, and all the meetings started with a safety note. Incentives were given to workers and contractors for the best safe performance.
8. The 'Beyond Zero' motto became a slogan for the project. This meant that the teams adopted a culture of continuous improvement, with a shift from preventing negative results to actively generating positive impacts. 'Beyond Zero' meant creating a safety culture of no accidents rather than just recording accidents and preventing them.

Some of the above-mentioned features have been incorporated in the implementation of Phase 1 extensions and Phase II construction work under the Kochi Metro project and in the Palakkad industrial cluster (under the Kochi–Bengaluru Industrial Corridor Project) and have led to positive results.

Recommended Policy Framework for Kerala

Based on my experience in major infrastructural projects, I would suggest developing a new policy/framework to mainstream programme/project management for all big projects in Kerala. Here are a few suggestions from my end:

1. Mega projects face challenges while managing stakeholders that cut across various ministries and departments in Kerala, as well as numerous infrastructure and regulatory frameworks. Therefore, it is recommended that a project management framework be developed, considering the specific issues and requirements of contracts in public, private and state sectors. Key areas to address include infrastructure, health, safety and environmental issues.
2. It is important to review and monitor the status of implementation of major public-sector, private or PPP projects undertaken across all sectors. Therefore, a high-level committee under the Chief Secretary, comprising the heads of top infrastructure ministries, can be set up.
3. A team of experts in infrastructure, project finance, delivery and legal sectors, with expertise in project and programme management, should assist this committee. This professional project management team will work with different ministries, departments and other stakeholders, monitoring these projects on a timely basis to ensure on-time delivery.
4. Sufficient funding should be allocated for project management support to successfully implement this project management framework.
5. The projects should be analysed based on their sizes and prioritised based on their importance, amount of investment, impact on society at large, etc.
6. NITI Aayog is working towards establishing the National Institute of Chartered Project Professionals, which will become the nodal agency for overseeing the growth of project management as a profession and creating competent project management professionals in India. This will help improve the availability of project management professionals for various projects, and they will be held accountable and responsible through a set of ethical and legal codes.

Infrastructure is the lifeline of economic development in a region. Timely implementation of projects, therefore, needs to be given due importance, and adequate steps should be taken to develop capacities, resources and skilled manpower to manage infrastructural projects.

Kerala's Way to Human Development

L.C. Goyal

The Indian Constitution aims to secure for all its citizens social, economic and political justice, liberty of thought, expression, belief, faith and worship, and equality of status and opportunity. It aims to promote fraternity among all, ensuring the dignity of the individual and the unity and integrity of the nation.

The essence of its Preamble denotes India's firm resolve to build and sustain an India in which all citizens, irrespective of their status, economic means, caste, creed or religion, shall feel equal and be given a decent standard of living and an India in which all communities shall live in harmony. Therefore, the core of the ideals and goals enshrined in the Constitution enjoins upon the State to pursue and achieve human development leading to a just society.

Human development is defined as a process of enlarging people's freedoms and opportunities and improving their well-being. The Nobel laureate Amartya Sen explains that aspects such as public education and healthcare are important in improving the quality of life, which impacts the capability of human beings to better fulfil their demands and needs as individuals and those of the economy and society. He says human development necessitates eliminating unfreedoms such as poverty, tyranny, economic and social deprivation, neglect of public facilities, and intolerance or overactivity of repressive states. The State plays a role in supporting human development by providing public education, healthcare, social safety nets, good macroeconomic policies and protecting the environment.

The human development index (HDI), launched by the United Nations Development Programme (UNDP), measures the average achievement in a country in three basic dimensions of human development: a long and healthy life, measured by life expectancy at birth; knowledge, measured by the adult literacy rate and the combined gross enrolment ratios for primary, secondary and tertiary schools; and a decent standard of living, measured by the gross domestic product (GDP) in terms of purchasing power parity.

An Atypical Model

It is in this background that Kerala's way to human development is to be viewed. The Kerala model was different in that it focused on human development indicators rather than on high growth rates. Kerala's high human development, with low per capita income during the very early years, earned international acclaim. In 2011, India's HDI rose by 21 per cent, with Kerala at the top of the chart. In 2021 too, Kerala helmed the HDI among the states with a score of 0.782.

K.P. Kannan, a social thinker and former director of the Centre for Development Studies (CDS) in Thiruvananthapuram, in his working paper for CDS in October 2022, states that Kerala enjoyed a historical advantage in terms of favourable initial conditions and the notion of public action, which emerged as critical factors in its human development trajectory. Public action, demanding the delivery of human development from the subnational state of Kerala, was made possible through social reform, radical politics, an active public sphere and a social economy. He finds that the early demographic transition and the large-scale emigration of adult males to the Gulf countries – both the direct outcomes of high human development – contributed to high per capita income growth and ensured its sustainability in the later years, from 1987–1988 to 2019–2020.

As far as I can discern, Kerala's high human development is attributed to a focus on public education, healthcare, social welfare schemes, budget provisions, land reforms, women empowerment, decentralisation, social capital, a politically active population, transparent public administration and political consensus.

Universal Public Education

There is ample evidence in the public domain to establish that Kerala has had a history of schooling since the pre-Independence era. Missionaries played a crucial role in making education accessible to all, irrespective of caste, creed or religion. Social reformers such as Sree Narayana Guru, Sree Chattampi Swamikal and Ayyankali encouraged various social groups to educate themselves by starting their own schools. Their teachings also empowered the poor and backward classes to organise themselves and bargain for their rights. The state also instituted what was popularly called the 'aided school system' to help schools through an annual maintenance grant for operating expenses such as salaries, utilities and maintenance.

The rulers of the princely state of Travancore were also at the forefront in the promotion and spread of public education. A school for girls was set up by the maharaja as early as 1859. In colonial times, Kerala had developed the culture of mass protests for social causes such as rights for Dalits and education for all.

Access to education was not confined to men. In the precolonial era, women – especially those coming from the matrilineal Nair caste – received education even in Sanskrit and other sciences. As assistant collector (under training) in 1980, I was amazed during my tours to interior rural areas to see old women reading newspapers. This was incredible for me, as I hailed from Haryana, where female literacy levels were abysmally low in rural areas. Kerala was way ahead in terms of female literacy and education at that time.

Even today, Kerala is widely recognised for nearly universal enrolment and retention, in terms of exceptionally low school dropout rates. It is noteworthy that Kerala's dropout rates are far better than the national average. However, I would underscore that Kerala's school education needs constant improvements, with special focus on ensuring better student learning outcomes at all levels. When I was Finance Secretary (2008–2010), we did away with a few uneconomic schools under the aided school system. It is heartening that parents have begun to embrace public-funded schools that have better infrastructure than private schools. This trend needs to be accentuated by the state government going forward.

Public Health

It is well documented that a long history of successful public health–oriented policies is at the core of Kerala's improved public health services. As early as 1879, vaccinations were made mandatory for public servants, prisoners and students. Missionaries led the efforts in setting up hospitals and schools in underserved areas.

After Kerala became a state in 1956, basic public health and education became its top priorities in terms of public policies. This was rather unique to Kerala in those early years of the country's independence. The state's high focus on social determinants of health, such as investment in clean water, sanitation, housing, access to food and public education, contributed to Kerala's relative success in establishing a public healthcare system (as compared to other Indian states).

In the 1970s, Kerala mounted an immunisation programme for infants and pregnant women; this was a decade before India initiated its national immunisation programme in association with the World Health Organization. Kerala was thus a clear forerunner in this domain for the rest of the country and a hugely positive outlier.

The foundational basis of Kerala's high health standards is its strong and expansive network of health infrastructure, in terms of its three-tier primary healthcare system. Kerala's life expectancy at birth, birth rate, mortality rates, palliative care, etc., rank not only the highest in the country but are also among the best across developed nations. For instance, Kerala had almost stabilised its population by 2011 and now has an infant mortality rate of 6 per 1,000 live births. No wonder Kerala has already achieved the 2030 Agenda for Sustainable Development targets set for mortality rates.

However, according to the State Economic Review 2022, infectious diseases, once eradicated, seem to be on the rise, along with a high prevalence of lifestyle-related communicable diseases. These challenges need to be effectively redressed through a set of mid-course corrections and suitable public policies.

Women Empowerment

Kerala has the highest score on the gender development index, as underlined by all social indicators. Historically, women in Kerala enjoyed relatively more autonomy and freedom, often attributed to the state's matrilineal structure. Later, their education and participation in the workforce led to their socioeconomic empowerment.

Kudumbashree, meaning prosperity of the family, is a landmark initiative launched by the Kerala government in May 1998 for the eradication of poverty and women's empowerment. It supports more than 4.3 million women as its members. It works through a vibrant women-centred three-tier structure anchored by neighbourhood groups, area development societies and community development societies. Kudumbashree has achieved multidimensional success and has been widely acclaimed. It is quite akin to the women's self-help groups (SHGs) formed under the Central government's National Rural Livelihoods Mission (NRLM). In June 2014, I had the privilege, as Secretary of Rural Development, to convince the new government of NRLM's criticality in the reduction of rural poverty and women's empowerment. The same year, I also convinced the top level of the new government that the Mahatma Gandhi National Rural Employment Guarantee Scheme (MNREGS) could play a critical role in rural employment generation and asset creation. Civil servants are required and expected to perform their duties in the larger public interest.

Land Reforms and Public Policy

Decades of struggle by peasants' associations led to land reforms in Kerala. These reforms were initiated by the elected communist government in 1957 and continued to be followed as the years progressed. Tenancy was abolished, benefiting 1.5 million poor households. The reforms also provided for the protection of agricultural workers and a pension for retired agricultural labourers.

Workers in the informal sector were organised quite early on in Kerala, securing higher wages than their counterparts in other Indian states. More importantly, they are now covered by collective care arrangements under thirty-two occupation-specific welfare fund boards (created by statutory legislation) that take measures for the welfare of their worker-members on a tripartite basis, comprising representatives of the state, workers/trade unions and employers. In fact, there was a broad consensus across the political spectrum to prioritise human development. Political parties had no choice but to continue with policies on human development and social welfare because the sustained pressure from a vibrant public sphere and the emergence of social capital were such that no political formation would dare displease the electorate and run the risk of losing the battle.

Decentralised Planning

Kerala's governance structure is marked by a rich history of decentralised planning and execution. Decentralised planning was initially attempted in a small way around 1990–1991, but a formal, extensive People's Planning Campaign was mounted in August 1996. It made far-reaching changes in the Panchayati Raj and community-level planning and implementation. A number of functions and functionaries were transferred to local self-governments (LSGs), such as the administration of schools, primary health centres (including sub-centres, krishi bhavans, etc.), along with the delivery of centrally sponsored schemes (CSSs) like the MNREGS. More significantly, there exists a sound and effective system of devolution of funds, backed by the recommendations of the State Finance Commission. Nearly 40 per cent of state funds are now leveraged by LSGs. We, in the Finance Department, decided in 2008–2009 that the earmarked funds for LSGs should in no case be withheld. Thus, functions, functionaries and funds – all the three Fs – are in large measure with local bodies.

Kerala was way ahead of other states in this regard. The decentralised planning and fiscal decentralisation in the state have been widely appreciated. I must, however, point out that local bodies need to be sufficiently capacitated to produce better results.

Stable Administration

Administration at the state and sub-state levels is a crucial component of the efficient design and delivery of public goods, including public education, healthcare and social welfare. It has to be responsive, transparent and accountable. My experience of working in the state has been that it is relatively better administered. The educated and informed people have made a big difference. What struck me most in 1991 was that even a young girl or an old woman during those days, and earlier too, would present her grievances to the district collector – and not to people below him/her, such as the additional district magistrate

(ADM) or deputy collector – and would come again if she was unable to meet the district collector on that particular day. The institution of the district collector and, for that matter, civil servants is generally well-respected by the political executive in the state.

Normally, a two-year tenure is given to a district collector. In 1991 there was a change of regime, and the political leadership that assumed office, though allegedly unhappy with me on account of misinformed feedback given by the local member of Parliament, retained me as district collector, Kozhikode, for a few months; in any other state, I would have been shifted immediately.

Also, Kerala has a culture of public protests to hold public officials accountable. This essentially creates bottom-up pressure to demand accountability from the administration in terms of the delivery of public goods. This is necessary to ensure citizen-centric, smart governance across the country.

State Budget's Role

Successive governments in Kerala have been allocating sizeable funds from their budgets to the social sector. This has led to enhanced human development in the state, including social welfare and all its indicators, laying a strong foundation of human and social capital. But the state's fiscal crisis from the mid-1970s to the early 1990s led to a drop in such outlays.

In recent years, state budgets have focused on consolidating the gains of human development and social welfare achieved hitherto, while creating a favourable ambience for sustainable agricultural and industrial growth and enhancing capital expenditure. As Finance Secretary from 2008 to 2010, I recall my discussion with the then finance minister. He had said that the 2008–2009 budget size could be increased to deal with the situation arising in Kerala due to the global financial crisis of 2008 because we could, in due course, grow our way out of debt. I told him that we could do so if we invested this money only on the capital side, to which he agreed.

It is gratifying to note that, as per the multidimensional poverty index (MPI) released by NITI Aayog in July 2023, Kerala has again figured as the least poor state in the country.[1] Ernakulam in Kerala is the only district in the country that has zero poverty. Kerala is also among the top ten states in the country in terms of per capita gross domestic state product (GSDP). The state's impressive scores across all twelve indicators of MPI are the result of its strong foundation in the domains of human development and social safety.

GOI's Role in Human Development

Ideally, schemes directly impacting the lives of common people are best planned and implemented by local-level governments. In fact, this is where they belong. Schemes of interstate importance can be taken up as CSSs, through funds in the Central government's budget, but implemented by states. However, over time, the number of CSSs increased and gradually, states were required to bring in a part of the requisite funds. This led to the states' substantial funds getting tied up in the CSSs (as a part of their annual plan outlays), thereby affecting their own specific goals and priorities.

This phenomenon, it appears to me, has a political underpinning. Given the parliamentary form of governance structure, involving members of the Lok Sabha directly elected by the people and their chosen leader as the prime minister, the ruling regime at the Centre reaches out to and connects with citizens through such schemes, creating a feel-good factor to woo voters during elections. Such schemes are essentially aimed at ensuring human development, social welfare and enhancing the ease of living for the people, especially those at the margins. This has become more pronounced in recent years, with different political parties ruling at the Centre and in the states.

The UNDP report of July 2023 noted that deprivation in all indicators had declined in India, and the poorest states and groups, including children and people in disadvantaged caste groups, had shown the most rapid progress. It further states that in 2005–2006, about 645 million people in India were in multidimensional poverty, and this number declined to about 370 million in 2015–2016 and further dropped to 230 million between 2019 and 2021. One may say that India is emerging as a social welfare state.

The Way Forward

The debate between human development and economic growth has been ongoing for some time. I do not intend to delve into this, as I firmly believe that India needs both. While the Central government continues to focus on human development coupled with social welfare, besides creating world-class modern infrastructure, a sharper push needs to be given by it to unleash the forces of enterprise, with a greater emphasis on micro, small and medium enterprises and private investment. This can be done by making it a lot easier, including at sub-state levels, to do business and generate good job opportunities, thereby enabling the GDP to grow at double digits in the coming decades.

Kerala needs to sustain its gains in the quality of human development and social welfare. On the other hand, policies are required by the state to reform loss-making public sector undertakings and, more importantly, to broaden its economic growth in terms of a continued boost to agriculture and industrial sectors rather than being satisfied with a vibrant service sector and construction activity (both of which are largely facilitated by foreign remittances). This calls for a durable fiscal condition, requiring actions by both the states and the Centre. It is hoped that the Sixteenth Finance Commission has studied the capacity and ability of states to raise their own tax revenues in a post-Goods and Services Tax scenario and recommended appropriate measures to provide more stability to Centre–state financial relations. Hopefully, it has also considered directly devolving more funds to the LSGs. In parallel, the states, including Kerala, will need to rationalise their priorities and control revenue expenditure.

Notes

1 'National Multidimensional Poverty Index', NITI Aayog, Government of India, 2023. Available online: India-National-Multidimentional-Poverty-Index-2023.pdf (accessed 26 September 2025).

Part 3
Local Self-Governance

Decentralisation and the Aftermath

K. Mohandas

THE 73RD AND 74TH Amendments came into effect on 24 April 1993 and 1 June 1993 respectively. The state laws had to be aligned with the amended Constitution within one year of the notified dates. In this chapter, I present the process followed by the Kerala government to achieve this. This is more like a personal memoir; it is not a theoretical study, critical analysis or value judgement on the decentralised democratic systems in the state (on which several books and articles containing different perspectives have already been written). I am writing something that ChatGPT cannot generate.

In July 1991, the new Kerala government appointed me Secretary of the Local Administration Department and Commissioner for Local Government. K. Karunakaran was the Chief Minister, and C.T. Ahammed Ali was the Local Administration Minister. Karunakaran had acquired a new halo around him as an influential national leader involved in the selection of P.V. Narasimha Rao as Prime Minister. However, Karunakaran's influence weakened after a major road accident and the obvious loss of clout in Delhi, and he was replaced after four years. Ahammed Ali was a fourth-time member of the Legislative Assembly (MLA) of the Muslim League and a first-time minister; he was – and continues to be – a decent and soft-spoken person, willing to listen to people, trying to learn more about new matters and wanting to act fairly (except for when he's under strong political pressure). The local self-government system comprised 991 panchayats, 54 municipalities, 3 municipal corporations and 1 township (Guruvayur). Then there were the district councils, constituted shortly before the Assembly elections, under the District Administration Act. In fact, in the elections for the district councils, the Left Democratic Front had won 13 out of the 14 district councils. The confidence gained from that victory prompted them to dissolve the Assembly one year ahead of schedule and hold the Assembly elections simultaneously with the Lok Sabha Elections of 1991, projecting V.S. Achuthanandan as the next Chief Minister. But then Rajiv Gandhi was assassinated, and the sympathy wave catapulted the Congress to power, both at the Centre and in Kerala.

The district councils envisaged in the Kerala District Administration Act (enacted by the P.K. Vasudevan Nair government in 1979) were to be a third tier of government. My additional job as Commissioner for Local Government was a statutory post under this act. The law was made 'pragmatic' before the elections were conducted in 1991, yet the district councils still had substantial functions. The District Collector was the ex officio Secretary of the council.

With the change of government, the district councils fell out of favour; the political choice was between killing them and crippling them. A constitutional amendment on local self-government was expected, as the Congress government at the Centre would respect the late Rajiv Gandhi's aspirations, and when it happened, the state would be forced to fall in line. The final political decision was to emasculate the district councils.

The always-busy Deputy Collector (general) was made the ex officio Secretary, and the functions were drastically cut down. Most of the District Collectors were delighted, as some overzealous district council presidents had earlier demanded petty things like getting the Collector's office, parking their vehicles on the main porch of the Civil Station, etc., to display their self-assumed numero uno status in the district. They seemed to have forgotten that the District Collector and District Magistrate is the state government's principal officer in the district.

Hatching the Devolution

With the 73rd and 74th Amendments coming into effect in 1993, new laws were required, considering the massive changes these amendments brought with them. My first self-assigned task was to identify the matters for which policy decisions were required. I listed a hundred such matters – administrative, structural and functional – and sent them to the Minister to gain the approval of the Chief Minister and then the Cabinet. While this was the formal route under the Rules of Business, which mattered for officers, the coalition system, which the state has had since 1967, required political decisions to be taken at the meetings of the Liaison Committee of the parties in the ruling coalition. And so, despite my follow-up with the Minister, decisions were not forthcoming, and time was running out. However, I did not want to bypass the minister. Finally, he himself asked me to go to the Chief Minister for approval.

When I met the Chief Minister, his initial response was totally unexpected. With his characteristic wink, he said, 'Make sure that maximum powers are given to the lowest level of panchayats.' Coming from a person who had a reputation for wanting to retain all power, this took me by surprise. When I gave him my views on the matters for which policy decisions were required, his reply was 'OK, come here on Saturday at ten o'clock.'

When I reached Cliff House, the Chief Minister's official residence, I saw a crowd there. The staff told me that the Chief Minister was chairing a Liaison Committee meeting. The Chief Minister's security person (known as a gunman!) then held the door open for me and said, 'Sir, you can go in.' I had no option but to go in and did not have the time to worry about the ethics of walking into an important political meeting. Senior ministers and leaders of various political parties were all there.

The deliberations during the meeting were as follows (originally in Malayalam), with only the Chief Minister and I speaking:

Chief Minister: So what are the points for decision?
Me: Sir, there are about a hundred matters, big and small. Some relate to the structure of the system, some are about the administrative arrangements and the most importantly are about the delegation of powers.

Chief Minister: Present them, one by one, with your recommendation.
Me: The first issue concerns the Panchayati Raj system. We need to have three tiers – village, intermediate and district. For the intermediate tier, the choice is between block and taluk; I recommend the conversion

of the block development office [BDO] into the block panchayat's office, as the intermediate panchayat's functions would be primarily developmental. The BDOs strongly oppose this. The Panchayat Department staff want it at the taluk level to expand the taluk-level office of their department.

Chief Minister: Let it be block only. Next?
Me: The election of gram panchayat presidents and municipal chairpersons can be either from among the elected members or chosen directly by all the voters.

Chief Minister: Our system is parliamentary and not presidential. Let us follow that. Then?
Me: The Constitution provides for three types of municipalities. We now have municipalities and corporations, but no nagar panchayats for the transitional areas. We may not really need them.

Chief Minister: Fine. Next?
Me: We have the township in Guruvayur. In the future, we can have only industrial townships where industrial establishments provide all the municipal services. The Guruvayur Devaswom may not be able to provide the municipal services there.

Chief Minister: Hmm.

The Chief Minister thought for a while. He was a staunch devotee of Lord Guruvayoorappan and went to the temple on the first day of every Malayalam month. I did not know much about the Devaswom at that time, but I became the Guruvayur Devaswom commissioner three years later and continued in that position for more than seven years. After some thought, the Chief Minister finally said, 'Let there be a small committee comprising the Liaison Committee's convenor, Sankaranarayanan [a senior leader who later became the Governor of Maharashtra], Minister Ahammed Ali [Irrigation Minister], T.M. Jacob [one of Kerala's best parliamentarians] and the Secretary. Start working tomorrow. Use my conference hall. No formal orders are necessary.' In effect, the Secretary to the government was made the Secretary of a political committee. But then I wanted quick decisions to do my work on time.

The newly formed committee was swift in its work and left several details for the department to finalise. However, it was not possible for my department to send a comprehensive paper to the Law Department to draft the bills, as matters were continuously evolving. Therefore, I got a small team of Law Department officers to work with us, as suggested by the law minister, K.M. Mani. This team was led by Deputy Secretary D. Saratchandran, a very competent officer. The only problem was that my Local Administration Department thought the team was part of the Law Department, while the Law Department considered them part of the Local Administration Department. Their drafts had to be formally processed in the Law Department – not that it created delays or conflicts. After all, procedures are procedures, and departments are watertight compartments, headed by different Secretaries, different ministers – and different egos.

The delegation of powers proved to be the biggest issue needing resolution. While the Chief Minister had privately given me a mandate for maximum delegation, the departments in question were not responding well to this order. A senior minister jokingly said, 'The CM can say so; he has only the Police Department, which will not see any delegation.' Another minister quipped, 'What will I do if all this is delegated? Nobody will come to meet me.' I told him that even though agriculture is a state subject as per the Constitution, the Central government has a huge Ministry of Agriculture.

Even with all this lack of enthusiasm in various quarters, one had a timeframe to adhere to. I thus sought the intervention of the Chief Secretary, K.V. Rabindran Nair. He was what one would call a perfect bureaucrat – a specialist in finance (having been Finance Secretary throughout his Secretary-level career in the state and Expenditure Secretary at the Centre), knowledgeable about most administrative matters, always balanced in thinking, fair and courageous in decision-making, with limited social contacts and no vested interests. He advised me to call the Secretaries and the heads of their departments in small groups, chaired by the senior Secretaries, so that, first, it would be manageable and second, there would be some peer pressure in every group. I was not fully convinced that this would work because there is no hierarchy between Secretaries, senior or junior, and each one is the boss of his or her department. However, to my surprise, this approach worked; where the ministers were reluctant, the officers gave pragmatic suggestions.

Finally, the Panchayati Raj Bill was ready. It was presented to the Assembly and referred to the Subject Committee of the Legislature. The Municipality Bill followed a few weeks later. The pressure groups of officers and others tried to influence decisions at this stage. The Rural Development Department officers (whom I rated as some of the best in government service) wanted the taluk to be the intermediate level of the Panchayati Raj system. They also wanted district rural development agencies to remain as independent agencies, distinct from the district panchayats. The Panchayat Department officers wanted all the additional posts for their own department. The Secretariat officers demanded that the Secretaries of district panchayats be selected from among Secretariat officials. And all general categories of employees wanted to continue as government employees without being transferred to the panchayats.

There was a seemingly minor matter on which there were lengthy discussions: the designation of the principal officer of the local body. The existing designations were executive officer of the panchayat and commissioner of the municipality. I favoured the continued use of these designations to avoid any confusion in the minds of the general public. However, the Municipal Chairmen's Chamber and the Panchayat Presidents' Association were keen on changing the designation of the principal officer to that of a 'Secretary'. They even asked me, 'Aren't IAS officers comfortable working as Secretaries? These are much lower officers, and their status will go up with this designation.' The Legislature Committee was unanimously in favour of 'Secretary' being chosen as the new designation.

A personal disappointment for me was with respect to the Poverty Alleviation Fund. Section 284 of the Kerala Municipalities Act, 1994, currently states that 'Every Municipality shall provide in its Annual Budget two per cent of the revenue receipts of the Municipality for constituting a separate fund to be called the Poverty Alleviation Fund for implementing poverty alleviation programmes in the municipal area, which shall be utilised subject to such guidelines as the Government may issue from time to time.'[1] I had proposed in the draft bill that this fund be placed at the disposal of the community development society (CDS) of poor women at the municipal level, but the final decision was that the municipality would manage the fund.

To provide some background, we had chosen the community structure to implement the Centrally Sponsored Scheme of Urban Basic Services for the poor. Poverty was defined based on physical parameters and not income or consumption (this was long before the multidimensional poverty index was introduced). Neighbourhood groups of twenty women from poor families were constituted, with a hierarchy of ward-level area development societies and a municipal-level community development society. The pilot project started in Alappuzha in 1992, with support from UNICEF and the National Bank for Agriculture and Rural Development, and it did so well that the CDS won the UN Foundation's 'We the Peoples' Award in 1995. It was a proud moment to see Valsala Sebastian, president of the CDS and a very poor housewife, travelling to New York to receive the award. A similar structure was created in all the municipalities from 1992 to 1994. In 1995, it was extended to the entirety of the Malappuram district. This initiative was taken by Collector James Varghese. I had attended the first meeting called by him – Health Secretary Gopal Krishna Pillai presided over it. The subsequent collector, T.K. Jose, furthered Varghese's endeavour and later became the face of this huge social instrument, which was expanded on a large scale and was given the beautiful name 'Kudumbashree' by the LDF government that came to power in 1996.

The municipalities – both political functionaries and officials – were either hostile or indifferent to the empowerment of the CDSs. The Municipal Chairmen's Chamber was totally against making CDSs autonomous. Their approach was clear – delegate and decentralise to our levels but not below that. The final consensus about the poverty alleviation fund was that its utilisation would be according to government guidelines.

The Legislative Committee spent a lot of time on the delegation of powers and functions to local bodies. In private, the Opposition members were surprised that the government had agreed to so much delegation. However, several matters in the 11th and 12th Schedules of the Constitution were not considered for delegation due to practical restraints. Rural electrification, urban water supply and fire services fall into this category. Therefore, the delegation of powers was neither complete nor comprehensive, even for matters that were only locally relevant.

Birth of the Law

The Bills went back to the Assembly to enact a new Panchayati Raj Act and a new Municipality Act to replace the existing Panchayats Act, Municipalities Act, Municipal Corporations Act, District Administration Act and Guruvayur Township Act. The Assembly sat until 7 the next morning to pass the Panchayati Raj Act. The Municipality Act was much longer, but it needed less time for legislative approval. The significant relief was that these could be enacted within the timeframe allowed by the Constitution.

The clause-by-clause discussions during the second reading of the Bill created challenging situations. Notices for amendments arrived late, and the minister had to be briefed on the government's stance on the proposed amendment. Some members on either side were effective speakers who gave the credulous minister the impression that their proposal was the only one to be accepted, but in reality this acceptance would have led to complications elsewhere. The minister then pleadingly looked back to the officers' gallery, and a note had to be sent to him shortly afterwards. Since there was no time to record the reasons for accepting or rejecting a proposal, the note often just said 'Yes' or 'No'. Then there were some official amendments to make last-minute corrections. The job was quite tough for a seasoned minister too.

Here, the local administration minister was ably assisted by the Irrigation Minister, T.M. Jacob, throughout the process. But then we also saw an unexpected official amendment to the Panchayat Raj Bill, substantially reducing the proposed delegation of minor irrigation work to the panchayats.

The laws created a constitutionally mandated structure for the local self-government system in Kerala. Now the implementation part came up. The State Election Commission and the State Finance Commission had to be set up. I still remember the Chief Minister saying in the Cabinet meeting, 'The Election Commissioner should be a retired senior IAS officer. Let us have M.S.K. Ramaswamy. Although Swamy is a simple person, the name will sound as if he is someone like T.N. Seshan.' The government chose P.M. Abraham, who had retired as Secretary of the Ministry of Surface Transport, as chairman of the State Finance Commission. The elections took place at the end of September 1995. In the meantime, A.K. Antony had become chief minister, and the Local Administration Department was divided into urban and rural and placed under two ministers – P.K. Kunhalikutty and P.K.K. Bava respectively. Their styles were contrasting: Kunhalikutty was quick to grasp matters and take effective decisions, while Bava was cautious and suspicious, concerned about correctness and probity.

Second Round and Quitting the Ring

I felt that it was time for a change but did not ask for it. With just a few months until the Assembly elections, a change in government was expected based on the electoral pattern in Kerala after 1980. However, even before that, the government made some illogical postings. I was appointed to the Local Administration (Urban), with the additional charge of Rural Development and part of Industries. Rural Development should logically have been under Local Administration (Rural). Anyway, this period was short; the elections came, V.S. Achuthanandan lost in his constituency, and E.K. Nayanar became Chief Minister for the third time. They appointed me Secretary of Local Administration again. The minister was Paloli Mohammed Kutty – a communist saint, if one may use that expression. The government wanted further reform in decentralisation, and what better way than to retain the officer who did the initial work. The government appointed a committee on decentralisation, chaired by S.B. Sen, with former minister V.J. Thankappan as vice chairman. The left governments always tried to harness the wisdom of left-wing intellectuals, especially from West Bengal, until 2011. S.B. Sen was a simple, sensible and mature person; unfortunately, he passed away before the final report by the Sen Committee was submitted.

A few months into my second cycle in Local Administration, I was sent abroad for a six-week training programme and did not want to come back to the same job. The government got an excellent successor for me – S.M. Vijayanand, who, with his strong personal commitment, is perhaps the most appropriate officer for this type of work. The government made me continue as a member of the Sen Committee. However, with the main charge of Industries and the additional jobs of land revenue commissioner, transport commissioner and Guruvayur Devaswom commissioner, the frequency of my attendance at the meetings reduced, and my world of local administration wilted gradually.

Why, Oh, Why?

Even after all these years, a few questions lie unanswered in my mind:

1. Why did the Constitution separate rural and urban areas as impermeable compartments, except for their coordination through the District Planning Committee? How urban are the smaller urban areas, and how rural are the large panchayats? Would it not have been proper to have a setup which covered the entire district?
2. Do we really need an elected body at the intermediate level, adding to the cost of governance?
3. The local bodies in Kerala have more than 50 per cent women members, and they are performing well, but is there a glass ceiling that stops them there without allowing them to advance to the state Assembly and Parliament?
4. Why couldn't corruption, both at the cutting-edge levels and at the decision-making levels, be eliminated in spite of democratic decentralisation?
5. Why do ministers continue to receive representations regarding matters within the purview of local bodies, and why are they processed in the Secretariat?
6. Why is the Ombudsman an invisible and ineffective body?
7. Solid waste management is a basic function of local bodies. Why have they failed miserably in that?
8. In the past, we had panchayat and municipal employees; now there is a huge, unified cadre of government staff under the local government system. Can we not create small cadres of local body staff again, at least in future recruitments? And aren't the panchayats overstaffed?

9. Village panchayat vehicles are seen in the state capital, and municipal vehicles are sometimes seen outside the state. Why are the local bodies splurging without concern for economy in expenditure?
10. Last but most importantly: are we ready to accept panchayats and municipalities as a third tier of autonomous government at the local level?

Notes

1 The Kerala Municipality Act, 1994. Available online: https://www.indiacode.nic.in/bitstream/123456789/17250/1/kerala__municipality__act_1994.pdf

Decentralisation in Kerala: A Retrospective

S.M. Vijayanand

AMONG THE STATES THAT have functional Panchayati Raj institutions, Kerala is the youngest in the sense that its efforts came in the wake of the 73rd Amendment. Ironically, for a state praised for its public action and known for its political consciousness and fierce political contestation, it did not have strong local governments until recently, even though local self-governance was advocated by influential political leaders like E.M.S. Namboodiripad. But when the Panchayati Raj system was finally adopted, it happened with a 'big bang', with most of the key decisions taken between 2 October 1995 and 17 August 1996 by two governments: the United Democratic Front government of A.K. Antony after K. Karunakaran stepped down, and the Left Democratic Front government under E.K. Nayanar, which took over in May 1996 after the Assembly elections.

Clearly, the top leadership of both political formations, especially E.M.S. Namboodiripad and A.K. Antony, had deep faith in decentralisation. They could provide the political justification for the same, one from a Gandhian angle and the other rather surprisingly from a communist viewpoint. Though communism avowedly believes in democratic centralism, E.M.S. could convincingly justify giving powers to local governments throughout his political career.

The literacy movement in the late 1980s provided Kerala with experience in people's mobilisation, and this was fruitfully harnessed during the initial days of decentralisation. Interestingly, the participatory planning method was first developed in the Kalliasseri Panchayat in Kannur with support from the Kerala Sasthra Sahithya Parishad.

Later, Dr K.N. Raj and Professor I.S. Gulati, proponents of decentralisation, through the Centre for Development Studies, attempted to validate the Kalliasseri model through pilot projects undertaken in about twenty-two village panchayats in 1995.

Thus, constitutional, political and intellectual factors converged and resulted in the launch of the People's Plan. Looking back, it is safe to say that this became possible only because of political and intellectual leaders at different levels, civil society activists and civil servants who stepped in and converted an opportunity into a deep-rooted and fundamental governance reform that has endured over time despite political changes.

The Approach

Kerala's People's Plan had clear objectives, which shaped its policy and practice. The key objectives were:

1. Democratisation and humanisation of the state
2. Widening and deepening participation, enabling people, especially the poor and disempowered including women, to have a role and a say in local developmental governance
3. Shifting from bureaucratic top-down planning and budgeting to participatory bottom-up planning and budgeting, with active involvement of professionals and practitioners from outside government as volunteers
4. Moving from official and political patronage to decisions based on societal norms
5. Enhancing the responsiveness of governance
6. Increasing transparency and accountability, especially social accountability and eliminating corruption
7. Transforming conflictual politics into a new politics of development that responds to local demand and potential
8. Facilitating cooperative and creative public action

The 'big bang' resulted in reversals of the conventional sequence. Of course, this approach brought with it several attendant teething problems which, by the end of 1998, the first full year of the People's Plan, threatened to seriously undermine the initiative. But concerted action by a small group of political leaders, officials and activists prevented lasting damage. The People's Plan Campaign, launched in 1996, helped in substantial social mobilisation, with high expectations.

Kerala chose participatory planning as the starting point for decentralisation. Though participatory planning clearly has Gandhian influences, it conforms well with the ideas of the left-wing thinker Paulo Freire, especially the idea of empowering the oppressed, which was also fundamental to Kerala's literacy movement.

There were some basic values and principles underlying the decentralisation initiatives which fortunately took root in the euphoric initial period of implementation. They included 'participation' in the sense of giving formal space to citizens in decision-making, giving special priority to marginalised sections. Another strongly held value was transparency and accountability. All these were incorporated into processes and systems. In this scenario, the role of the government was clearly delineated. It included:

1. Creating capacity
2. Setting up interim operating systems of governance – because traditional Indian administrative systems had been designed for centralised governance and were not appropriate for decentralised participatory governance
3. Providing a policy framework without restricting the freedom to respond to local needs
4. Guiding local governments without controlling them; enabling them without directing them
5. Proactive troubleshooting. Considering that local governments were bound to make innumerable mistakes in the early stages, mostly out of ignorance or enthusiasm and very few of them would be mala fide, the government provided easy access to the elected leaders and activists and set up a remarkably successful system of fast-tracking responses to issues called the coordination committee, which was empowered by the Cabinet to sort out all operational issues without moving files to different departments in the government including finance and planning.

What Kerala Got Right

Other than big politics and the associated 'big bang', Kerala got several things right, some of them by design and some by serendipity. In the transfer of functions to local governments, most human and social development functions at the district level and below – including health, education, nutrition, Scheduled Caste (SC) and Scheduled

Tribe (ST) development, women and child development and social security – were moved to local governments, with gram panchayats, municipalities and corporations getting the largest share, considering their proximity to people. In economic development, a significant portion of agriculture and allied sectors went to the local governments. In infrastructure, roads other than highways and major district roads became a local government responsibility, as did the maintenance of assets, mostly buildings and roads, which were transferred to them.

Thus, most functions related to human and social development, which constitute the core of the so-called Kerala model, are now local government mandates, and the sustainability of the model depends on their performance.

During the floods of 2018 and the Covid-19 crisis, local governments became the de facto frontline of governance, even though disaster management has not been devolved to them. They spontaneously coordinated departments like Revenue, Police and Labour effectively, laying a strong claim to having become real local governments in the fullest sense of the term, beyond expectations.

Surprisingly, along with the delegation of functions, the transfer of functionaries too was achieved with considerable success despite the existence of powerful employee unions through a simple formula: the work and the worker going together. Using this principle, the state transferred the different institutions and their staff to the local governments concerned. More impressively, it was able to create a new cadre for engineers by carving out surplus engineers from the Public Works and Irrigation departments, a cumbersome task.

There is documented evidence that over the years the transferred officers have aligned themselves closer to their respective local governments, fostering stronger working relationships there. For example, in the initial years of decentralisation, allopathic doctors could not work closely with the elected bodies. However, around 2005 this started to change slowly, and by 2011 the change was palpable, with positive results.

In terms of finances, Kerala's decentralisation can be termed 'classical'. The noteworthy features are: the local governments mobilise a significant amount of money as part of their own-source revenue; the village panchayats collect approximately ₹500 crore as their own tax and another ₹500 crore as non-tax revenue. Municipalities and corporations together collect a little over ₹800 crore as own tax and a little over ₹500 crore as non-tax revenue. These figures, especially the rural ones, compare very well with the rest of the country.

Among all the states in the country, Kerala's devolution is by far the fairest in terms of the sharing of resources between the state and local governments.

No Stacking the Deck – This Is 'Pure' Money

The state devolves 26.50 per cent of the state plan to local governments under the People's Plan. This amounted to ₹8,048 crore during 2023–2024. Of this, ₹1,341.30 crore was reserved for the Scheduled Caste Sub Plan (SCSP), constituting 45.50 per cent of the state SCSP, and ₹201.50 crore for the Tribal Sub Plan (TSP), constituting 23.40 per cent of the state TSP. The budget allocates these funds accordingly.

In addition, the state contributes ₹928 crore towards Centrally sponsored schemes implemented by the local governments. It is expected that the Central share would be around ₹5,600 crore. Further, ₹1,411 crore is earmarked for state schemes implemented by local governments, and ₹7,500 crore is the likely expenditure for different social security pensions, where the beneficiaries are selected by the local governments.

The state also devolves 4 per cent of its own tax revenue as a general-purpose fund, which is an addition to the own resources of local governments and is non-lapsable. Also, 6.5 per cent of the state's tax revenue is passed down to local governments for maintenance of the transferred assets – 4 per cent for roads and 2.5 per cent for buildings. The expected amounts for the general-purpose fund and the maintenance fund for the current year are ₹2,244.30 crore and ₹3,646.99 crore respectively.

Unlike many other Indian states, the devolution does not include the salary component, which is fully paid for by the state government separately. One can say that the funds given to local governments constitute 'pure' money, and all of this can be invested by local governments. Here are some highlights of Kerala's devolution:

1. Even during the worst times of fiscal stress, the shares of the local governments were not disturbed.

2. The fund flow is assured because it is budgeted and cannot be reappropriated. Allocations are transparent. Since 1 April 1997, every rupee has been devolved through non-discretionary, formula-based systems.
3. The devolution is equitable, with significant weightage for backwardness.
4. The devolved funds are 'fungible', which means they are not allocated against a scheme but as a lump sum under broad categories, and local governments can use them for their top-priority expenditure requirements.

During a financial year, the funds flow freely and automatically, with monthly allocations made in most cases without waiting for expenditure reports and claims, as was the case at the beginning of the Ninth Five-Year Plan.

Most importantly, the state has been prompt in constituting state finance commissions (SFCs). In 2019, when the Sixth SFC should have been constituted in every state, Kerala was one of only six states to do so. Further, in 2021, Kerala was the first to operationalise the Sixth SFC's recommendations relating to devolution. This was just three and a half months after the recommendations were submitted.

A strong framework is required for decentralisation to endure. Kerala has robust Panchayati Raj and Municipality Acts, with innovative features like a Citizen's Charter, an absolute right to information, an Ombudsman and Appellate Tribunal for local governments, and a state development council on the lines of the erstwhile National Development Council.

A Homage to Kerala's People's Plan

The framework for decentralised planning has been accepted nationally. More or less following the methodology developed for the People's Plan in Kerala, more than 2.5 lakh gram panchayats in the country are preparing gram panchayat development plans. Interestingly, the Government of India christened this exercise the People's Plan Campaign with effect from 2018.

The planning framework is quite inclusive. Forty-five per cent of the SCSP and 23.40 per cent of the TSP funds are planned.

Of the annual allocation of funds, 10 per cent is set apart for women, and another 10 per cent is allocated for vulnerable groups such as the elderly, children and person with disabilities.

For local governments to be effective, they need well-defined freedoms and clearly demarcated limits. The local governments of Kerala can approve any scheme within their financial allocation, with no ceiling. Their decisions cannot be overruled by the government. Even if they violate the law, the government can only stay the decision and take a final call after getting the views of the Ombudsman, who is a serving or retired high court judge. The same procedure, including giving a detailed charge sheet, must be followed for dissolving a local government or removing any elected head or member.

The experience of over a quarter of a century shows that all governments have facilitated the smooth functioning of local governments without infringing upon their autonomy.

Kerala is unique in having local government associations for village, block and district panchayats as well as for municipalities and corporations. These bodies facilitate government interaction on policy issues. For instance, they once commissioned Dr M.A. Oommen to develop a memorandum for the Union Finance Commission and they occasionally conduct action research on priority themes.

Partnering with Kudumbashree, the women's network rolled out in 1998, has had several positive effects:

1. Kudumbashree runs several social enterprises to which many functions of local governments are outsourced, especially waste management and the running of budget hotels.
2. Considerable funds have flowed from the local governments to Kudumbashree for livelihood activities.
3. This partnership has ensured that Kerala is the highest spender under the Mahatma Gandhi National Rural Employment Guarantee Scheme when compared to its poverty levels, with the annual expenditure crossing ₹5,000 crore, of which nearly 70 per cent flows to Kudumbashree members as wages, arguably the most critical factor in reducing absolute poverty in Kerala. According to the latest NITI Aayog estimate of multidimensional poverty, absolute poverty in Kerala is only 0.7 per cent.

4. Kudumbashree members play an active role in the state's participatory planning.
5. Nearly two-thirds of the elected women representatives in local governments, urban and rural, are from Kudumbashree, an unexpectedly powerful outcome of cooperation.

For local governments to convert their capabilities or potential into effective functioning or performance, capacity-building is critical. In the early days of the People's Plan, there was a three-tier system of resource people, that is, about 600 key resource people at the state level, about 10,000 district resource people and about a lakh local resource people. They were involved in different types of capacity-building. Soon the capacity-building programme became institutionalised through the Kerala Institute of Local Administration (KILA), which has gained national stature as an institution of excellence in training elected functionaries. Curiously, KILA was started in 1990 using donations from each village panchayat. Its governing council has representation from all local government associations.

Analysing the functioning in terms of attainments, panchayats and municipalities are recognised and respected as local governments; they have become the frontline of governance. People know of their functions and are able to exert demands.

This has expanded the democratic space. Decentralisation has ensured equitable fund distribution to local governments, resulting in a 'diffuse' economic stimulus. Local governments focus on pro-poor expenditures, enhancing basic infrastructure like housing, sanitation and roads. Improved supply and demand have boosted public service performance, with a rise in government school attendance for the first time in three decades. The public health system has also seen significant improvement, with government health facility usage rising from 29 per cent at the start of the People's Plan to 47.50 per cent in 2018.

Another outstanding performance is in care and compassion. The palliative care movement of Kerala has become an international best practice as a local-government-led, community-managed system with the full involvement of health professionals. The Ashraya scheme, catering to the needs of the poorest of the poor, comprises destitute individuals who form less than 2 per cent of the population and has achieved wide acclaim. The community-based education of children with mental disabilities through BUDS schools in Kerala has also been well recognised.

Abject poverty has decreased rapidly, with the latest figures of multidimensional poverty in India by NITI Aayog indicating that only 0.7 per cent of Kerala's population is poor, as against the national figure of 25.1 per cent. The social security net has widened and, as of now, there are 51.35 lakh people benefiting from pensions for the elderly, widows, persons with disabilities or agricultural labourers.

An unexpected but impressive performance of local governments was their proactive response to the devastating floods in 2018 and 2019, involving excellent relief activities and initial rehabilitation. The performance of local governments in leading the efforts against Covid-19 from the front also received considerable attention across the country.

Natural calamities and pandemics have brought out the best in local governments. Though a detailed study needs to be conducted, impressions gathered in the field and from experts indicate that the following factors made local governments perform beyond expectations:

1. Responsibility assigned with trust and expectation
2. Clarity on the roles to be performed
3. Wide dissemination of information about the responsibilities entrusted to them
4. People's expectation of help close at hand, creating a kind of demand-and-pull factor
5. Intensity of work resulting in the push factor
6. Incentive for total performance, as there is a huge risk even in a small slip-up and the services constitute a non-rival public good
7. Joined-up functioning at the cutting-edge level without political differences and working closely with civil society organisations, non-governmental organisations (NGOs) and volunteers
8. Local-government-wide action beyond electoral constituency
9. All functionaries at the local level coordinated by the local governments
10. Visibility and recognition

11. Results and satisfaction motivating quality of performance and heralding a new politics of development, quite different from the politics of profit, whether in terms of votes or money or both

All these positive features have significantly contributed to Kerala earning the top place in the Devolution Index, and that too well ahead of other states, as revealed by the following figures:

State	Index
Kerala	0.72
Maharashtra	0.54
Karnataka	0.50
Tamil Nadu	0.47
Gujarat	0.45

Table 1: Figures from the Devolution Index prepared by the Tata Institute of Social Sciences in 2016

Now, after more than twenty-five years of the People's Plan, it is time for a critical reassessment.

What Kerala Didn't Get Right

Traditionally, water supply and street lighting are local government functions globally, yet Kerala has failed to transfer these responsibilities to local governments effectively. The declaration of the Kerala Water Authority as a local authority to overcome certain legal challenges, despite it being the sole statutory body for water supply, is notable. Furthermore, while village panchayats, municipalities and corporations manage street lighting, they lack control over personnel. The labour unions' resistance to local government control explains this anomaly.

While the capacity-building of elected representatives has been remarkable, the attempt to professionalise the bureaucracy of local governments, especially the Secretaries of village panchayats and urban local governments, has not been very successful.

Recently, the government integrated officials under different categories of local governments into one service. Though it is a welcome step, there are serious defects. For example, without any rhyme or reason, the Secretary of the block panchayat is given the same status as the Secretary of the village panchayat, even though, since the beginning, the block development officer was a kind of supervisory authority over the executive officers of panchayats. Another inexplicable decision is the removal of the cadre of village extension officers, even though much of Kerala's rural development is due to the field-level efforts of these functionaries. There is no denying that, since the 1980s, they have become distanced from the people, and some of them even become corrupt. But they retain their deep, collective understanding of field-level realities and the capacity to interact with the lay public. Another serious deficiency is that all departments have been brought under one principal director, seriously affecting the identity and self-respect of heads of technical departments like the chief town planner, chief engineer and LSGD.

Even though the transferred officers have moved closer to local governments, some critical departments like Agriculture, Social Justice and SC/ST still maintain some kind of distance from the elected panchayats.

Realising that the operating systems of governance in India were designed for centralised rule, it was decided to develop appropriate systems for local governments, facilitating transparency, participation and ease of operation without compromising on fairness, integrity and due processes. This effort, called institutionalisation, is nearly twenty years old but remains a work in progress. It is high time that appropriate systems are put in place for personnel management, project management, institutional management, financial management and so on.

While the capacity-building efforts of Kerala are among the best in the country, it has not yet moved on to governance and management; the focus is still on rules, procedures, processes and development concepts.

Though the hallmark of Kerala's decentralisation has been its participatory planning, it is still based on the negotiated and impressionistic priorities of the elected representatives. There is hardly any use of data in fixing priorities, and spatial planning is not integrated into the planning system, even though nearly two decades ago the Kollam district developed a viable model of participatory spatial planning.

When nearly one-third of the state plan is devolved to the local governments for planning and implementation, there is a need for active convergence with the state plan and convergence across the tiers in the true spirit of multilevel planning. This can at best be said to have been only partially successful.

District planning is at the core of the constitutional amendments. In spite of two sincere efforts, district planning as a viable methodology has not emerged in Kerala.

A unique feature of Kerala's People's Plan Campaign was the harnessing of the voluntary services of experts from outside the government using the concept of a voluntary technical corps, an innovation that was nationally applauded. But gradually, due to silent opposition from the local-government bureaucracy and a lack of enthusiasm from the elected representatives, the utilisation of non-government experts declined rapidly and was formally abandoned in 2012.

It is intriguing that the state which has the largest number of NGOs in the country, the most active media and a relatively concerned academia could not attract their interest and involvement in the decentralisation initiatives to the extent desired.

Second-Generation Challenges of Decentralisation

While agriculture and allied sectors, especially animal husbandry, have received considerable attention and allocations from local governments, more needs to be done to generate jobs and incomes, which are central to local economic development.

In terms of social justice, especially for marginalised sections, performance has been very poor.

Hydra-Headed Corruption Still Reigns

When the People's Plan was started, it was reckoned that corruption had decreased over the years; however, corruption seems to have crept up, as evidenced by the number of cases registered by the Vigilance Department. This is confirmed by the informed opinions of activists in the field of decentralised planning. Local government corruption is less than corruption in state departments – there is enough evidence to show that the unit cost of any work done by the good local governments is less than that of similar work done by state departments. However, it has to be acknowledged that decentralised corruption is more dangerous than corruption at higher levels, as it weakens people's faith in representative democracy.

Another negative feature is the fixed, ward-wise division of funds, irrespective of unique development needs and priorities. This hyper-democratic effect was never expected, and there is no system to counter it.

Kerala's ageing population is actually a sign of its development, for it captures the state's all-round development performance in one indicator. But handling an increasing share of the elderly population in a sensitive manner requires adequate preparation and carefully modulated local action. The current efforts of local governments need to be pushed further.

Another long-term challenge is environmental degradation and the consequent threat of climate change. Though local governments started addressing these problems nearly ten years ago, the pace is too slow; there is a need for concerted rapid action on this front.

State Finance Commissions have noted that local governments are under-collecting taxes and non-tax revenues, with an estimated 40 per cent of taxes having 'escaped'. This needs to be addressed through technological measures like geographic-information-system-based tax mapping and punitive actions for careless assessment and evasion.

Similarly, though local governments have proved themselves to be good at raising user charges, they tend to fix them in an ad hoc manner.

Opportunities

1. Riding on the success of Kudumbashree, the government has announced a policy decision to set up self-help groups of the elderly and persons with disabilities, without any distinction like male, female, above poverty line, below poverty line, etc. These need to be immediately operationalised, considering their potential.
2. A policy decision was taken to convert the Kerala State Audit Department into an autonomous, professional local-government

audit commission that would focus on performance audit, in addition to routine audit. This needs to be actualised at the earliest.

3. In the context of decentralisation, local statistics need to be developed, mostly using the statistics generated during administrative processes. Kerala can show the way in developing a coherent local statistics system, as it has the biggest Department of Statistics in the country. This is critical for local planning.
4. The Government of India launched a promising programme with great fanfare in 2014 called Unnat Bharat Abhiyan, which mandated that every institution of higher education, starting from Indian Institutes of Management, Indian Institutes of Technology and Central universities up to graduate colleges, do something in a village panchayat in the vicinity.
5. Recently, the Ministry of Panchayati Raj launched the initiative of localising sustainable development goals (SDGs). Kerala is in the best position to develop an international model to show how local governments can facilitate the attainment of the SDGs.

Conclusion

If one were to judge the performance of Kerala's decentralisation vis-à-vis the ideals that motivated the policymakers at the beginning of the People's Plan, it would be difficult to give it more than a passing mark at this point in time. But when Kerala's performance is compared with that of other states or its local governments with those of other developing countries, the state can hold its head high and claim to be developing a new Kerala model of development. So the time has come to look back, learn from the successes and failures, and move forward rapidly. But this calls for strong political signals.

Part 4
Personal Reflections

Not All Were God's Creatures Once

Madanamohan Rameshkumar

Travails of My Grandfather

Sometime in the mid-eighteenth century, my great-great-great-grandfather Vaikom Ramakrishna Pillai had secured, by outright sale, more than 200 acres of land. Though it was criss-crossed by small streams, bisected by a thodu,[1] pock-marked by ditches and uneven with mounds and bushes, it was fit for cultivation. He was more worried about the vast expanse of forests, thorny scrub lands and marshes in the vicinity of his private acquisition, and he made repeated requests to the Vadakkumkoor Raja to gift him the land via a grant. He would have to put in massive efforts, including extensive deployment of slave labour, to reclaim the impenetrable stretches to make it cultivable. When the raja issued a proclamation granting him those lands, around 300 acres, on a lease of 99 years, he was more apprehensive than happy because the deed stipulated that the grantee should make the lands arable and start raising crops within two years. It was a win-win situation for the raja, for agriculturists of the area frequently complained of marauding wolf packs, thieving jackals and droves of wild boar killing cattle and destroying crops.

Ramakrishna Pillai was already cropping sufficient paddy, with the surplus being carried by his slaves, under the supervision of his Karyasthan, or manager, to nearby markets for sale. His properties abounded with mango and pepper, jackfruit and anjili or wild jack (a relative of jackfruit; fruits are small drupes with spiny skin) and punna (calophyllum) with leathery, dark-green leaves and fruit that look like huge, dark-green grape clusters. Punna seeds yielded oil when crushed. It was used for lighting lamps and purposes other than cooking. There were a few marotti trees (*Hydnocarpus pentandra*) in one corner, near the scrublands and near the huts of slaves, with globose berries. Seeds of marotti fruit also provided oil for non-edible uses. Marotti oil was used as an Ayurvedic medicine for many skin diseases, including leprosy. Pillai's properties contained some coconut trees, the oil of which was precious and used only for cooking.

Pillai debated at length with his peers, Karyasthan and family members on how to put to use his newly acquired land after reclamation. From the time his ancestors had started settling in Vaikom, exotic plants such as papaya, guava, pineapple, breadfruit tree and cashew or paranki pazham (literally Portuguese fruit) had been introduced there, largely piloted by Jesuit missionaries from Portugal, belonging to the Society of Jesus. His 'puraidom' had quite a few cashew trees and breadfruit trees. It is said that before the advent of the Portuguese, 'Mappila vargam', that is, the Arabs, had introduced tea, and the Dutch opened the taste of coffee to Hindustan. But the only organised, extensively cultivated crop in the kingdom was paddy.

Agriculturists like Pillai had heard that the Dutch had established a number of coconut plantations. There were dozens of them spread across various locations in Travancore and Kochi. Some had been leased for a compensation of around 14,000 rupees for twenty-seven years or so. It was incumbent upon the lessees to cull old and sterile trees and plant new ones. The Dutch would inspect the plantation every year. They also wanted the lessees to erect fences around the plantations to prevent stray cattle from entering the plantations. The young saplings were especially vulnerable to the cattle. Pillai had heard about a Dutch farm, situated in Arookutty, near Kochi. He wanted to establish a large plantation and wanted to study how the Dutch did it, even though he would have to wait almost seven years to start realising regular incomes. Coastal areas were ideal for growing the coconut crop. Vaikom was not by the sea. It was along the Vembanadu lagoon, the largest backwaters of Travancore, and it had significant salinity because of the sustained organic contact with the sea. People would use coconut trunks and fronds as house construction materials. But more importantly was the demand for coir.

The spread and popularity of coconut in the coastal strip of Kerala as a plantation agricultural crop had an organic linkage with geographical and hydrological upheavals in the past few centuries. The historian Kosambi speculates that the coconut, a native of Malaysia and probably Indonesia and the Philippines, had arrived on the east coast in the early centuries after Christ, facilitated by seaborne migrations. The western coast, on the contrary, was in many places full of forests, and even Alleppey, the 'Venice of the East' and a famed centre of coir trade later, became habitable only in the eighteenth century, during the times of Raja Kesavadas. P. Sankunni Menon in *History of Travancore*[2] describes how Kesavadas got a port constructed at Alleppey, having realised the locational advantages of the place. Slaves toiled for months to clear scrub jungles and bushes along the seashore. His successor, Velu Thambi, too cleared scrub jungles in a number of small islands or 'thuruthus' north of Alleppey to make them fit for cultivation. Coconut saplings were planted in parts of the cleared areas and other areas were leased for paddy cultivation. This was in 1805. Coconut cultivation on a large scale along the west coast of Travancore was therefore a recent development.

It was a determined Pillai who came back from Arookutty after visiting the Dutch coconut plantation. He was impressed by the circular bunds around each tree and in the open spaces between the bunds soil was gathered in one-and-a-half- to two-feet-high conical heaps to conserve water and prevent runoff. Between rows of trees were narrow channels which served the purposes of drainage and irrigation. All around the plantation was a fencing of illimula, a species of bamboo with thin stems, and pandanus (kaitha), light-yellow flowers of which exuded a heady fragrance. Pandanus clumps had grown quite dense in places, some of them bearing massive yellow fruit that looked like hypertrophied pineapples. The leaves served as good raw material for weaving mats and baskets. The spiny margins on the sides of the leaves were removed, and after dipping them briefly in boiling water to make them supple and strengthen the fibres, the leaves were dried.

Lord's Creatures as Chattel

If he had to clear all these scrublands, the forests and thorny bushes and reclaim marshy stretches to make them fit for cultivation within two years, perhaps the raja would not mind extending the period, Pillai thought. He surmised he would soon have to mobilise or purchase an adequate number of additional slave labourers. The tharawad,[3] 'Cherickaparambil', already had ownership of around a hundred slaves, some of whom had come along with the properties purchased by him.

Slavery was fundamental to agrarian relations in Kerala. There were three categories of slaves.[4] First were 'agrestic serfs' who were slaves by birth, bought and sold like cattle and most of whom were transferred along with the land sold. 'They were literally like trees or oxen' and many sale deeds would explicitly allow the buyer to kill them or sell them. Though some legal provisions evolved later which protected slaves from being put to death, they were mostly ignored. Still later, officials were appointed to mete out punishment to slaves to ensure that the slave owners did not go overboard in inflicting punishment. The punishments were meted out at suitable locations in the property to male and female slaves separately. According to a sale deed of 1788, 'aalu vela olakkaram'[5] described in P. Bhaskaranunni's iconic study of Kerala sociology, *Pathombatham Nootandile Keralam*,[6] Moothedathu Narayanan of Valankara desam sold a Pulaya woman named Polinna and her children to one Mathunni Mathunni with absolute rights and permission to kill if necessary, to sell if necessary and to use them as draught animals if necessary.[7] All slaves in Pillai's stock were agrestic slaves by birth and belonged to the Paraya, Pulaya and Kurava castes.

Pillai avoided the next two categories like the plague. The second category consisted of prisoners of war sold into slavery and women criminals condemned to slavery because they could not be given capital punishment. One may recall Marthanda Varma's ruthless extermination of his rivals, the Ettuveettil Pillamar[8] and the sale of inconsequential relatives as slaves and the sale of women and children to fisherfolk in perpetual bondage. The second category also included women of higher castes found guilty of intimacy with lower-caste men. To the third category belonged people who sold themselves or their children during scarcity and famine. Many belonging to the Ezhava caste were slaves of this category.

In *The History of Travancore*, R.N. Panikkar says that agricultural operations were entrusted to Pulayas.[9] They were considered integral parts of the lands, like goods bought and sold. If a Pulayan belonged to one master and a Pulayi to another, the first offspring of the Pulayi would be owned by the master of the Pulayan and the later offspring of the Pulayi would be owned by her master. But the Pulayi's master had a right to acquire the first offspring by paying a fixed price. When exceedingly hard pressed, the Pulaya couple could sell their children or sons- or daughters-in-law at a cost not exceeding 60 fanams (8.5 rupees). Since any amount beyond 60 fanams was the master's right, they had no incentive to sell at a price above 60 fanams. According to Bhaskaranunni,[10] a cow was safe in Kerala and killing a cow or violence against a cow was one of the five crimes undeserving of pardon. But slaves could be killed with impunity, and notwithstanding legal provisions which forbade such killings, authorities would ignore such atrocities.

Another source of slaves had a nexus with weird rituals and practices like 'Pulappedi' and 'Parapedi' ('fear of Pulaya' and 'fear of Paraya'), writes Bhaskaranunni.[11] On certain days of the year, such as the days of 'Pooram' and 'Vela' festivals, the local raja used to grant permission to the 'lower castes' to move about freely in certain sacred groves ('kaavu'). They were even permitted to touch or molest higher-caste women they encountered on the roads. Any higher-caste woman subjected to such 'touch pollution' by the Pulayas or Parayas running amok on that day had to go with them and she would be excommunicated. These women, in consequence, became slaves.

In Pillai's properties, huts of slaves were situated near the border fence at the rear. There were two groups of huts, one for the Parayas and one for the Pulayas, but at a shouting distance. Pillai found it extremely odd that the most wretched of the earth too had their own untouchability code and distance regulations. Of Pillai's agrestic slaves, the Parayas would not work alongside the Pulayas; they considered themselves superior. The two groups of huts had been constructed strictly in accordance with the distance prescriptions. There was a pond near one cluster for Parayas and the other group used a thodu at a distance for bathing and washing clothes. Logistics of allotment of work of the day had to be carefully designed lest they run into each other, which would result in acrimony and consequent waste of time. The Ezhava slaves would only work keeping a distance of more than 32 feet from Pulayas. These amazingly weird practices and scarcity of efficient draught animals affected agricultural productivity. The inviolable practice of untouchability precluded the use of slave labour for domestic purposes.

Pillai would provide rice gruel and a vegetable curry, usually pumpkin, ash gourd, red spinach or bottle gourd, to all slaves at noon. In addition, monthly wages consisted of a 'parah'[12] of rice for every able-bodied slave and half a parah for children. It is not as if the children only made merry and ate. They were deployed for less arduous duties like weeding and contributed to the family's nutrition by catching fish or digging out mice from bunds separating the paddies.

Abbe Dubois was a Christian missionary from France who spent three decades in India, from 1792 to 1823. His seminal work, *Hindu Manners, Customs and Ceremonies*,[13] is unrivalled in recording the sociology of those times. It is said no other work on Hindus 'combines a recital of broad facts of Hindu religion and Hindu sociology and many masterly descriptions of the "vie intime" of the people among whom he lived for so many years'.[14]

The description of Parayas, a caste name immortalised in the English language by the word 'pariah' in the lexicon, in Dubois's scholarly treatise holds a mirror to the appalling social conditions of those times. He writes:

> There are certain classes, however, who owing to the depth of degradation into which they have fallen, are looked upon as another race of beings, altogether outside the pale of society.
> … Best known and most numerous of these castes is the 'parayer'.
> … Throughout the whole of India the pariahs are looked upon as slaves by other castes and are treated with great harshness.
> … The idea that he was born to be in subjugation to other castes is so ingrained in his mind that it never occurred to the pariah that his fate is anything but irrevocable.[15]

According to Dubois, some Europeans kept Parayas as servants because persons belonging to other castes would not do menial tasks like cleaning chamber pots or cooking beef. Some 'pariahs' were allowed to enlist in European and native armies. But they are 'absolutely deficient in all sense of honour and one might almost say that in the matters of vice they outstrip all in brutality, as the Brahmins do in malice'.[16]

About their abominable living conditions, Dubois writes: '[They] are much addicted to drunkenness … what chiefly disgusts other natives is the revolting nature of food which the pariahs eat. Attracted by smell they will collect in crowds around any carrion and contend for spoils with dogs, jackals and crows … Then they divide the semiputrid flesh and carry it away to the huts ... Sometimes they secretly poison cows and buffalos.'

Dubois also writes about 'pulich' (Pulaya), whose 'degradation and squalid misery' are worse than that of pariahs. He says Pulayas were not allowed to build themselves huts for protection from the vagaries of the weather. A lean-to, supported by four bamboo poles, open from all sides, served as their dwelling place. Many of them lived in nest-like structures set among branches of trees with thickset foliage where they would perch like 'birds of prey'. 'A hundred paces is the very nearest they may approach anyone of a different caste. If a Nair who always carries arms chances upon one of these unhappy people on the road, he is entitled to stab him on the spot.' In some areas Pulaya slaves had to wear stone garlands or 'kallumala' to identify themselves.[17]

Slave Trafficking

'Slavery in Kerala', a document forwarded by senior revenue officials to the Board of Revenue in 1818, explained prevalent types of slave transactions.[18] 'Jenmom'[19] right over a slave could be transferred to another person in an outright sale transaction. A slave could be mortgaged in a 'kanom' transaction (lease or 'otty'), wherein the owner would receive two-thirds of the value of the slave in cash and the remaining value in rice. The mortgagee was liable to provide a replacement if a slave died in his employment. The original owner was legally entitled to reclaim the slave on repayment of the consideration paid. A slave could also be transferred on 'pattom' or rent. Possession of slaves could be transferred by these methods either accompanying a land transaction or independently. The number of slaves in possession was an indication of the social standing of a landholder. For maintaining a stock of slaves, the slave owners had to pay a certain amount per slave every year to the Naduvazhi, the local raja. It was called 'adimappanam'[20] and was a source of revenue to the royalty.

Prevalent conventions governing slave transactions in the society enjoined the owners not to sell members of a family separately. Transactions were humane(!) enough to ensure that the wife was sold along with the husband and children with their parents. In a report on the nature of some slave transactions, Koman Sirdar, a tehsildar, writes:

'When a cheruman takes a cherumi belonging to another proprietor, it is not customary for either the cheruman or cherumi to undertake anything for maintenance of one another reciprocally. All the children together from them are to belong to cheruman's proprietor provided such children are brought forth during the lifetime of the cheruman. Any child born after his death or before marriage to that cherumi would belong to cherumi's proprietor.'[21] Prices of female slaves depended on their childbearing capacity too and differed from area to area. A judge of a court in Calicut, E.B. Thomas, writes that the price of a slave woman is 'very high if she is very productive'.

The memoirs of James Forbes, an oriental scholar who spent eighteen years in the service of the East India Company including as manager of a British godown at Anchuthengu (formerly known as Anjengo),[22] mentions waves of poor moving to in times of agricultural distress where he witnessed a young man offering to sell himself in return for only food and shelter and a mother trying to sell a child for a sack of rice. The cheapest commodity in Anjengo was children. He bought a boy and a girl of eight to nine years as a gift for a woman friend in Bombay at a price less than what it would cost him for two pegs of Scotch in London. Their travel to Bombay, which took two months, food and four sets of clothes together cost him only 20 rupees. He felt that the children were fortunate that he bought them to be sent to a place where they would be looked after well.[23]

Rev. Henry Baker Jr writes[24] that on all market days either guardians or relatives brought children for sale to Changanassery market for prices ranging from 6 to 18 rupees. Of the foreigners, the most profitable trades used to be conducted by the Dutch from Kochi, Kollam and Calicut ports and the most profitable commodity for the Dutch was slaves, including Nair and Thiya slaves who had become slaves upon being convicted by the local king. Some organised gangs used to indulge in the abduction and kidnapping of children of Thiyya and other castes and sell them to agents in Mahe and Kochi, under the control of the French and the Dutch respectively, from where those children used to be sold as slaves in French island colonies. Their vile predecessors, the Portuguese, had not only rivalled them in the slave trade but also displayed wanton cruelty. A large number of slaves were captured by the Portuguese from the Malabar Coast and sent to Batavia (Jakarta),

Ceylon, Mauritius and Cape Town till the Dutch seized their settlements in the mid-seventeenth century. Thikkodiyan's *Chuvanna Kadal* (Red Sea), a celebrated work of historical fiction published in 1963,[25] set against the background of naval wars between the Portuguese, the Zamorin and Kunjali Marakkar, traces the romanticised adventurous journey of a fisher boy, Pokkan, enslaved by the Portuguese after a war and exhibited in the slave market in Goa for auction. Evocative descriptions of the slave auction include 'blue-eyed black beauties and hardworking fishermen with great physique from Malayalakkara'.

There was also a huge population of Sircar slaves (government slaves). They came into the possession of the Sircar when sometimes properties were forfeited for the realisation of government dues such as land revenue. It was also a widespread practice to auction slaves of revenue defaulters. Feudal rulers (Travancore kings, for example) possessed huge armies of slaves to till their lands. So did the temples that owned vast tracts of land. The Sircar used to lease slaves to other needy landowners and did roaring business. The rulers (Sircar) and gods themselves were integral parts of a slave-owning society and were top predators of the food chain! In 1848 there were 6,760 adult Sircar slaves and 1,266 child slaves in Kochi. Besides, 573 adults and 141 children were attached to properties in the possession of Sircar. Together, the labour of these slaves fetched a revenue of 4,041 rupees a year to the Sircar.

My Grandfather's Travails: Redux

Pillai had once transferred on kanom eleven Pulaya slaves to a Nair landholder, Gangadharan, securing a price of 300 fanams. The slaves were not unhappy with Pillai; they were well fed and healthy. In lieu of the balance price, he was paid 100 parahs of paddy. A few years later, finding that he needed more manpower, he decided to terminate the mortgage by repaying the consideration he had received. He summoned his Karyastan, Kunjan Nair, to convey the message that he would be sending the money back by the following week and that the slaves needed to be 'prepared' to be dispatched to the parent 'tharawad'. By his assessment his land stock would be tripled and, given the land-use pattern he had in mind, mostly of coconut and paddy and also some banana, he may need an additional hundred on his permanent roll. For clearance and reclamation, keeping in view the seasonal nature of agricultural operations, an additional fifty on mortgage would be enough to supplement his available stock of 'adimakal' (slaves).

He had an enormous task on hand. But slaves were abundant in the markets and freely available. The weekly markets of Kaduthuruthy and Kottayam would present plenty for sale. All landowners had a judicious mix: there would be some children and hardworking men and women. Some women were quite fecund, very good for the perpetuation of the stock. Some in his stock always bore male offspring. In the markets plenty of Ulladas and Kuravas too would be on display. But most of them were lazy and they detested the hard labour involved in agricultural operations. Some of them were adept weavers and woodworkers, though. Pillai decided to depute two of his trusted overseers to the Kaduthuruthy and Changanassery markets to replenish his stocks. He always preferred Malabar Cherumans. They were sincere, loyal, hardworking and healthy specimens.

Kunjan Nair reported, 'Angunne [Master], people say that the situation in Tamizhakom is quite precarious. Slaves are selling cheap.'

'Famine? Drought? No rains?' Pillai quizzed. Across the hill ranges of the west lay the rain-shadow areas of Tamizhakom. During times of drought, the parched lands and hunger would displace hundreds of poor families. Landowners saddled with idle slaves and with no income, no tilling and no sowing would put slave stocks on distress sale. Traders and middlemen would greedily scour the sun-battered villages of Ramanad, Porulatchai, Kovai and Madhurai for purchases. Very often it did not involve even fanam transactions. What would money buy if there were no goods to buy? The sellers would be paid in kind: parahs of rice and coconuts.

'I cannot send you or others to places so far away,' Pillai said doubtfully. Kunjan said, 'There is a vyapari in Trippunithura. He is a trustworthy slave trader. He goes every year to Tamizhakom. We have to pay edanilappanam[26] and some costs.'

Pillai agreed. 'Send a message to him to see me after two days. Also, we need to call Chakkunni too, that margam koodiyavan,[27] from Vechoor.' Chakkunni and his gun would be integral parts of the plan for exterminating wild fauna from the royal grant. Traps, poison and expertise of slaves, even of the Vattuvan (Hunter) tribes, of which he had two, would be inadequate. Chakkunni had converted to Christianity a few years ago and was the proud owner of a rifle gifted to him by the king for the display of exceptional bravery in saving the life of a deputy tehsildar from some 'goons'. That the 'goons' were some embattled citizens fed up with his atrocities and gross misconduct was another matter.

Emancipation: A New Tortuous Dawn

Political initiatives of the British administration, compassion on the part of the rulers of Travancore and Kochi, advocacy of abolition by liberals and the proselytising religious zeal of Christian missionaries had started having an impact on the inhuman practices of trafficking in slaves by the early nineteenth century. Many missionaries purchased slaves from their owners, converted them to Christianity and gave them freedom. There were also en masse conversions to Islam, which helped the slave castes to break the shackles of bondage. Overnight a 'Cheruman' would cease to become an untouchable (in theory); he would earn instant recognition as a member of the human species. The whole Muslim community would stand solidly behind any convert if he faced any harassment or threat. However, Christian missionaries were able to arrest these waves of conversions to Islam by offering various incentives like remission of 'thalavari' (head tax) and 'oozhiyam' (an amount a bonded labour owed to his creditor) and educational facilities by influencing British administrative policies.

The Dutch and the French were infamous for being complicit in organised rackets of abduction of children and smuggling them out of their colonies in Kerala. According to Dr Francis Dey, in the Dutch colony of Kochi, churches served except on Sundays as godowns of slaves to be exported.[28] Consequent to the establishment of British rule in Malabar, a proclamation had been issued in 1792 against such practices. Punitive measures contained in the proclamation included distraining the slaves if found, the levy of a fine at five times the cost of the slaves, the declaration of the seller as a thief and the confiscation of transport such as boats used for such activities. But trafficking in slaves went on unimpeded notwithstanding such orders because many loopholes were left unplugged and rehabilitation of slaves, including linkages for ensuring alternate livelihood, was not taken care of. For example, an order stated that 'the traditional practice' of adiyalars selling their children to 'reputed savarna families' could continue, with the condition that children could be taken back when the condition of the poor families improved!

In 1819, the practice of the Sircar disposing of slaves by auction to realise government dues was stopped. Rani Lakshmi Bai had also issued an order in 1812 prohibiting all forms of slavery except those attached to the soil in agriculture. The order prescribed severe punishment for breach thereof, including banishment outside the state. This too had not served the desired objectives. Though hailed as reformatory, it did not engage with the central issues. These steps only slowed down the pace of trafficking at best and slaves themselves were unhappy about the uncertain future these orders entailed in the absence of alternative livelihood and rehabilitation. Therefore, they often connived at their own trafficking.

The arrival of Protestant missionaries in Travancore in 1816 heralded a new era of rationalism and liberalism, and they worked zealously against these evil practices. But their primary aim was conversion, and they had a gargantuan pool to pick from. But for the converts it was not as if their new lease of life was peaceful, though they achieved a higher social status, protected by the Christian missions and having benefited from education, training and employment. Some of the emancipated women started covering their chests, which had earlier been prohibited. Many converts were threatened and subjected to physical assault by the erstwhile slave owners and some of the prayer halls and school rooms were burnt down.

E.B. Thomas, a judge in Calicut, wrote a strong letter on 24 November 1841 to 'Sadar adalat' regarding the unceasing trafficking in slaves. He described therein the prices of slaves and some transactions. The price of boys below 10 years was 3 rupees and 8 annas, and girls fetched less. On 10 August 1841, an infant of 10 months was sold in a court auction for 1 rupee and 10 annas. He had recently adjudicated on the ownership of 27 slaves. The judge also pointed out, by way of a letter dated 24 August 1842, that as per the census of 1835, the number of slaves was 1.44 lakh and it had increased to 1.59 lakh as per the 1842 census, which clearly indicated that slavery was not on the decline in Malabar (though various orders to control and eradicate the slave trade had been issued in the past). Apparently, Thomas's letters prodded Company directors to write to the British government to enact anti-slavery legislation. Following this the Indian Slavery Act, 1843, was enacted by the British Parliament, which contained provisions to regulate slavery in British India. The Act, however, had fundamental flaws and was largely ineffective. It did not abolish slavery or criminalise the ownership of slaves. It did ban the sale of slaves for debt and granted property rights to slaves. The courts were not empowered to adjudicate on claims to ownership of slaves. But the pernicious social and economic structures basic to the system could continue unhindered. These provisions were widely publicised by the collectors. The Collector of Malabar, however, advised the Cherumars that it would be expedient not to leave their owners if they were being treated kindly. He even said it was their obligation to do so. Basically, therefore, the aim was to ensure that attempts to eradicate slavery did not lead to negative repercussions to both owners and slaves, and to tread slowly and carefully. Every time a reform was discussed, landowners and feudal lords would be up in arms, highlighting its adverse effects on agriculture and productivity, including possibly the collapse of agriculture.

In 1847 missionaries including Charles Mead and Baker submitted a representation to the Government of Travancore to ban slavery. Their demands included:

1. Slaves should not be allowed to travel outside the state as slaves.
2. Slavery should attract punishment as provided in the Indian Slavery Act 1843 (as applicable to British India).
3. Slaves should be allowed to possess property.
4. Hereditary slavery should be abolished forthwith.
5. Sircar slaves should be released from bondage to start with.

General Cullen, Resident of Travancore, was an administrator with progressive views and a fervent supporter of conversion. He forwarded the memorandum to the diwan and pursued the matter forcefully. He insisted upon the government that an enactment on the lines of the 1843 Act be promulgated to the extent that it related to slavery.[29]

Even before the anti-slavery proclamation was issued, in some places slaves had begun asserting themselves by being aggressive to their owners. Some slaves fled to places far from the areas of their owners' influence and took refuge in villages in the high ranges like Mundakkayam and Ranni. Some incidents were militant in nature. Armed agents of landlords raided the camps of fugitives and carried them back to their owners. In some cases the missionaries 're-retrieved' the Pulaya slaves and sent them to their sanctuaries. Many schools were opened by missionaries; Rev. Mead's wife, Johanna Mead, had opened boarding schools for slave girls. The slave owners felt that the slaves when taught would cease to work, a classic concern of every oppressor that the educated were no longer amenable to oppression. The slave owners realised that anti-slavery campaigns were antagonistic to vested interests in agriculture. According to Rev. George Mathan of the Anglican Church, 'Strong fears existed among all classes of people that enlightenment will be followed by liberation.'[30] Syrian Christian and Nair landlords, often in unholy alliances, would burn down schools and unleash violence at conversion ceremonies. Many felt that the missionaries had 'usurped landlords' position of authority over the pulayas'.[31] In some cases, the influential missionaries ensured that these miscreants were punished by law and some were even made to reconstruct vandalised school rooms and chapels. There was tremendous enthusiasm among Pulayas to see themselves converted and they went in droves, confident and enthused about the protective and beneficent role of missionaries. After centuries of subsistence as something equivalent to cattle, it must have been a draining emotional catharsis when they were reborn as humans. This transition from subhumans was indeed a tortuous process.

Children of Sircar slaves were freed from slavery in 1853, but the Government of Travancore was still vehemently opposed to the abolition of slavery. They were apprehensive of the opposition from influential slave owners, public unrest and loss of revenue. A proclamation however was issued in 1853 regarding the abolition of slavery, but it was full of self-defeating clauses and designed to be ineffective. In 1854 a number of articles appeared in the 'Church Missionary Records' about the abject conditions of slaves. They came to the notice of the British government, which felt that effective interventions were immediately needed. In the same year, Lord Harris, a vehement opponent of slavery, assumed the Governorship of Madras and it was reportedly consequent to his firm but forceful requests that Kochi and Travancore issued proclamations banning slavery. Finally, in April 1855 an effective anti-slavery landmark order was proclaimed by Kochi. All Sircar slaves were freed. Slaves could acquire property. Penal provisions were incorporated to take adequate legal cognisance of persons dealing in slaves. In June 1855 Travancore followed with a proclamation banning slavery.

But adequate publicity was deliberately not given to the proclamations. Rev. Baker published copies of the proclamation in Malayalam and ensured their dissemination among the slaves, notwithstanding the opposition of landlords. However, even after this momentous step, the trafficking in slaves continued, both openly and secretly. Obviously, clandestine arrangements between owners and slaves could not be controlled by the government. Under Sections 370 and 371 of the Indian Penal Code the sale and purchase of slaves were made an offence in 1862, but this did not lead to the eradication of slavery altogether. It would take decades more for this scourge, passing off in many areas as 'bonded labour', to disappear completely. For example, in 1902, the king of Kurumbranad sold thirteen slave families that belonged to his palace to Muppathinadamsadesom in Wayanad by a written sale deed.

But the proclamations banning slavery eventually resulted in radical changes in the age-old social and agrarian relations and they led to the erasure of a dark blot in Kerala's collective conscience, though it would take a century more for collateral scourges like untouchability to make an exit.

Slave Statistics

Bhaskaranunni gives some estimates of the number of slaves in Kerala in the nineteenth century. In 1847, there were 60,000 slaves in Travancore. In 1857 Kochi also had around 60,000. In Malabar, only in Palakkad, Valluvanad and Ponnani, there were around 89,000 slaves. Based on these figures, he concludes that Kerala had a slave population of around 5 lakh in the nineteenth century.[32] According to Francis Buchanan, Travancore had 1.64 lakh slaves in 1836 out of a total population of 12.80 lakh.[33]

Notes

1 Stream.
2 P.S. Menon, *History of Travancore* (Trivandrum: Kerala Bhasha Institute, 1973).
3 Ancestral home.
4 Adoor K.K. Ramachandran Nair, *Slavery in Kerala* (New Delhi: Mittal Publications, 1986).
5 Palm leaf agreements of the price of slaves.

6 P. Bhaskaranunni, *Pathombatham Nootandile Keralam* (*Kerala in the Nineteenth Century*) (Kerala Sahitya Academy, 1988).
7 'Kettukil kettamarum, kollukil kollamarum, poottikil poottamarum'.
8 Chieftains of eight houses.
9 R.N. Panikkar, *The History of Travancore* (Trivandrum: Vidya Vilasini Book Depot, 1951).
10 *Pathombatham Nootandile Keralam.*
11 Ibid.
12 Measure equivalent to 8 kilos.
13 Abbe J.A. Dubois, *Hindu Manners, Customs and Ceremonies*, H.K. Beauchamp (trans.) (Oxford: Clarendon Press, 1906).
14 Ibid.
15 Ibid.
16 Ibid.
17 Ibid.
18 Adoor K.K. Ramachandran Nair, *Slavery in Kerala* (New Delhi: Mittal Publications, 1986).
19 Hereditary.
20 Slave money or slave tax.
21 Adoor K.K. Ramachandran Nair, *Slavery in Kerala* (New Delhi: Mittal Publications, 1986).
22 East India Company's first trade settlement in Kerala, 1694.
23 James Forbes, *Oriental Memoirs* (London: Richard Bentley, 1934).
24 Rev. Henry Baker Jr, *Slavery in Kerala: Banning of Slavery in 1855*.
25 Thikkodiyan, *Chuvanna Kadal* (1963).
26 Brokerage.
27 'Margam Koodal' referred to joining the path to attain salvation. Colloquial usage for conversion to Christianity was described as such.
28 Francis Dey, *The Land of the Perumals* (Gantz Books, 1863).
29 Renjini P. and C. Natarajan, 'Rani Gowry Lakshmi Bai: Abolition of Slavery in Travancore', *International Journal of Home Science* 3 (3): 336–339. Available online: https://www.homesciencejournal.com/archives/2017/vol3issue3/PartF/3-3-84-673.pdf (accessed 25 November 2025).
30 G. Oomen, 'Dalit Conversion and Social Protest in Travancore, 1854–1890', *Bangalore Theological Forum*, 27 (3 and 4): 69–84.
31 Ibid.
32 Bhaskaranunni, *Pathombatham Nootandile Keralam.*
33 Francis Buchanan Hamilton, *A Journey from Madras Through the Countries of Mysore, Canara and Malabar* (London: T.Cadell and W. Davies, 1807).

The Accidental Educationist

T.P. Sreenivasan

KERALA HAD PRODUCED MANY brilliant diplomats, but there was no tradition of the Kerala government utilising their services in any capacity. Therefore, I had not expected any assignment from the state when my family and I moved to Thiruvananthapuram in 2004. Apart from family and friends, I was banking on the golf course to keep me trim, and the KIMS hospital, if golf did not work, to provide health cover. So it was a surprise when Chief Minister Oommen Chandy called and offered me the post of Vice-Chairman of the Kerala State Higher Education Council, an institution of which I had no knowledge. I suggested to him that I had extensive experience with diaspora matters and that might be an area I could help with. But the chief minister was determined. He wanted someone with deep knowledge of global trends in education to give a new direction to higher education in Kerala as he wanted to liberalise it. I accepted the offer but did not know how to go about it. It was with considerable effort that I prepared myself for my role as an accidental educationist. I recalled how several diplomats had made a mark as educationists in other states and thought I would follow in their footsteps.

In the initial briefings by my predecessor, the Department of Higher Education and the education minister, I gained the impression that nobody expected me to do anything substantial – I would essentially be the twelfth man. I was expected to continue my predecessor's unfinished agenda and expand it. The Department of Higher Education was initially friendly, but it was more interested in protecting its own turf. The minister saw me as the chief minister's person and trusted the department more. Fortunately, the council had some experienced educationists. Even though all of them had been selected primarily for their party affiliations, we came together and formulated a six-point agenda consisting of infrastructure, teachers' training, use of technology, autonomy, research and internationalisation. Nobody objected to these, but the department had its own work plan in which the council was not involved, and fortune seekers in my own office were more loyal to the department than to me. This chaotic situation continued till the very end, and the Opposition exploited the situation to their advantage.

Stirring Up a Hornet's Nest

The situation was further confounded when the Government of India shifted some education funding from the University Grants Commission to councils in the states. The department was desperate to retain the funding. Our efforts to take over the new responsibility of the Rashtriya Uchchatar Shiksha Abhiyan (RUSA) were undermined by the department, which misinterpreted the rules and even questioned my credentials for being the vice-chairman. The Opposition, which had an ideological opposition to liberal education, exploited the rift and opposed the reform proposals, arguing that we were commercialising and commoditising higher education.

The chief minister was keen to grant an autonomous status to some of the arts and science colleges. We worked on the regulations for autonomy, but many students, teachers and even the management opposed them on various flimsy grounds. Nonetheless, we were able to secure autonomy for twenty colleges under different universities, with a supervising body to ensure proper implementation. Both the department and the concerned universities created several impediments. But some of the better colleges performed very well and introduced innovative courses, though they had to be self-financing. Now, with the Pradhan Mantri Uchchatar Shiksha Abhiyan being introduced, it appears that state-run universities will continue to retain control of the autonomous colleges and will use funds that were originally gathered through RUSA.

Our proposal to allow private and foreign universities in the state was specifically targeted by the Opposition. We argued that massive private investments were required to raise the level of education and that competition with foreign universities would be beneficial. However, nine former vice-chancellors issued a statement against these reforms. They virtually instigated the students to revolt against these proposals. Their concern was that the new institutions would be more enlightened and would not be amenable to strikes and campus politics. Our proposals were purely exploratory, but the threat of violence spread across the state as the students did not realise that they were acting against their own interests. I was personally targeted because I tried to explain the new policy in every forum. The politicians in the ruling front did not publicly defend the new policy as elections were close and a change of government was in the air. They were also preoccupied with allegations of scandals and corruption charges against the government.

Global Meeting, Local Action

A Global Education Meeting (GEM) had been under preparation for a long time, but its announcement was projected as the onset of harmful reform. It was forgotten that private investments had led to the growth of the education system in Kerala. The political atmosphere, which was already vitiated by scandals, worsened as students began to agitate against reform. A movement started against the reform, which resulted in physical violence against me when I arrived at the venue of the GEM to open the meeting. The attack was politically motivated and no consideration was given to the merits of the proposal. The demonstrators did not seem to know that the reforms were necessary to rescue the state from a decadent educational system. I was not hurt, but a photograph of me lying on Kovalam Beach after the attack by students appeared in the media. The attack became viral, symbolic of the politicisation of education and the extreme intolerance towards change. The violence vitiated the discussion and most delegates from outside Kerala left the state in disgust, proclaiming that they would never return to discuss education.

It transpired that the chief minister and the education minister had kept away from the GEM because of an understanding between the government and the Opposition – the Opposition had agreed not to disrupt the meeting if the chief minister and the education minister weren't present. And though they kept their word, the Opposition disrupted the meeting. The chief minister revealed this several months later when he released my book, *Education of an Ambassador*.

In the book I have recorded our efforts and experiences, detailing our proposals and drafts for legislation. The book was presented to my successor, but it did not receive any serious consideration. Fifteen years after those events, the current government has voiced plans to implement some of these proposals and drafts. Even so, there was no acknowledgement of the work done by the council under the Oommen Chandy government. In 2025 the Kerala Assembly approved the legislation to permit private universities, but precious time has been lost and damage already done because a lot of our students have left the country for higher education. Since its existing universities do not have enough students, private universities may not be enthusiastic about investing in Kerala.

The reasons for this sad state of affairs are not hard to see. First and foremost, the over-politicisation of the education sector is a curse. Political parties must develop a consensus on what reforms should be attempted, how much private investment should be sought, how much autonomy should be given to colleges and universities, what the medium of instruction should be at different stages of education, the level of skill development to be included at different stages and what kind of foreign universities should be invited to the state. Without consensus on such issues, successive governments will try to reinvent the wheel and the dream of Kerala becoming a hub of higher education will remain a mirage.

The National Education Policy 2020 contains a specific plan to liberalise, modernise and internationalise education. However, the Kerala government has not accepted the policy as a whole. Therefore, Kerala is likely to fall behind other states in educational progress. Educational systems around the world have changed more in the past ten years than they have in the past century, and we have no choice but to redouble our efforts to catch up with the rest of the world.

To Kerala via Nagaland: My Entry into the IAS and the Journey Through Thick and Thin

Vinod Rai

THE MOST ANTICIPATED EVENT after an aspirant qualifies for the Indian Administrative Service (IAS) is the cadre allotment. Received in Mussoorie, cadre allotment evokes mixed feelings. The 1972 batch – my batch – was no exception. My allotment was to the Nagaland cadre. Belonging to Uttar Pradesh, being schooled in Delhi and then being allotted to the Nagaland cadre … Need I say more?

I derived solace in the fact that five of us were allotted to that cadre. While my family and I were slowly processing this news, there came another bolt – the Nagaland government informed the Department of Personnel (DOP) that they would not accept five officers together. As the state had three districts then, they argued to be allotted only two – or at most three – officers. However, there was no way the Government of India could let this happen; it was, and always has been, the big brother, the more powerful entity, and so its writ must prevail. So after an exchange of numerous messages – the internet had not made its presence on this earth and far-off Nagaland was accessible only by the police wireless network for rapid-fire exchange – all five of us were packed off to Kohima, the state capital. After two days of travelling by the chugging Assam Mail and another day by the metre-gauge AT Mail, we landed at the Dimapur Railway Station. No sooner had we disembarked than a gentleman approached us and inquired if we were the five IAS probationers allotted to the Nagaland cadre. We saw hope, we saw sunshine. Indeed, we were being welcomed. On our confirming our identities, he handed each of us a sealed cover. It was from the state government, so we immediately got down to reading its contents. It was a single piece of paper, not even addressed to us. On reading through it, we realised that it was a copy of a police wireless message from the Chief Secretary to the Secretary of the DOP. It read: 'Five IAS probationers reported to Dimapur railway station today. Since the state government has not agreed to accept them in the Nagaland cadre, they have been directed to go back and report to the department of personnel, Government of India.'

Not being experienced in the ways of government, we decided to go to the circuit house and weigh our options. We looked for the bearer of those five sealed covers and realised that he had pulled a disappearing act. To cut the saga short, after fifty-three days of being in limbo, it was decided that we would do our district training in Nagaland, and the Central government would reallot our cadres. We were then sent to different districts in Nagaland; I was sent to Tuensang.

Fast forward to the second phase of training, and five IAS probationers are still in search of cadres! Eventually, the reallotment was completed and I had been allotted to far-off Kerala because the Indian government couldn't send me to any other place that was closer to Nagaland! Badal Das, a Kerala cadre batchmate, had got married and was transferred to Madhya Pradesh, and so I was going to be his replacement. Another Nagaland cadre batchmate was reallotted to Manipur purely because Falguni Rajkumar from that cadre had married his batchmate and shifted to Karnataka!

So Kerala it was for me.

My Entry into Kerala[1]

When I reached the Thycaud guest house on 21 July 1974, I realised that I still hadn't been allotted a cadre. I had joined the IAS with dreams of rapidly climbing the rungs of the ladder and rising to the post of district magistrate in a well-known district. Yet, here I was, unable to find a state that would accept my services. And what was my fault? I couldn't really think of any.

After reaching the Secretariat, I was advised to call on the Chief Secretary, K.P.K. Menon, who also happened to be a former air force officer. I was promptly ushered into his room. While I had just settled down in the chair offered to me, I was a trifle baffled to find a glass of pale-yellow liquid on Menon's table. This was at about 11 a.m. Coming from Tuensang in Nagaland, where my district collector, the redoubtable John F. Halliday, started his early lunch with a glass of beer, I had not expected to witness the same trend in distant Kerala. It was only after spending many days in the state that I came to identify the real contents of that glass – cooled cumin water! And of course I took to the drink in a big way over time.

K.P.K. Menon was intrigued by my 'species', that is officers who had been allotted to certain states without being trained there. I had supposedly completed my two-year probation. However, I had not the foggiest idea of Kerala's geography, let alone its language and laws. Quite amazed by the situation, Menon exclaimed loudly in his clipped accent: 'Oh, oh! You are going to be fairly indigestible material for us!' This was a rather strange interpretation of my predicament. Nevertheless, I mustered some courage and offered a solution: 'Sir, please attach me to any district collector for two months and I will make myself digestible.' If 'digestibility' was indeed going to be the criterion for my getting a regular assignment, I had to highlight my employability in those terms. Menon then decided to send me to the Cannanore (now Kannur) district.

My two-month stint in Cannanore was immensely enjoyable and professionally beneficial. John Mathai, the sub-collector of Tellicherry (now Thalassery), taught me the basics of revenue administration (especially during our Jamabandi trips to Kasaragod and Taliparamba); K.M. Chandrasekhar, project officer of the Small Farmers Development Agency (SFDA), trained me in development administration; M.K. Ravindranathan, the additional district magistrate, coached me in general administration; and K. Srinivasan, my district collector, schooled me in Malayalam and also taught me basic survival skills. These were the best professionals and colleagues I could have asked for.

An eye-opener for me was that on Independence Day in 1974, the district collector was to unfurl the flag and review the march-past. I was quite surprised to find that while the district collector drove to the parade ground in his official jeep, his wife followed in their personal car. This would be quite unheard of in the northern states, where the district collector and his wife driving together in the official car was the accepted practice. Nobody would look askance at it. In Kerala, no family member of an official ever travelled in an official vehicle. This culture of integrity was an excellent initiation for me.

After two months, I was posted to Thrissur. Located in the centre of Kerala, this compact, semi-urban cultural capital of Kerala has become my second home. I was first posted here as assistant collector, then as project officer of the SFDA, and later as district collector.

I Finally Get a Posting: Thrissur

K.S. Nair was the district collector of Thrissur when I arrived there as the assistant collector. He was thorough in his approach, popular in the district and very affectionate towards me. In fact, when I wanted to shift from the rest house to the residence earmarked for the assistant collector, he would not allow me to do so on a Tuesday, ostensibly because it was not auspicious!

Over time, I earned my spurs in this job and slowly gained confidence in managing officials and dealing with the public in Malayalam. One of my achievements was the successful organisation of a ganamela (music fest) to collect funds for flood relief; a part of the funds collected was utilised to build an indoor stadium.

I Move on to the Secretariat: Trivandrum

My next posting was at the Kerala Government Secretariat in Trivandrum (now Thiruvananthapuram). I was appointed as Deputy Secretary in the Revenue Department. It was also here that I got to witness the functioning of the bureaucracy at the state level.

The state was reeling under a severe monsoon; there was loss of life, property and crops. As is customary in such situations, the Government of India sent a damage assessment team. The visit of the team to the flood-affected areas went off well, and its leader conveyed the team's appreciation for the arrangements we had made. After the team's departure, on returning to Trivandrum, Revenue Secretary S. Padmakumar and I briefed the minister for cooperatives, Baby John. On hearing the favourable feedback, Baby John conveyed his satisfaction. I was then amazed to hear Padmakumar tell him: 'At least give us a good treat for a job well done, Sir.' The minister dug into his kurta pocket and pulled out a few crinkled currency notes. No sooner had he put the money on the table than Padmakumar grabbed it and counted it

– it totalled ₹700. 'It will buy a meal for two,' he said, pleased. We drove off to Mascot Hotel, the only decent restaurant in Trivandrum back then. After a hearty meal, when the bill arrived, Padmakumar tipped the waiter and told the manager to send the bill to his house. I was surprised since he had the cash to settle the bill there and then. Padmakumar's justification, delivered in an analytical, 'elementary-my-dear-Watson' style, was: 'Vinod, when this bill goes home, my wife will pay it. In the process, my ways and means position has gone up by seven hundred rupees!'

Brilliant budgetary management, isn't it?

Taking on a Political Stalwart

After a few months, I was posted as the managing director of the Kerala State Cooperative Marketing Federation, the designated agency for the procurement of raw cashew nuts. The raw cashews procured by the agency were allotted to cashew processing factories by the government's cashew special officer. This was to ensure that all cashew processing factories got enough raw cashew to process, thereby providing the labour force in each factory with gainful employment and stalling the monopoly of a handful of factories. This move would also ensure that all cashews were processed in the state and not smuggled to neighbouring Tamil Nadu or Karnataka, where Kerala's cashew processors had set up factories to reap the benefits of cheaper labour.

My batchmate Gopal Pillai was the cashew special officer back then. He was a stickler for norms, and both of us had a pathological dislike for misplaced political pressure. He was in perennial pursuit of lorries smuggling cashew to neighbouring states and quite enjoyed the task. On one such occasion, he caught a lorry load and after confiscating it promptly got it sent to our godown. Not to be outwitted, the lorry owner pressured the industries minister, concocted a case of mistaken facts and accused us of overenthusiasm. The minister started searching for Gopal, who by then had made himself scarce – the age of mobile phones was still to come. The minister then did the next best thing: he summoned me and told me to release the lorry. However, since he was not the minister of my department, I refused to budge. Besides, there was a written order in place for the lorry's confiscation, and I could not release it based on the industries minister's verbal instructions. He was livid. Here was a young officer, with precisely seven years of service, openly defying him. He voiced his opinion of IAS officers who were irreverent towards ministers and ended by saying, 'If you do not release that lorry, I will suspend you.' Such a threat did not appeal to the young, still idealistic and upright officer in me. In chaste Malayalam, I retorted, 'Sir, you cannot do that to an IAS officer.' The minister's eyes grew to the size of footballs and his jaw dropped open! It dawned on me that these were not welcome signs and I beat a hasty retreat. I realised I had put myself in an unenviable situation: the then chief minister was a Communist Party of India (CPI) leader and so was this minister; IAS officers were available a dime a dozen and suspending them was child's play. Panic was soon getting the better of me. Post-haste, I made my way to the residence of Baby John, the minister for my department. I found out that he was indisposed. Nevertheless, I got an audience with him. His comment on hearing my account was: 'You have not done the wisest of things.' Wise or otherwise, I left it to him to fix the situation. Poor man! Despite his state of indisposition, he went to the chief minister's office as he realised that the situation could spell difficulty for me. The industries minister, I believe, was already there and was fuming. Thankfully, with Baby John's intervention, the problem got sorted and I survived to tell the tale!

Back then, Kerala's politicians were benevolent and statesmanlike. In present times, no politician will raise a finger to help a young officer.

Back to Thrissur

Thrissur's architecture is unique, having been developed around the ancient Vadakkumnathan Temple. Around the temple runs a radial road, with smaller arterial roads feeding into it – quite like Connaught Place in New Delhi. This whole area is called the Swaraj Round. This round was usually congested, with a succession of buses halting at the bus stand and creating a nightmarish traffic jam. With the support of like-minded people, we managed to relocate the bus stand. We also created a new fish and vegetable market away from the round, which substantially eased the clutter near the temple. The entirely new township, comprising the bus stand and the market, was named 'Sakthan Thampuran Nagar', after the most popular ruler of the Cochin dynasty. Though the relocation of the bus stand and the market was initially seen as an inconvenience, its benefits far outweighed the temporary hassles and the move was hailed by the people as very progressive. Having said that, one group dissented – the students of Vimala College, a popular women's college, who now had to walk an extra 200 yards to catch a link bus. I received a 'testimonial' from a student and have preserved it to this day as a reminder that even the best of plans meet opposition. The 'testimonial', on a page torn from a notebook, reads: 'I have seen a lot of fools in my life but never a fool like the present district collector. He has caused so much difficulty by shifting the bus stand. Someone please put some sense into the DC.'

Sadly, I never got to meet the author of the letter.

This brings me to the 1987 National Games of India, which were hosted by Kerala. The chief minister wanted the swimming events to be conducted in Thrissur. However, there was only one minor hitch: Thrissur did not have an Olympic-size swimming pool! But since this was the chief minister's wish, we had no option but to comply and build a new swimming pool. We got to the job with barely a year and a half left for the games. Government land near the indoor stadium was identified; it was low-lying and had to be filled. However, filling it up would stop the natural drainage of a cluster of houses unless good alternative drainage mechanisms were created. Now, the successful conduct of the games in Thrissur would be a huge achievement for the ruling Congress, and so its competitor, the Communist Party of India (Marxist) or the CPI(M), chose to dispute the site selected for building the new pool. We managed to thwart the protests, but to our ill luck, one fine evening, while the pool was being dug, there was a heavy downpour. This immediately caused waterlogging in the houses in which we had created only temporary alternate drainage channels. E.K. Menon, a CPI(M) member of the Legislative Assembly (MLA), led a mob to break some of the embankments, ostensibly to help waterlogged households. Thousands of gallons of water poured into the area dug out for the pool, inundating the machinery. There was obviously a huge clash between the folks whose houses were waterlogged and the larger community seeking to have an Olympic-sized pool in the town. I decided to have photographs taken of the inundated swimming pool area. These were then plastered in all the local newspapers with the help of well-meaning and development-oriented citizens and journalists such as K. Radhakrishnan and K. Balakrishnan, so the public could decide for itself if it wanted the work on the pool to go on. People, as a rule, respond sensibly if taken into confidence, and Thrissur has always had a tremendously cooperative citizenry. On the photographs going public, there was a groundswell of opinion against E.K. Menon's actions and widespread support for the creation of a new swimming pool. House owners also cooperated, and so work was restarted. The swimming pool was completed in time for the National Games. Radhakrishnan and Balakrishnan still remain good friends of mine.

In this episode, there was a huge learning experience for me. Modern citizenry seeks participation in administration. Implementing public policy becomes simpler and accelerated if progressive citizens are associated with the development process. There is a desire in such people to contribute to the development and well-being of their kinfolk, and they can thus be a huge force multiplier in building opinion towards public policy initiatives. Good governance requires a participative approach and today's citizenry looks for opportunities to be associated with governmental initiatives. It is incumbent upon the administration to recognise such individuals and assimilate their cooperation.

From Thrissur to Harvard

As a consequence of the Kerala Legislative Assembly elections held in April 1987, the Congress-led United Democratic Front (UDF) alliance, of which K. Karunakaran was the chief minister, lost to the Left Democratic Front (LDF). Ordinarily, when governments change, certain bureaucrats in selected posts (such as the Secretary to the chief minister and the district collector of the chief minister's district) and other so-called favourites end up as bureaucratic casualties. I had reconciled myself to this, more so as I had already completed two years in the district. But a different kind of crisis awaited me.

Bureaucrats usually undergo mid-career training. I had applied for the same and been shortlisted for a one-year training programme at the Harvard Kennedy School, popularly known as the Mason Program. This is a prestigious course. In April, I was informed that I had been chosen. I was thrilled.

After the change of government in the state, I paid a routine visit to the new revenue minister, P.S. Sreenivasan. In the course of the conversation, I told him about my selection for the Mason Program. He immediately responded: 'Don't presume that we propose to remove you from Thrissur and therefore try to leave for a course. We do not plan to remove you from Thrissur, so go back and complete the projects you have initiated. Forget the course!'

I panicked. Going to Harvard was a once-in-a-lifetime opportunity. I was among the five selected candidates from about a hundred applicants. How could I give it up just to remain a district collector for another six months or so? I politely explained the significance of the course. The revenue minister wished to hear no more and dismissed me from his presence. A feeling of terror slowly began to engulf me. What was I to do?

I could not blame the minister, as he was being kind to me and did not know the significance of the training programme. Out of desperation, I made a beeline for the Chief Secretary's office, waited my turn, met him and narrated my tale of impending woe. He did appreciate the situation and reassured me that he would take care of it. I remained on tenterhooks until I took the flight for Harvard, leaving Thrissur in June 1987.

My love affair with the town and the district, however, continues.

All's Well That Ends Well

I had another stint in Kerala as the Principal Secretary in the Finance Department. The LDF government, led by the CPI(M), was in power. E.K. Nayanar was the chief minister, and T. Sivadasa Menon the finance minister. Menon was an exceedingly affable and warm person. He was considerate towards his officers and receptive to new and progressive ideas.

The state's ways and means position was precarious and it was quite a struggle to collect resources to cover its development and administrative expenditures. I was fortunate to have colleagues such as A.K. Dubey, K.M. Abraham and V.S. Senthil to help me within the different branches of the Finance Department. These officers were professionally outstanding, dedicated to their assigned duties and objective in their approaches. Having such a dedicated team lessened the burden on me. Moreover, the minister trusted us and would not make any major decisions without consulting us.

For the Finance Department, the most importantly period is the budget preparation time. In 2000 we had a peculiar problem that could have caused great embarrassment. The state budget is always read out in the Legislative Assembly in Malayalam. According to the prevailing practice back then, the budget speech was first written in English and, after being okayed by the finance minister, was translated into Malayalam on the day preceding the presentation. This was done at the eleventh hour to avoid the possibility of any leakage of information. That year, we decided to complete the entire process in-house. While transcribing the translated portion, the computer malfunctioned and portions of the transcribed Malayalam speech were irretrievably lost. Panic ensued.

Unfortunately, these kinds of catastrophes always have more onlookers on the sidelines than problem-solvers. The Kerala Secretariat is also a battleground of political unions, owing allegiance to the ruling and opposing coalitions. And so, by morning, word spread like wildfire that the Malayalam text was unavailable and that the finance minister would be forced to read the English version instead. And obviously, the Opposition, looking for an opportunity to embarrass the government, would not allow the speech to be read in English, thereby orchestrating a first-class constitutional crisis.

K.M. Abraham and I sat in the office the entire night. As a measure of abundant caution, I had earlier photocopied and preserved every page of the translated speech shown to me for approval. This became the very document that was available to us and it saved the day, indeed. I apprised T. Sivadasa Menon of the situation at about 7 a.m. He was unflustered, perfectly willing to read from the photocopied text as opposed to the normal, neatly printed speech. We assured him that by the time he completed the speech in the Assembly, we would have redone the entire process and that the printed versions would be ready.

The Assembly convened; fireworks and theatrics were expected. Just as the Speaker gave permission to the finance minister to present the budget, the leader of the Opposition got up to protest in advance against any attempt by the minister to read his speech in English. There were shouts and counter-shouts. T. Sivadasa Menon played along, enjoying himself thoroughly as he had the (photocopied) Malayalam version – something the Opposition was not aware of. Every minute spent on such wrangling gave us additional time to finish our work. After a good forty minutes of hurling allegations and counter-allegations, the minister was allowed to read his speech. And the Opposition received a huge surprise on hearing Malayalam – their intelligence reports through union representatives had suggested otherwise!

By the time all the formalities in the Assembly were over, Abraham and his team had redone everything, and the printed version of the speech and the budget documents were in the pigeonholes of the MLAs in the MLA hostel. All's well that ends well!

Far-off Kerala: A Blessing in Disguise

I have provided these detailed vignettes to portray the fact that despite the change of cadre – 'in public interest', as bureaucratese would put it – my landing in Kerala was the best thing that happened to my career. The administrative culture in the state was distinct. Outsiders were welcome, and learning the language was encouraged. Politicians and officers had respect for one another and gave each other space. Interactions were courteous and deferential. Punctuality was remarkable – a team from the Asian Development Bank visiting me was amazed to find everyone at their desks by 10.15 a.m. The state was progressive in every respect. Besides the usual markers of progress – namely, standards of education, primary health and rural infrastructure, land reforms and local self-government – the state also had the following: a nimble-footed government machinery that performed with military precision in times of any emergency; a well-informed and good-intentioned citizenry that was ever willing to cooperate with the administration when taken into confidence with regard to developmental issues; Christians, Hindus and Muslims living in harmony, with respect for each other's places of worship; and an agile and often overdriven media which kept a hawk's eye on officials, ensuring transparency and accountability – the basic edifice for good governance. My journey in Kerala from 1974 until retirement has been enriching. I am proud of my time in the state and owe much to it.

Notes

1 This section contains extracts from my earlier book, *Not Just an Accountant*, published by Rupa Publications in 2014.

The Rubicon Crossed

Vijay Chandran

I WAS AS MUCH a rationalist as any young man growing up in Kerala in the 1960s. Faith was always blind and anything that would not go through the hard sieves of reasoning was to be rejected straight away. I used to feel ashamed of myself as an undergraduate who borrowed money to travel the great distance of twenty kilometres to listen to Swami Chinmayananda's Geeta Jnana Yajnas. How could this postgraduate take in a theory that depended on illustrations and metaphors to prove itself and had no substantive basis of its own? Every phenomenon must have its scientific explanation. If science cannot find an explanation today, it will certainly have one tomorrow. The rationalists' group that I had a brief honeymoon with reassured me that such a tomorrow would not be far off, given the way science was advancing.

This was the dominant view in the 1970s and 1980s, when preoccupation with career left me little time to think of such things. However, the doubting Thomas in me would occasionally raise his head, asking if science would indeed be able to explain everything. But career was a hard taskmaster and my focus was on excelling in it.

My Central deputation was also in Kerala as development commissioner of the Cochin Export Processing Zone (CEPZ), now known as the Cochin Special Economic Zone, under the Ministry of Commerce. After succeeding in persuading an American company, one of the 500 largest companies in the world, to start its facility in CEPZ, I was taking a laid-back approach and had plenty of free time. The doubting Thomas in me got more opportunities and his questions became more nagging. My wife, Geetha, a solid support all through, had little time for the raging conflict in me as she had started her own Montessori school. But she was aware of it. One day a small item in the newspaper caught her attention. A priest in the Catholic church nearby was arranging a two-day workshop on pranic healing on the weekend. We thought this might provide some answers and registered for it. But on Saturday, my wife developed cold feet, saying it was her washing day.

And so I went alone.

The teacher, a physics lecturer in a college, explained that everyone has an energy field, or aura, around them, which can be seen only by some people called clairvoyants but can be felt by everyone by energising their palms. He asked us to hold our palms facing each other and to concentrate on them. Within no time most of us could feel some tingling sensation in our palms. That was interesting.

He then asked us to feel the aura of another participant with our energised palms. Nearly all of us could feel some resistance about two to four inches away from the other's body. He said that this was aura, not visible to the naked eye but 'feelable' by the energised palms. Every living being has this aura and its depletion or excess is a sure sign of illness in the corresponding part of the body. He explained that any illness first affects the aura and reaches the body only later. So if you can keep the aura balanced, you can prevent many illnesses. He said that the energy field can be photographed, thanks to Kirlian photography, the invention of a Russian scientist. I took him at his word. I had to wait a few more years to get the aura of my fingers photographed in the Kirlian way.

In the afternoon he divided the sixty of us into pairs and asked us to feel the other's aura. I felt some congestion of the aura around my partner's abdominal region, and he said he had some problems with digestion. The rationalist in me dismissed this as a coincidence of no significance. But I could not conceal my excitement from Geetha in the evening. She too was curious to know more and we decided to do an experiment.

Sitting at the dining table, she extended her palms facing each other and gradually brought them closer to each other. With her eyes closed and concentrating on her palms, she said she could see a white light between them. Not knowing what to do, I asked her to bring her palms closer. She did and saw the light hardening like a solid block.

'Press closer,' I said.

She did and felt the light hitting her chest and an old breathing problem returning. She opened her eyes and went to the bedroom to take a puff from her inhaler. We decided to go to the class together the next day.

Sunday's class was more of practicals and was over by lunchtime. Hearing about Geetha's experience, the teacher decided to test her further. The priest and a few other participants gathered around Geetha and the teacher. The teacher asked Geetha to close her eyes and imagine that someone was standing next to her. She told me later that the person she had imagined was me.

The teacher held his palms facing each other vertically, the hand on top a little above Geetha's head. He asked, 'What do you see?'

'I see a vertical column of white light,' came the answer.

He then held his palms facing each other horizontally. 'Now what do you see?'

'The column of light has become horizontal.'

Now he brought his palms closer together and moved them towards Geetha's face, between her eyebrows. 'Any change in what you see?'

'Now the light is hitting my forehead.'

He moved them closer and closer and she started shaking her head, saying, 'It is getting stronger and I can't bear it.'

Afraid she would fall, I inched closer, ready to catch her. Then she opened her eyes. The teacher said she had clairvoyance-like abilities and that he would discuss this with the Grand Master of pranic healing from the Philippines when he came visiting. I found this mind-boggling.

The next day Geetha had a couple of men visiting her at her school. One of them had seen the teacher's experiment with her at the workshop and had brought along his friend, who had been complaining of problems with his heart. She said, 'Take him to a doctor. Why are you involving me in this?'

The visitor said he knew me and pleaded with her to have a look at his aura. His earnestness made her agree and she felt his aura. She said she didn't feel any congestion in the chest region but felt some in the abdominal area. The visitor said that a doctor too had told him that there was no problem with his heart but some problem with his digestive system.

Did the rationalist in me cross the Rubicon and become a 'believer' that day? No. I put it down to just one more coincidence. Little incidents like this continued to take place in our lives, but none strong enough to make the rationalist budge. We had to wait for a few more years for my final transition.

Geetha's ancestral home in her village has a small temple. Its maintenance was far from ideal, though some mandatory poojas were held without interruption. When some misfortunes happened in the neighbourhood, the people there started attributing those to the poor maintenance of the temple. The news reached us and we had to respond. Geetha, her two brothers and I decided to renovate the temple. But we had to first know what was on the deity's mind. And that could be known only by conducting a Deva Prasnam, an elaborate affair that goes on for a minimum of three days, with a main astrologer and his assistant on one side and an independent astrologer on the other questioning their findings.

A pandal had to be put up, the local people were to be invited and all attendees fed. In spite of the expenses, we decided to hold one.

Though the main conclusion of the Deva Prasnam was to rebuild the temple, which we did, what happened on the sidelines was inexplicable. The main astrologer, who lived about a hundred kilometres away and was a total stranger to the place, started speaking about Geetha's ancestors. She had two uncles. Both had passed away. The moment he brought up the younger uncle, he asked, 'Did he marry twice?' That was true. He had divorced his first wife and married another woman. How did the astrologer know? A sceptic said he might have sent some informant earlier. But in a village, any stranger collecting such information would be known.

About the elder uncle, he asked, 'Did he have some connection with another temple and did he end that connection angrily?' That was also true. He was the tantri of another family temple about thirty kilometres away and had left that in a huff when some local people rejected some of his suggestions about the rituals there. How did the astrologer know?

Similarly, he spoke about three more generations of Geetha's uncles. There was no way of verifying what he was saying. But some seniors in the crowd who remembered these uncles validated some of the things he said.

Among the many other things he spoke about, he said there was a pond in the compound. No one there remembered this. But a couple of years later, when I visited a relative who was the daughter of one of the uncles the astrologer had mentioned, she told me, without any prompts from me, about a pond that had been there in the compound.

But the most striking thing the astrologer said was that he could find the presence of Nagas (serpent deities) on the property. He said there was an abandoned well with clear water in the northeastern corner of the property, which was visited by the Nagas. I didn't know about the well. But during a break we went to that corner and we were not surprised to see a well there, covered by overgrowth but with clear water.

The astrologer asked if a Nagaprathishta had been conducted nearby recently. We didn't know. But a person in the audience said there had been one in a nearby temple on the northwest side of the property about six months ago. The astrologer said that a Naga from this property had gone to that temple because we were neglecting it. He stipulated that we must do a proper prathishta for the Naga first, indicating that it could solve any childlessness in the family.

We did a proper prathishta later. There was a woman in the family with no children even after nine years of marriage. She was asked to come down and be present throughout the three days of the Nagaprathishta. The priest gave her a small bottle of coconut oil energised by mantras. She and her husband were to take it together for twenty-one days. That was not possible as the husband was living in a different town due to work. So on her way back she stayed with him for one night and got pregnant. Their child is now sixteen years old.

No more proof was required. As Shakespeare has it in *Hamlet*: there are more things in heaven and earth than are dreamt of in one's philosophy. The Rubicon had been crossed. I became a believer, convinced that science, be it today's or tomorrow's, will not be capable of explaining everything. Interestingly, when I got a chance to give a short speech in the presence of the Dalai Lama, I made this exact statement. When he spoke, he deviated from his written speech and made a reference to my statement, strongly supporting it. I was thrilled! This is the most cherished memory of my public speaking.

With the enthusiasm of a new convert, I started reading avidly everything I could get on alternate healing, like acupressure, pyramidology and magnetotherapy. I studied Reiki, even trying it out with good results on some of my yoga students in the UK, where I lived with my wife after my retirement. From there, moving towards spirituality was a natural progression.

My fifty years of yoga and some twenty-five years of meditation have been of great help. Life is an abiding joy. The eternal conflict of bhakti versus yukti, which raged in me in the beginning, is all gone. I realise that both have their place. In this the great Shankaracharya has been my role model. These days I am engaged in translating his Sanskrit commentary on the Bhagavad Gita as well as Swami Chidananda Puri's Malayalam explanation of Shankaracharya's commentary into English. Three volumes corresponding to the first three chapters of the Gita have been published. The first two are available on Amazon.

A Slice of Kerala

M.P. Joseph

I HATED IT WHEN my bosses in Geneva, where the International Labour Organization has its headquarters, informed me on Christmas Eve, which also happens to be my birthday, that I was being transferred and posted to Cambodia.

Those were the days before Google Maps and the internet. I therefore looked up Cambodia in the atlas, though I knew I would not find it easily. Having heard many dark stories about Cambodia, I told myself that it would be easier if I searched for it in the heart of darkness (pun intended). Then a friend of mine from school, more knowledgeable than the rest, told me not to worry. 'Cambodia is right next to Virginia,' he said. He had concluded that places that rhyme must be close to one another. He guaranteed me that Cambodia, being next to Virginia, was a fine little place that I would like very much.

He was wrong about the location but right about the description. For when I landed in Cambodia, the land of the Khmers, the Khmer Rouge and Pol Pot, I found it beautiful and full of joyous people.

A Mirror-Image of Kerala

Strangely, Cambodia is a slice of Kerala in Southeast Asia, an oriental version of Kerala, complete with coconut trees, jackfruits and delicious mangoes. Its natives are rice eaters who love to eat rice three times a day and have rice porridge for breakfast – their word for that lovely, refreshing morning rice gruel is, hold your breath, 'kanji', which they eat with a bit of dried fish or pork. Like us Malayalees, they are meat lovers, with an abundance of vegetables in their diet. And like us, their first love is fish, all types of fish: dried fish, fried fish, pickled fish, fish paste, fish sauce that stinks to high heaven, fish boiled or steamed whole, fish cooked deliciously with pickled lime, etc. And, like in Kerala, their plantation crops include rubber and cardamom. There is a whole mountain range in southern Cambodia called the Cardamom Mountains, home to ginger, Kampot pepper (a geographical indication product) and a whole lot more.

Cambodians hardly ever call themselves Cambodians, just as we hate to call ourselves Keralites, which sounds artificial and contrived. We proudly call ourselves Malayalees and similarly they call themselves Khmers. Our language is Malayalam; their language is Khmer. Our Malayalam months are Chingam, Kanni, Thulam, Vrishikam, Dhanu, Makaram, Khumbam and so on. I had never heard of these Malayalam months anywhere else in India or in the world. But when I landed in Phnom Penh – Cambodia's capital – for the first time, my taxi driver greeted me with, 'Welcome to Cambodia, Sir. Welcome on Valentine's Day, Dop-Boon Khumba, meaning the fourteenth day of Khumba or fourteenth February.'

Unlike us, for whom only half of January is Makara, the Khmers regard the entire month as Makara. The entire month of February for them is Khumba, our Khumbam. March is Mesa, our Meena Masam. November is Vrichika, August is Kanni and December is Dhanu. It is amazing that of all the outlandish places in the world, the Khmers in Cambodia have the same names for months as we do in Kerala.

It is not merely the months that are similar; many other Khmer words too have a Malayalam connection. Phnom Penh literally means 'the lady's hill'. You get my drift. Like the word 'pennu' in Malayalam, 'penh' in old Khmer means woman. And a synonym for 'penh' is 'strei', our 'sthree'. A street in Khmer is a 'veedhi', a school is a 'vishyalay', a university is a 'moha vishyalay', a man is a 'log', an office is a 'karyalay'. The medal I received from the prime minister of Cambodia was called the Saha Meitrei Seva Medal, 'seva' being our 'sevanam' or service, 'saha' meaning auxiliary and 'meitrei' meaning friendship. The prime minister, Hun Sen, who just handed over power in a bloodless transfer to his son Hun Manet, has a long title starting with 'Mohasenapati', which in Malayalam means 'the Supreme Commander'. The list of connections is endless.

While I am told we have forty-four rivers in Kerala, Cambodia has just three. The first is the mighty Mekong, which has strong Indian roots, arising from the Himalaya and then flowing north and east into China. It later moves into Myanmar, Thailand and Laos, before it flows majestically through Cambodia and finally moves on to the neighbouring Vietnam. It eventually flows into the South China Sea. The two other rivers are the Tonle Sap and the Tonle Bassac, which are mere tributaries of the Mekong.

The Tonle Sap is unusual, for it is both a tributary and a distributary of the Mekong. During the monsoons, much like the kalavarsham (rainy season) of Kerala, when rain falls in torrents, the Tonle Sap River becomes a tributary of the Mekong, feeding its already swollen waters. Tonle Sap is unusual in another way – it is both a river and a lake. The river originates from the Tonle Sap Lake, on the shores of which sits the town of Siem Reap, which literally means 'the town where the Siamese (or the Thais) were defeated'. This town is also famous for Angkor Wat, the largest Hindu temple in the world, even though a thousand years ago the king of Cambodia, Jayavarman VII, converted to Buddhism along with the whole country. At the entrance of Angkor Wat, you can still see a statue of Lord Vishnu, with one arm broken by an overzealous Buddhist.

I have heard that a zealous organisation in Bihar is building another Angkor Wat in the state, twice as big as the original. Meanwhile, the Cambodians are laughing. Angkor Wat belongs to Cambodia; no one can take it away or replicate it. It is their national symbol; it is on their flag and everywhere else. Even Pol Pot, the communist dictator who wreaked destruction throughout Cambodia, did not dare destroy Angkor Wat.

But I am digressing. The Tonle Sap Lake is a freshwater lake – the largest in Cambodia and across Indochina – which, during the rainy season, swells up to four or five times its previous size. The Tonle Sap River arises from the Tonle Sap Lake and flows southward through the Khmer countryside into the mighty Mekong at Phnom Penh. It is the swollen waters of the lake, along with the incessant rains in the nearby countryside, that flow into the Tonle Sap River. Flowing southward from the lake, the Tonle Sap River makes the Mekong basin a rich rice bowl. For six months of the year, the Tonle Sap River flows south and empties itself into the Mekong.

Then, when the dry season sets in, the Tonle Sap Lake becomes a shadow of its former self, while the mighty Mekong continues to brim with water due to the melting snow of the Himalayas. As the Tonle Sap Lake – especially since it is almost emptied during this period – sits somewhat lower in height than the Mekong, the Mekong's waters start to flow into the Tonle Sap River, which in turn flows into the Tonle Sap Lake. Thus, for the next six months of the year the waters of the Tonle Sap River flow in the opposite direction, this time from the south to the north.

A Fest à la Indian Mela

Between the six months of the southward flow and the subsequent six months of the reversed northward flow, there are about three days when the Tonle Sap River stands still, like a car that has to be stationary before the gear can be put in reverse. It is on these three days that the Khmers, as we do in Kerala, hold their annual water festival, which really is a pseudonym for boat races. Just like the Tonle Sap River, Phnom Penh also comes to a standstill, with hundreds of thousands of people, cars, two-wheelers, land rovers, bullock carts, bicycles, tricycles, tuk-tuks and people crowding the river's banks. More and more people descend on the city. The city stands still; no one, no traffic, nothing – not even the Tonle Sap River – moves, except the Mekong and the Tonle Bassac. The city comes to a gridlock, and all is set for the boat races.

If, like me, you thought that the chundan vallam or the snake boats (I wonder who mistranslated the word 'chundan', meaning 'beaked', into 'snake') were found exclusively in Kerala, you are wrong. The acme of the boat races on the Tonle Sap River are the races of the snake boats, which are rowed by hundreds of men dressed in uniforms, just as they are during the Nehru Trophy Boat Race is Alappuzha. The only difference is how punctual, thorough and perfect the boat races in Phnom Penh are: no confusion, no pushing or shoving, no false starts, no arguments, no fights. There are quite a few drunk people everywhere, but they all behave well. Everything is carried out methodically and professionally. What else could be the case when the king is in attendance? And, more importantly, when Prime Minister Hun Sen himself is present? Everything would then be as it should be, or else many heads would roll. And I am not talking figuratively. That is the first difference I could see from the matters here in Kerala.

But Agh, the Menu

And then there is another difference. That is in some of the food that is eaten there: from the stinking fish sauce that, like the curry leaves here, finds its way into every menu, to their love for pork and pig entrails, fried and spiced chicken feet, beef, which is very expensive here and, most of all, their love for fried cockroaches and spice-fried beetles, flies and other crawlies, all of which are eaten neat or as 'touchings' with the local brew or their Black Labels and single malts.

But the one fruit that they love the most is the durian, which is foul-smelling and the colour of a child's excrement. It is both the god of fruits and the fruit of the gods, and you can be killed for sacrilege if you say anything bad – let alone nasty – about it. Durian is very expensive, and if even one of the five oval-shaped, pulpy, jackfruit-like segments of the durian were to be offered to you, it would be offered as though it were the food of the gods, carried up to you as the priest in our Catholic churches carries the body of Christ – the 'bread' or the 'host', as it is called – up to the altar. It would be desecration if you refused the offer and you would have to pay a heavy price for any such irreverence shown to the fruit of the gods.

The Khmer Rouge and the Apocalypse

Undoubtedly, the greatest similarity between us and the Khmers is our fascination with communism. The Khmers carried that fascination to its logical conclusion with a communist revolution, overthrowing the US-backed Lon Nol government in Phnom Penh in April 1975. The Khmer Rouge or the Red Khmers, under Pol Pot, took complete control of the city and the country and imposed pristine communism on the land. Their first decision – much like Muhammad bin Tughluq's – was to order that everyone, yes, *everyone*, should leave the city within seven days. Anyone who questioned the order was shot and killed in full public view. So began one of the strangest migrations that the world has seen. Men, women, children in their guardians' arms, grandmothers, grandfathers, great-grandfathers, great-grandmothers, the sick, the disabled, the hungry, the poor, the rich, the middle class – everyone began a trek out of the city. No one knew where they had to go, for no one had been told. They were just asked to walk, walk to the countryside, and walk they did. There was no food, and there was scarce water; the April sun was hot, but walk they did. After travelling many tens of kilometres, some were told to stay in a nearby village and grow rice. City dwellers as they were, they knew little about agriculture and least of all about rice cultivation. Those who demurred, answered back or did not walk fast or sincerely enough were shot on the spot, for disobedience was to be squashed when its first signs emerged. The others moved on. If they lingered by the lifeless bodies of their loved ones, they too would be shot.

Many thousands died of exhaustion, starvation and dehydration. The weak were left on the roadside to perish and for the vultures to feast on. The Long March ended with tens of thousands dead and the others put in agricultural camps where they were all told to grow rice.

There was no need for any relationships. The party was all that was necessary. Everyone's relationship was to be with the Khmer Rouge or the 'Angkar' or 'Onka', as it was locally known.

Rice was important not because it was the staple that would help the country get out of hunger and poverty but because the Chinese needed it. Pol Pot had come to power with the help of the Chinese, and Beijing demanded rice in return. So rice had to be grown and everyone had to grow it. However, those who grew it received none to eat. They would be given a gruel in the morning – kanji with lots of water and a few grains of rice in it. The menu would be the same for lunch and dinner.

The Onka didn't spare anybody. Men were all put in one camp, women in another, pre-teen girls in one, pre-teen boys in another, young men in one camp and young girls in another. There could be no mingling among the sexes. Sons and daughters were separated from their fathers and mothers, brothers from sisters, babies from mothers and husbands from wives. The party was father and mother. It would provide all that was necessary, and anything that it could not provide was unnecessary. It would also decide who would do what, who would marry whom, when they would marry, when they would be allowed to sleep together and for how many nights, when they could have children and how many.

If anyone disagreed or showed the slightest hesitation to carry out anything they were asked to do – including sleeping with and procreating with someone they hardly knew – the punishment was instant death.

And when the only objective of its citizens was growing paddy, the party decided that nothing else was required, so all other businesses and commercial enterprises were shut down. Markets, shops and radio stations were closed down. Professional workers of any kind, such as painters, chartered accountants and lawyers, were all asked to go and work in the paddy fields. All workshops and industries were done away with. Newspapers, magazines and books were burnt, libraries sealed and bookshops, of course, were bourgeois and thus closed. Anything printed was destroyed, and printing presses, unnecessary, of course, were closed down. To cut a long story short, just about everything except the party and its offices was closed down.

Everyone except the high and mighty was asked to go and grow paddy. So everyone worked in the paddy fields, hot, sweaty, weak and tired. Thousands died from overwork and exhaustion, from hunger and starvation, from beatings and punishments.

Wives had to spy on husbands and husbands on wives and report to the party. Grandmothers had to spy on grandfathers. Children had to spy on their own parents; brothers had to spy on sisters and vice versa. If they did not, they were finished off. Survival became the order of the day, so they had to succumb to the party's orders. And when they did, the brother or the sister whom they reported on was killed. Killing became the order of the day. The old and the sick were taken away, ostensibly for treatment, and were killed off. They were, of course, a drain on the party and the State as they could not work in the rice fields.

The greatest enemies of the party and the country were, of course, those who were educated. So the party ordered that every educated person be killed. Anyone who had completed schooling was done away with. Everyone therefore tried to look rustic and uneducated, but most couldn't escape their fates. Anyone who could either read or write was ordered to be killed. Next, anyone wearing glasses was ordered to be killed, for if you wore glasses you could be educated or you could read or write and therefore, by definition, you were the State's and the party's enemy. So those who wore glasses took them off and destroyed them.

In response, the party's next order was that its officials were to check everyone's noses. Anyone whose upper nose carried the telltale marks of having worn spectacles was killed.

The killings took on a momentum of their own. If, for instance, I was found to be an enemy of the party solely because I wore glasses, I would be taken away and killed immediately. Once I was killed, the party officials would then identify ten other persons – friends, former colleagues, family members, relatives, even complete strangers – whom I may have been close to, talked to or simply greeted. These ten persons would then be brought for questioning for being friends with the State's enemy. And no one who was brought in for questioning went on to live. Those ten persons would also be killed. And thereafter, ten more persons whom these people may have been close to, or simply interacted with would be brought in for questioning and then killed.

And thus, as in a money chain, the killing chain would expand outward to capture more and more enemies of the party, all to be finished off – multi-level killing.

The killing of hundreds of thousands of such enemies soon became a strain. Guns were scarce and bullets scarcer. So innovative ways had to be found to kill people. And, of course, these people also included children and infants who had met or played with the enemies of the party and were therefore enemies of the party themselves. Killing infants and children was inexpensive and easy. The child or infant would be held by one leg or foot, and its head swung against a coconut tree. The child would die instantly and, most importantly, inexpensively and would be left there to rot or for the vultures to feed on.

A cheap way to kill grown-ups too had to be found. It would be difficult to hold men or women by their feet and swing them so that their heads would smash against a tree. So for such grown-ups – and these included people who were seventy to eighty years old – a large pit would be dug. It was not dug by the executioners but by the victims themselves. These people would then be told to sit in a row, one behind the other, on their haunches. The one at the top of the row, next to the pit, would be asked to bend with their head bowed forward. The one behind them would be given a strong piece of wood or a tree branch. They would then be asked to stand up and bring that piece of wood down on the head of the person sitting at the edge of the pit, awaiting death. This blow would crack open the person's skull; blood would be spewed as though it were leaking from a high-pressure pipe and, without a word, the person would fall forward into the pit, dead.

The stick would then be passed to the next person in line. The person who had just stood up and hit the first person on the head would be asked to sit on their haunches at the edge of the pit. The third person in that row of death would then have to bring the stick down heavily and crack the head of the second person, who was occupying the position of the person they had killed. They would die instantly, falling lifeless into the pit before they could utter a cry. The queue would thus move forward, one hunched step at a time, to be killed with a blow on the back of the skull. The last person would be killed with a blow to the head by the executioner.

None of these persons would raise their voices. Why? For they would otherwise be tortured for a couple of days before being killed. An instantaneous death with a quick blow to the head was so much more preferable.

Thankfully, in 1979 a Vietnamese army with some former Khmer Rouge soldiers, including Prime Minister Hun Sen, liberated Phnom Penh from the Khmer Rouge on Pram Pee Makara, the 7th Makara or 7 January, which is Cambodia's Independence Day.

In less than four years, from 17 April 1975 to 7 January 1979, about 40 per cent of its population was either killed or died of disease, starvation, dehydration or exhaustion. During this time, Cambodia's population decreased from about 11 or 12 million to about 7 or 8 million.

… And a Thought

A sad country with a lot of happy people, or a happy country with a lot of sad people? In my many years in Cambodia, I could never be sure.

Let us hope that the similarities between Kerala and Cambodia do not grow further lest we become a full-fledged communist state.

In the Service of Kerala: Lessons That Shaped My Life and Career

Amitabh Kant

As I reflect on my journey, I can't help but feel a profound sense of gratitude for the opportunities and challenges that have shaped my life. Kerala is the birthplace of my career in the Indian Administrative Service. It was in 1980 that I became part of the Kerala cadre, marking the beginning of a professional voyage that would profoundly shape the course of my life. Looking back now, I realise that the lessons I learned in Kerala have been a lighthouse throughout my journey. I carry the spirit of resilience, innovation and community knowledge with me in everything I do.

From Grassroots to Governance

My initiation training in Thrissur offered a glimpse of Kerala's uniqueness. This state was different, with a Marxist government and robust labour unions. When you carried your luggage off the train, the union demanded 'nokku-coolie', which essentially meant payment for merely watching you handle your bags. It was a cultural shock, to say the least. This was balanced by the fact that my district collector, V. Vijaychandran, took a keen interest in my training, making me feel welcome and ensuring that my learning experience extended beyond the classroom. He encouraged me to deliver speeches in Malayalam at all public functions, helping me immerse myself in the local culture and community.

In 1982, I received my first posting in the Tellicherry (now Thalassery) sub-division, situated in the historic Malabar region, which spans from Kannur to Kasaragod. Tellicherry was a small, congested town steeped in history, with a unique character all its own. The town's fish market, located at its heart, posed quite a challenge due to its overpowering stench. One of my initial decisions as sub-collector was to relocate it to the beach area. But we didn't stop there; we embarked on a mission to widen roads, remove encroachments and take some tough, albeit necessary, actions.

In life, success isn't solely determined by academic excellence but by diverse interests and the fervour to create a positive impact. As a young and enthusiastic officer, I didn't always weigh the consequences of my actions. I was fortunate that the people of Tellicherry supported me in my endeavours. It was during this time that I began to believe that good work was both achievable and appreciated.

One evening, I received word that a local fisherman had fallen into the Arabian Sea from the top of a rocky alcove. I rushed to the scene and oversaw his rescue. As sub-collector, I directed that he should be taken to a local hospital, with the assurance that the district administration would cover the medical expenses. However, a delay in treatment due to a lack of advance payment to the doctor claimed his life. I called in the drug inspector and ordered a raid on the doctor's clinic. The inspection unearthed spurious drugs and expired medicines, prompting the registration of a case.

This incident escalated into a major controversy, with the medical fraternity accusing me of exceeding my authority as a young sub-collector. They sought intervention from the minister, who halted further proceedings and demanded an explanation from me. Meanwhile, another crisis unfolded as a group of Naxalites surrounded the doctor's clinic, conducting a 'public trial'. I hurried to the scene to rescue the doctor. Eventually, despite the minister's support, the doctor had no choice but to cease practising in Tellicherry. The support of the local population taught me a valuable lesson about the influence of 'people power' and public awareness in Kerala.

Amid these challenges, there were moments of sweetness and unity during my time in Tellicherry. To foster communal harmony, I initiated the Tellicherry Carnival. This event aimed to bring together people from various religious backgrounds through cultural celebrations. It sought to revive the traditional art forms of the Malabar region, promoting unity and cultural exchange.

Among all the cherished memories, one stands out – eating the unforgettable biryani from the Paris Restaurant (old) in Tellicherry. Served on a banana leaf and accompanied by papadam and pachadi (raita), it remains the most delectable biryani I've ever had, surpassing even the famed Hyderabadi and Lucknowi biryanis. I also cannot ever forget the evenings we spent with Moosa and his wife, Faiza, at their beautiful mansion by the sea.

Empowering Fisherfolk

After my time in Tellicherry, I received a remarkable opportunity through the recommendations of K.M. Chandrasekhar and R.C. Choudhary. Their recommendations led the then chief minister, K. Karunakaran, to select me to work in the fisheries sector as general manager of the Kerala State Co-operative Federation for Fisheries Development Ltd, also known as Matsyafed. This role placed me at the helm of the organisation dedicated to the welfare and progress of the region's esteemed fisherfolk community. My career was marked by a strong commitment to bring about a positive difference in the lives of those I served.

Matsyafed was no ordinary organisation; it had sprung to life just six months earlier, driven by the noble goal of enhancing the lives of traditional fisherfolk. As I stepped into this role in September 1984, a rush of ideas surged through my mind, accompanied by a profound sense of purpose.

One critical issue that had plagued fisherfolk for far too long needed immediate attention – the omnipresent 'middleman'. These intermediaries left fisherfolk with a mere 20 per cent of the market price for their hard-earned catch. To tackle this issue head-on, we introduced the concept of beach-level auctions, ensuring that the producers received a fairer share of the proceeds from their daily catch.

We also opened bank accounts for fishermen for direct payments. Back then, opening a bank account was a lengthy process, often taking seven to eight months. However, it was essential for fishermen to have access to loans for modern fibreglass boats equipped with outboard motors and efficient disc nets.

I spent countless hours travelling from one fishing village to another, engaging with fishermen, forming self-help groups and gaining their support and confidence for our transformative project. You might wonder how a North Indian earned the trust of Malayalee fishermen. The secret was the local lingo. By mastering the local language and speaking Malayalam fluently, I gained a 'superpower', which intrigued the locals and allowed them to truly become insiders.

Of course, the success of our scheme rested primarily on its merits. For every ₹100 earned from fish sales at the auction, 50 per cent was directly transferred to the fishermen's bank accounts, while the remaining 50 per cent went towards loan repayment. The financial structure of a project can be its making or undoing, and this principle would later underpin many of my future endeavours.

We also addressed the transportation woes of fisherwomen, who faced difficulties while transporting their catch from coastal towns to cities. To solve this issue, Matsyafed introduced special buses exclusively for fisherwomen, complete with space for their fishing baskets at the rear. This initiative gained popularity and led to the introduction of several similar buses.

Looking back, those were truly exhilarating days, and I often consider them the best days of my life. It was during this time that I began to understand the immense potential of coastal and marine tourism, an economic sector that could thrive while promoting environmental stewardship – a theme that would continue to influence my career.

Furthermore, our journey of transformation was rooted in real-time data utilisation, continuous feedback, rigorous monitoring and evaluation – a foundation I would carry with me into my future endeavours. Evidence-based policy frameworks became paramount, grounded in data that had been converted into actionable intelligence. Without this, the path to meaningful change would remain obscured.

Taking Flight: The Collector of Calicut

In the summer of 1992, I found myself stationed as district collector of Calicut (now Kozhikode). It was a pivotal posting in my career, one that would leave an enduring mark, still recognised and appreciated by the local citizens.

Calicut held historical significance. Vasco da Gama's arrival in Calicut back in 1498 had left an indelible mark on history. It was often said that if da Gama were to return, he would find the city almost frozen in time – narrow streets and a complete absence of modern urban planning. What struck me the most was the lack of public spaces and recreational areas, and tackling this issue became my top priority.

In the heart of Calicut lay the Mananchira Maidan, choked with encroachments. Armed with my powers, I initiated the removal of more than a hundred illegal structures and transformed the maidan using the traditional red laterite stone of the Malabar region, after which it shone as a fabulous green lung in the town, with beautiful illumination, featuring a musical fountain. The Mananchira Maidan quickly became the city's pride, a place where people could gather, relax and unwind in the evenings.

Another challenging endeavour was the widening of Calicut's narrow roads. A total of twenty-six roads were expanded, and the Calicut bypass project, albeit fraught with personal risk, was pushed forward. The then chief minister, K. Karunakaran, ensured there was no political interference, and large-scale encroachments were demolished. As a consequence, Calicut got improved roads and a much-needed bypass that continues to benefit the city to this day.

However, the real game-changer was the transformation and expansion of Calicut Airport. Perched atop a hill, it featured a runway suitable only for smaller aircraft and was of little use to locals who worked in Saudi Arabia and Oman. Their journeys to and from Calicut involved passing through Bombay (now Mumbai), and they had to deal with immigration hassles, customs scrutiny and touts. When the minister for civil aviation, Ghulam Nabi Azad, expressed an inability to fund the airport's expansion, I proposed a novel solution to Karunakaran – raising our own resources. This idea galvanised the Malayalee community working in the Gulf, many of whom hailed from the Malabar region. To manage these funds, we established a special purpose vehicle called the Malabar International Airport Development Society, with me serving as its first chief executive officer (CEO). Funds secured through user development fees facilitated the repayment of a ₹120-crore loan from the Housing and Urban Development Corporation Limited, enabling the expansion of the Calicut Airport's runway to 9,000 feet.

During my time in Calicut, a cultural renaissance unfolded. Next to the Mananchira Maidan stood a dilapidated building that housed a forgotten library. I orchestrated the demolition of this structure, employing innovative thinking. The lower floor was transformed into shops that fetched substantial rents. The income, in turn, funded the creation of a world-class library on the upper floors. Calicut had been home to some of the greatest Malayalam writers – Vaikom Muhammad Basheer, S.K. Pottekkatt, Thikkodiyan and M.T. Vasudevan Nair – and the local population took immense pride in Malayalam literature and its authors. The library swiftly became a meeting point for all writers and intellectuals in the city.

Going beyond the confines of bricks and mortar, I initiated a festival called Malabar Mahotsav. Renowned musicians and artists such as Amjad Ali Khan, Zakir Hussain, Allah Rakha, Shiv Kumar Sharma and Sivamani graced the occasion, captivating large crowds that primarily consisted of locals who sat on dhurries along the beach. It was a harmonious convergence of diverse cultures.

One of the most challenging moments during my tenure as district collector was the need to maintain law and order on 6 December 1992 – the day the Babri Masjid was demolished. I invited Kerala's leading artists to Calicut, urging them to express the concept of communal harmony through their artwork. A massive, 100-metre-long canvas was procured and set up in the Mananchira Maidan. Just two days before the event, I managed to contact the legendary M.F. Husain, who graciously accepted the last-minute invitation.

After three transformative years in Calicut, my next assignment led me to serve as managing director of the Kerala State Industrial Development Corporation. This phase witnessed the initiation of several critical infrastructure projects, including the BSES power project, Vallarpadam container terminal and the Southern Gas Grid, all executed under the public–private partnership (PPP) model. I also played a pivotal role in the construction of a second bridge connecting the Cochin mainland to Willingdon Island. Mattancherry was the state's first build-operate-transfer bridge, with Gammon India securing the project through competitive bidding.

Recognising that Kerala's true strength lay in tourism rather than in heavy industries, I began actively supporting and financing tourism entrepreneurs. Many of Kerala's experimental resorts and tourism initiatives emerged as a consequence of this effort, marking the state's emergence as a leading tourist destination.

Celebrating God's Own Country

One chapter in my professional history exemplifies the power of resilience and invention. I was in my early forties and had run into political problems for no fault of my own. I was unnecessarily harassed and almost ten months had elapsed without a posting, leaving me questioning whether my career had come to a standstill.

Call it providence or serendipity, but in September 1997, I assumed the position of Secretary, Tourism, Government of Kerala – a posting that many in the bureaucratic community considered less than desirable. At that time, Kerala was largely unheard of as a tourism destination, known primarily for its strong communist regime and trade unions. Kashmir and Rajasthan were the prominent tourist destinations for both Indian and foreign travellers. Little did I know that this posting would alter the course of my career. My mission was clear – to transform Kerala into a global brand known as 'God's Own Country'. To achieve this, it was evident that Kerala as a destination had to be elevated up the value chain, and a PPP was essential for this.

Collaborating with private entities, we took traditional art forms such as Kathakali, Theyyam and the martial art of Kalaripayattu to the forefront of Kerala's tourism offerings. We rebranded Ayurveda, highlighting it as not just a massage but a comprehensive twenty-one-day treatment regimen. Kerala's cuisine, including dishes like appam and fish moilee, took pride of place in our efforts.

One remarkable initiative involved the Periyar Tiger Reserve, where we partnered with the Forest Department for an ecotourism development programme. We trained twenty-one former poachers to serve as forest guides – an out-of-the-box idea that required substantial positive thinking and rigorous monitoring to succeed. Another innovative concept was the introduction of tree huts, crafted by locals in the hilly Wayanad region.

The turning point arrived in November 1999 when the millennium edition of *National Geographic Traveler* listed Kerala as one of the fifty must-see destinations of a lifetime. The publication declared Kerala a 'paradise found' for its exotic beauty and the intellectual and social equality it offered, standing shoulder to shoulder with any first-world country. 'God's Own Country' had firmly established itself on the global tourism map.

The next challenge was to amplify this success through a meticulously crafted mass media campaign. However, funding was a significant hurdle. I made my case and presented it to the Finance Secretary, tourism minister and the chief minister. I understood that without unanimous support, the plan would never come to fruition. Creating consensus, though, is no easy task.

With the green light from the progressive Tourism Minister E. Chandrasekharan Nair, we embarked on a mission to create an inspirational campaign. To accomplish this, we needed a visionary artist. I set my sights on the renowned cinematographer Santosh Sivan, fully aware that Kerala Tourism did not have the budget usually associated with his work. It was a Sunday afternoon when I received an unexpected phone call, rousing me from my siesta. The voice at the other end declared, 'Call from the Prime Minister's Office.' It was Brajesh Mishra, Principal Secretary to Prime Minister Atal Bihari Vajpayee. He informed me that Mr Vajpayee would be vacationing in Kerala and that I was tasked with making all the arrangements. His visit was indeed a recognition of all our efforts.

Fourteen months later, however, I applied for the Central pool and was slated to join the Finance Ministry. I was informed by Brajesh Mishra, Principal Secretary to the prime minister, that I would be joining the Ministry of Tourism as Joint Secretary, even though there was no vacancy in the department. The incumbent officer was eventually transferred, creating an opening. This twist of fate placed me in the right place at the right time and armed me with the proper skill set to orchestrate the Tourism Ministry's most successful campaign: 'Incredible India'.

I've realised that, in addition to hard work, destiny plays a significant role in one's life. This journey exemplifies the unforeseen twists and turns that can lead to significant milestones, often driven by passion and dedication to a cause. In the growth of tourism in Kerala, I must pay tribute to the invaluable work done by Dr V. Venu, who was then director of Tourism.

The Birth of 'Incredible India'

As I embarked on my role as Union Tourism Joint Secretary in July 2001, my first task was to organise a chief ministers' conference. However, fate had different plans. Just one day before the event, the Twin Towers in New York City fell victim to a devastating Al-Qaeda attack, which set tourism back globally. This horrifying incident marked the beginning of a tumultuous period in global history.

In the face of this monumental challenge, the Ministry of Tourism took a creative approach. It offered to purchase advertising space in brochures produced by travel companies, even though the prevailing sentiment was that no one would want to travel to India in such turbulent times. Countries like Singapore, Malaysia and Thailand too had scaled back their advertising efforts. The travel industry was grappling with uncertainty and fear.

However, opportunities for innovation and change often emerge in the darkest moments. It was during this crisis that I made the audacious decision to launch the 'Incredible India' campaign. In 2002, India had eighteen tourism offices abroad, but there was a lack of precise positioning, common branding or a concise and precise message. Each foreign office seemed to promote a different aspect of India, be it 'Spiritual India' or 'Cultural India'. Our advertisements lacked the sophistication and emotional appeal seen in campaigns like Malaysia's 'Truly Asia' or Thailand's 'Amazing Thailand'. Kerala's 'God's Own Country' campaign had set a shining example, providing me with the confidence to determine what would work and what wouldn't.

The print campaign for 'Incredible India' was brilliantly conceived by the creative director, V. Sunil. Each frame told a unique story, moving beyond clichés to capture the essence of India. Simultaneously, we commissioned Bharatbala Productions to create a soul-stirring 'Incredible India' film. We adopted headlines such as 'Not all Indians are polite, hospitable and vegetarian', accompanied by an image of a Royal Bengal Tiger, to convey the idea of an optimistic and extroverted India and challenge rigid global stereotypes. However, Union Tourism Minister Jagmohan remained sceptical, emphasising the need to work on infrastructure before advertising. After persistent discussions and rounds of interaction, Jagmohan reluctantly agreed orally to launch a centralised marketing campaign, and the concept of 'Incredible India' came into existence through a massive campaign initiated in 2002. By the end of 2003, its positive impact was evident. The campaign resulted in a 16 per cent increase in tourist traffic within its first year. Jagmohan, a phenomenal minister, focused on improving infrastructure, revamping heritage sites and fostering convergence between the Ministry of Tourism, the Archaeological Survey of India and the Central Public Works Department. I also had the privilege of spearheading the Atithi Devo Bhavah campaign in 2005, which celebrated the belief that the 'Guest is God'.

This period in Kerala and at the centre of Indian bureaucracy solidified my reputation as a marketing maverick. It drove home the importance of confronting crises with innovative thinking and seizing opportunities for disruption and fresh, creative ideas.

Forging a Transformative Path for India

During my tenure as Secretary of the Department of Industrial Policy and Promotion, I spearheaded initiatives like Make in India, Startup India and Ease of Doing Business to realise the vision of Prime Minister Narendra Modi. These efforts simplified regulations, making India an attractive investment destination. The result was a remarkable shift in India's economic landscape, propelling it into a global powerhouse. This journey showed the immense potential of our entrepreneurial ecosystem.

Startup India has empowered entrepreneurs and created a dynamic ecosystem – with over 1,50,000 recognised startups and 115 unicorns (as of 2024) – and several job opportunities. India now boasts the world's third-largest startup ecosystem, with rapid growth in unicorns. The digital landscape is thriving, showcasing immense potential. This success story, driven by innovation and governance, exemplifies India's entrepreneurial spirit.

Initiatives like Make in India, Production Linked Incentive schemes and corporate tax cuts have catapulted India into a global manufacturing hub. This transformation has significantly increased the manufacturing sector's contribution to the country's gross domestic product. Infrastructure development and business-friendly policies have further supported this shift.

NITI Aayog: A Surprise Opportunity

As CEO of NITI Aayog, the Aspirational Districts Programme (ADP) became a landmark project for me. Inspired by my learnings from Kerala, we aimed to uplift India's most backward districts. Innovative approaches such as the Poshan app and mobile health ambulances transformed healthcare and well-being. The success of the ADP, recognised globally, demonstrates the power of data-driven policies, collaboration and compctition.

The success of the ADP received global recognition, and the United Nations Development Programme described it as a 'catalyst for expediting development'.[1] The ADP not only improved socioeconomic outcomes but also empowered local governments and fostered partnerships with the private sector and philanthropic organisations. Looking ahead, the programme's principles of data-driven policies, collaboration and competition, reinforced by the innovative spirit I encountered in Kerala, should continue to guide India's development efforts.

India's Leadership on the Global Stage: G20 Presidency

In July 2022, I was appointed as India's Sherpa to the G20, an assignment that initially seemed devoid of substantial content or scope for implementation. However, my perception swiftly changed. As I immersed myself in this role, I encountered a dynamic team of young officers who transformed what I had initially considered uninspiring into the most challenging and captivating experience of my life. We took our G20 presidency to all the states of India, hosting over 220 meetings in 60 cities. We converted the G20 into a people's presidency by involving the citizens of India.

The mandate from Prime Minister Narendra Modi was clear: our presidency must be ambitious and inclusive, with a strong focus on representing the interests of the Global South. Under this directive, we faced numerous hurdles, which we turned into opportunities, ultimately achieving a 100 per cent consensus on all our priorities, aligning the world's major economies. The New Delhi Leaders' Declaration, with its eighty-three paragraphs and no dissent, symbolised this remarkable global consensus. It took 200 hours of negotiations, 300 bilateral meetings and the circulation of 15 draft documents among Sherpas to navigate these challenges successfully.

Our presidency was a pivotal moment for global cooperation, especially at a time when faith in multilateralism was eroding. We successfully shifted the focus from conflict to development and collaboration, showcasing India as a global leader committed to enhancing policy and regulatory coherence among G20 countries.

One of the most significant outcomes of India's G20 presidency was the expansion of the G20's scope to include the African Union, bringing in a coalition of emerging markets and expanding representation to encompass 80 per cent of the world's population. This shift reflects our commitment to ensuring that the Global South plays a leading role in global growth.

It has been an honour for me to serve as Prime Minister Narendra Modi's Sherpa to the G20, and our presidency will be remembered as a beacon of hope for a more united and prosperous world.

Lessons Learnt in God's Own Country

My journey from the heart of Kerala to the heart of Indian bureaucracy has been a profound and humbling experience.

The state of Kerala has had a significant impact on my life and career. Fairly early in my career, I had the privilege of working alongside a visionary civil servant, K.M. Chandrasekhar, who instilled in me the art of thinking on a grand scale and planning decades ahead. Under his guidance, I learned the importance of delegation, empowering junior colleagues and building strong, cohesive teams dedicated to delivery. During my endeavours to improve the livelihoods of traditional fishermen in Kerala, I discovered that community participation and the strategic use of technology were pivotal in leapfrogging developmental progress.

As district collector in Calicut, I learned that files were merely a means to an end and that transforming a city required meticulous planning, unwavering commitment to quality and implementation, and active collaboration with local citizens as partners.

Kerala also served as my classroom for the fundamental lesson that if India is to achieve a developed-nation status by 2047, states with lagging social indicators must undergo radical transformations in education, healthcare and nutritional standards. The human development index emerged as the linchpin for sustained growth over three decades.

Perhaps the most profound lesson Kerala imparted was resilience. When I was without a posting for over nine months and faced political harassment, I found solace in the state's enduring spirit. Kerala taught me never to lose hope, remain optimistic and always believe in myself.

My tenure as a Kerala cadre officer allowed me to witness the incredible potential of government-driven change. I realised that effective governance transcends policies and regulations; it hinges on our ability to comprehend the aspirations and challenges of the people we serve. It requires us to foster collaboration, engage with stakeholders and harness public awareness to usher in positive and enduring transformations.

Notes

1 PIB Delhi, 'UNDP Report Lauds Aspirational Districts Programme, Recommends Replication in Other Parts of the World', 11 June 2021. Available online: https://www.pib.gov.in/PressReleasePage.aspx?PRID=1726315 (accessed 7 October 2025).

A Malayalee Officer in Bihar Unravels a Curious Scam

T. Nandakumar

I JOINED THE INDIAN Administrative Service (IAS) in 1972. Unlike today, cadre allotments were finalised rather late – about six months into our training at the Lal Bahadur Shastri National Academy of Administration (LBSNAA). I was allotted Bihar. My initial instinct was to resign and return to my previous job at the State Bank of India (SBI). But due to the gentle insistence from family and friends – and because the SBI position was no longer available – I stayed on. Plus, the academy had a policy: any trainee who chose to quit had to bear the cost of their training. In effect, there were no real options.

So in 1973, I reluctantly left for Bihar, an unfamiliar terrain. I 'landed' at the Ranchi Railway Station en route to the Administrative Training Institute – and received my first shock. There were no taxis, no autorickshaws, just cycle rickshaws pedalling through a quiet, unhurried town. Over time, I adjusted to the laid-back atmosphere.

After two months in Ranchi, I was posted to Munger (then Monghyr) for my district training. Incidentally, Munger was infamous at the time for its thriving trade in illegal firearms. I stayed at the Circuit House nestled within the historic Munger Fort, right on the banks of the Ganga – a quaint, peaceful spot with a remarkably skilled cook on staff.

The collectorate and sub-divisional office there housed a surprisingly large number of officers – far more than I'd seen in similar establishments in Kerala. Naturally, they were intrigued by the arrival of a South Indian assistant collector, a freshly minted IAS officer and, to their amusement, a bachelor.

The Caste Question: And They Found Out!

Over the course of a few days, camaraderie blossomed among my colleagues. Conversations shifted from formal exchanges to quiet laughter and informal chatter. But with familiarity came curiosity, and soon, the inevitable question arrived, cloaked in discretion: 'Which caste do you belong to?' I sidestepped it tactfully. 'I'm unfamiliar with Bihar's caste structure, so I couldn't say for sure.' My evasions were met with persistent probing. 'Kuch toh hoga? Brahmin? Kshatriya? Vaishya?' They would stop short of mentioning Shudra – as if hierarchy lingered even in speculation.

Unable to elicit a clear answer, they turned to deduction. My name became their first clue. 'T' for 'Thakur' – a title loaded with layered connotations. In Bihar, 'Thakur Sahib' implied a Rajput identity, yet most Rajputs preferred the sturdier 'Singh'. The surname Thakur was shared not only by Maithil Brahmins and Bhumihars – a prominent caste in Bihar and Eastern Uttar Pradesh – but also by barbers, as in the case of Karpoori Thakur, Bihar's former chief minister. The guessing game continued, fuelled by caste calculus and regional stereotypes.

Three years later, I was posted as district collector of Madhubani – a district so deeply rural it was labelled 'backward' even by Bihar's generous standards. Tucked near the Nepal border, Madhubani was scattered with modest temples and mutts. Word came from seasoned insiders: steer clear of most priests. Power in those spaces wasn't just spiritual or religious – it was transactional.

My wife, however, found peace in temple visits. Deeply religious, she would often go alone. I, preferring discretion, usually stayed away. This sparked a fresh round of local speculation: why did DM Sahib chauffeur madam to temples but not step inside himself?

Soon a new narrative emerged. The public had cracked the mystery: DM Sahib was a Malayalee Christian named Thomas Nandakumar. In their eyes, this explained everything. And perhaps it was the neatest answer to every doubting Thomas.

Understanding caste equations in Bihar wasn't just difficult – it was vital. And I learned, often uncomfortably, that navigating identity here required both tact and quiet resilience.

Conversations with JP

In July 1974 I joined as sub-divisional officer (SDO) in Katihar – a single-subdivision district nestled just north of the Ganga and sliced by the unpredictable Mahananda rising from the hills of Nepal. To the west, the formidable Kosi loomed, known grimly as the 'Sorrow of Bihar'. The name wasn't metaphorical.

I arrived amid chaos. The Mahananda had breached its right embankment. The Ganga was in full spate. Nearly half the district lay underwater, families displaced and huddled on embankments in makeshift shelters. Connectivity was dismal and railways became our lifeline. Relief efforts felt Sisyphean. I still recall rumbling across submerged fields aboard a goods train towards marooned villages and desolate landscapes.

As if floods weren't enough, this was also the dawn of Jayaprakash Narayan's (JP's) Chhatra Andolan – a student-led movement against the government's corruption that was quickly gaining muscle. Names that would shape national politics – Lalu Prasad Yadav, Nitish Kumar, Ram Vilas Paswan and Sushil Kumar Modi – were involved and already commanding attention. The unflooded parts of the district were caught in agitation, and law and order teetered on the brink. The district collector and I felt hemmed in, disaster and dissent pulling us in opposite directions.

Then came the idea: a public appeal to JP and his 'boys' to suspend agitations while we tackled flood relief. The students dismissed it outright. But fate was kind – JP himself was visiting Katihar the following day. As his security fell under our purview, I took a chance to speak with him directly. I made my appeal again – not as an administrator but as a fellow citizen in crisis.

Within the hour, news arrived: the agitation was suspended for two weeks. Not just that – the students were instructed to join hands with the administration to aid relief efforts. JP had reportedly told them: 'The agitation is not against the district collector or the SDO. They are doing public work. In a crisis, don't undermine those who serve the people. The battle is against a corrupt system.'

Our conversations began on that generous note. JP was frail, bound by strict dietary rules. He avoided the standard government fare.

His niece was married to the superintendent of police, and JP preferred home-cooked meals. Over quiet dinners, he would talk, his voice still strong with conviction.

His favourite subject? The recall of elected representatives. Members of the Legislative Assembly (MLAs) and members of Parliament (MPs), he argued, turned indifferent the moment votes had been counted. Power, patronage and privilege replaced public service. His formula was simple but audacious: after two years, if one-third of an electorate demanded it, there should be a recall. Fresh elections. No excuses.

We pointed out the cost, the logistics, the turbulence. JP was unmoved. 'No price is too high to keep democracy clean,' he would say. What became of that idea – and of the movement that followed – is another story. But the question lingers: is it time to reconsider 'recall' as a constitutional instrument? In today's climate, it may provoke powerful possibilities.

Eradicating Smallpox from India

In Pachera village, Kadwa block, Katihar district, 17 May 1975 marked India's final indigenous smallpox case. It was a quiet village, but that day it became the epicentre of a global milestone. What preceded it was the most intense public health mobilisation India had seen: the 'Smallpox Zero' campaign, backed by the World Health Organization and formally known as the Intensified Smallpox Eradication Programme.

In 1973 India accounted for nearly 58 per cent of the world's reported smallpox cases. This grim statistic shattered the illusion that vaccination alone would suffice. The new approach – search, surveillance and containment – demanded precision and vigilance. While it was initially only the Health Department's domain, it quickly became clear that medical expertise couldn't stamp out the disease.

On 21 June 1974 Bihar's Chief Secretary sent an urgent directive: district magistrates must take full charge of operations. The baton had been passed to the IAS. Lawrence B. Brilliant, in his account of smallpox eradication, noted:

> On June 21, 1974, the chief secretary of the state of Bihar sent a special letter to all district magistrates informing them that they were to assume

> complete responsibility for carrying on and organizing the campaign in their districts. In effect, the Indian Administrative Service (IAS) – India's very competent district magistrates – had given up hope that doctors alone could handle the epidemic and smallpox eradication in India took over command of the emergency epidemic control activities from the normal medical authorities, relieving the civil surgeons and district medical officers.[1]

Surveillance expanded beyond hospitals – into marketplaces, schools, homes. Every corner mattered. In this zero-error campaign, one missed case could undo years of effort.

While the search and surveillance machinery gained momentum, containment remained a thorny challenge. It was enforced by administrative fiat: strict protocols, house quarantines and limited movement. We believed we were protecting lives – but we overlooked livelihoods.

During one of the containment operations, we discovered a woman from an infected household working in nearby fields. Her quarantine breach jolted us. When questioned, her response cut deeper than any report ever had: 'My children have nothing to eat. My husband is sick. We earn each day to survive.'

Her words exposed a blind spot in our otherwise rigorous campaign. We had enforced the rules but failed to anticipate human need. From that moment, the relief fund was tapped to provide four weeks of free rations and nutritional supplements to every quarantined household. Policy adjusted to compassion. The lesson, however, was etched not in directives but in her face – tired, determined and burdened by choices no parent should have to make.

Even today, whenever I hear the word 'containment', I remember her. That woman, those children, the quiet anguish behind our grand success story.

When the Patna Railway Platform Was Pledged

It was 1976. I was wrapping up my tenure as SDO, looking ahead to a promotion and a posting to Patna. The promotion came, but the posting was impacted by a scandal that erupted around the Patna Urban Cooperative Bank. A question in the Bihar Legislative Assembly, amplified by a blitz of headlines exposing blatant misappropriation of funds, forced the government's hand. A liquidation order followed – and I was appointed joint registrar of cooperatives and liquidator of the bank at Patna.

My first visit to the bank remains etched in memory. The gates were crowded with desperate depositors – daily-wage earners, pensioners, small traders – who had parked their meagre life savings there. With tearful eyes, they asked the one question that I couldn't yet answer: 'Will we ever see our money again?'

I began with what I could control: recovering loans, fast and firm. Then another scandal broke. Someone had allegedly pledged the Gandhi Maidan and Patna Railway Station's Platform No. 1 to secure a loan. It sounded laughable. Until I saw it myself – a plain sheet of paper, signed off by three board members, declaring them as mortgaged assets. It was surreal. But there it was, neatly filed.

The chairman of the bank was a sitting MLA from the ruling party. The Opposition seized on this as political dynamite. The chief minister, shaken, gave us a free hand. We wasted no time. My assistant registrar and I, alongside a police inspector, lodged first information reports under every section of the Indian Penal Code we could think of.

The chairman and bank secretary fled the city. We filed more FIRs, secured arrest warrants and invoked surcharge provisions of the Bihar Co-operative Societies Act to recover losses. Attachment orders followed, targeting the bank secretary's hotel and shops. In a twist almost cinematic, the law allowed the attachment of fixtures – windows, doors, anything removable.

We began with the windows of the hotel owned by the bank secretary, and he eventually surrendered.

The chairman assumed I would hesitate. He misread inexperience for timidity. But sometimes, not knowing limits helps one push harder. We proceeded with the same tactic – this time, his residence. His supporters tried to provoke unrest. We remained calm. One window – that's all we needed.

By afternoon, he surrendered in court – on a stretcher, flanked by private doctors in a theatrical flourish. Anticipating this, we had government doctors, including a cardiologist, ready. The court saw through the charade. The health plea was dismissed. His plan to transfer to a posh private hospital was denied.

After that, the message was clear. Recoveries gained momentum.

The chief minister was furious, but he held his silence. In those landline days, staying away from the phone was a strategy. No calls meant no instructions.

We recovered enough to pay back every individual depositor – principal, not interest. Government institutions weren't so lucky. As for me, I wasn't suspended. I wasn't punished. And I am alive to tell the story. In Bihar, that felt miraculous.

Perhaps I was shielded by something intangible – the blessings of the poor, maybe.

I thought of this story again, nearly five decades later, when the Karuvannur and Kandala cooperative scams shook Kerala. Another tragedy. Another cycle. We haven't moved the needle – not enough.

Notes

1 L.B. Brilliant, *The Management of Smallpox Eradication in India* (Ann Arbor: University of Michigan Press, 1985), 54.

A Heady Mix of Math, Science and the Baton

Rajan Medhekar

WHAT DO YOU GET when you blend physics, mathematics and policing? A perfect recipe for disaster? Or a thrilling adventure? I discovered it was both – and infinitely more – in my improbable journey from a nerdy researcher to a uniformed guardian of peace.

In the early 1970s, as a fresh graduate just out of BITS Pilani, with stellar marks in mathematics and applied physics to boot, I supposedly had the world at my feet. Did I say 'feet'? I hadn't the foggiest notion where to take the next step. Career options in those days were depressingly finite: engineering, medicine, law or teaching. None appealed to my restless, clueless but creative mind.

So after completing postgraduate studies at Bombay University in solid state physics, I began pursuing a PhD in theoretical physics under Dr V.G. Bhide, then deputy director of the National Physical Laboratories, Pusa, New Delhi. (Dr Bhide went on to become the chief scientific adviser to the prime minister. He retired as vice chancellor of Pune University.) We explored liquid crystals – the technology behind modern digital screens like those on your smartphones, which at that time, of course, were not even a distant dream; digital watches were just making their appearance. I did rather well, even winning the 'Physicist of the Year' award in 1974–1975. Then disaster struck. Despite the award, a crucial equipment grant slipped out of my grasp, being granted to another team amid whispers of nepotism. Devastated, I told Dr Bhide I was quitting.

He gave me that curious look seasoned mentors reserve for overwrought, impulsive protégés. 'What's next?' he asked and I mumbled something appropriately vague. He shrugged with magnificent indifference. 'Try UPSC. Be a bureaucrat, diplomat, cop or an auditor.' I laughed at the absurdity. Little did I know that's exactly what fate had in store for me!

I reasoned I had nothing to lose by taking the exams: pass them and reject the offer or fail them and return to research. But destiny, as it often does, had other plans entirely. I was selected for the Indian Police Service (IPS) in my first attempt, even scoring, despite being from the science stream, the highest marks in the subject of ancient Indian history that year. My secret? Reading Amar Chitra Katha comics on the exploits of Pulikesin-2, Harsha and the like. To be fair, I had also scanned through R.C. Majumdar's authoritative *Ancient India*, but illustrated comic books have a way of sticking in the memory that plain text does not.

I was clueless about what the IPS had to offer, even though my father was a well-known IPS officer of the 1949 batch. Though from Maharashtra, I barely understood my home state's police setup. My father's Intelligence Bureau (IB) postings had taken him to Delhi and the Northeast. He also had a stint in Bhutan as India's first police adviser. In this beautiful kingdom at the base of the Himalayas, he advised King Jigme Dorji Wangchuck, the founder of modern Bhutan, on police matters and helped train and set up the country's first police force. He retired in 1984 as Maharashtra's first director general of police (DGP) – a rank introduced in 1982 when he was appointed to that post. Before that the Maharashtra State Police Force was headed by an inspector general of police (IGP). But he kept his policing work in his office, hardly discussing it at home. However, the allure of independence drew me to the Lal Bahadur Shastri National Academy of Administration, Mussoorie, for the Foundation Course. This training course is compulsory and is attended by all All India Services (AIS) and Central Services officers who have successfully cleared the UPSC selection process.

I took my first first-class overnight train ride, having previously travelled only third class – yes, we had three train classes back then besides the 'unreserved' compartment. At the Dehradun railway station, I was uncertain about how to get to the Lal Bahadur Academy. I spotted a lanky fellow sitting on his trunk, smoking a cigarette, and decided to ask him. He appeared equally lost and told me that he too wanted to go to Mussoorie to join the Indian Railways Traffic Service. We, two strangers embarking on parallel adventures, decided to share a taxi. Who was he? Have patience – you'll discover soon enough!

After the Foundation Course at Mussoorie, we, rookie officers, scattered to specialised academies. In Mussoorie, we made wonderful friendships across services, some of which endure even after half a century. Sadly, however, sometime in the late 1980s, bureaucratic wisdom deemed it appropriate to scrap the combined Foundation Course format. This retrograde decision destroyed the format's primary purpose: fostering early familiarity among officers of different services. Whoever conceived this notion inflicted lasting damage on inter-service camaraderie and administrative harmony, and the results in the field are plainly visible. Fortunately, better sense prevailed and the Combined Services Foundation Course in Mussoorie was reinstated.

The IPS probationers proceeded to the Sardar Vallabhbhai Patel National Police Academy (SVPNPA) in Hyderabad via Nagpur. We completed a disaster management training course at the National Fire Service College, which is managed by the Ministry of Home Affairs (MHA), Government of India. Incidentally, the 1975 batch was the first to get fully trained in this splendid new facility; earlier batches had trained at Mount Abu since 1948.

During training, we were sent in small groups on a veritable Bharat darshan to the north, south, east and west to enjoy and appreciate India's diversity. I was part of the group sent north, and we met President Fakhruddin Ali Ahmed and the iconic Prime Minister Indira Gandhi. I served as the group leader, guided by B.S. Sastry, then an assistant director at the National Police Academy, who went on to become DGP of Kerala.

The audience with the President proved stiff and formal, but tea with Mrs Gandhi was delightful. She chatted freely and asked, 'What should I speak about?' Our brave guide, Mr Sastry, blurted out, 'The Twenty Point Programme, Madam!' Mrs Gandhi then spoke about the programme eloquently, fielding our questions with practised ease. But when I asked about the police's role, she flashed her signature smile and said, 'Join me for tea on the lawns!'

In the lawns, she mingled without the usual phalanx of staff or security – just her, regal yet warmly accessible. Returning to the hostel of the Indian Institute of Public Administration, where we were put up, we mercilessly ribbed poor Mr Sastry for referring to the Twenty Point Programme as the Twenty-One Point Programme when he spoke to Mrs Gandhi. He panicked, fearing retribution in those perilous Emergency times, until we revealed that we had been joking, and he bounced back splendidly.

Cadre allotment resembles winning – or losing – a lottery. I drew Kerala, a state about which I knew absolutely nothing. I'd never even ventured south of the Godavari! Madras (now Chennai), I'd heard of, but Trivandrum (now Thiruvananthapuram) and Kerala? Not a clue other than seafood, pickles, Kathakali and spices.

A Wily Ticket Collector and a Fast Train

The only route to Trivandrum, where I was directed to report by the MHA, was by train: from Delhi to Madras by the GT Express, and then onward by a connecting train. On reaching Madras I was settled in the first-class lounge for a six-hour wait with an Irving Wallace novel when a wily ticket inspector tempted me with an 'earlier' train going to Trivandrum. I jumped at the offer, only to discover from fellow passengers that I'd been magnificently deceived – this train would reach Trivandrum a full day after my original train! However, there was no turning back, and so I embraced the journey and savoured Kerala's lush green welcome once we passed Palghat (now Palakkad).

Reaching Trivandrum, I found no trace of my batchmate Jacob Punnoose, who was meant to receive me. He had of course stuck to my original schedule and come the previous day, and must have thought that I had fled on not seeing me on the train! I grabbed a taxi, and the driver, spotting fresh prey, treated me to a scenic detour of Shanmugam Beach, East Fort, etc., before dropping me at the Police Training College (PTC) in Thycaud, which turned out to be just two kilometres from the railway station.

Our quarters were spartan, with not even a ceiling fan – quite the downgrade from the luxury of the National Police Academy's independent room with an attached bathroom. At PTC, we shared rooms and every morning had to dash across a corridor to reach the bathroom before PTC's staff streamed in. The food in the mess introduced me to Kerala's cuisine, cooked in aromatic coconut oil, and I was soon addicted. Kattan kappi, kappa meen curry, egg roast with appam, and puttu and kadala, I had and savoured all these first in that humble mess.

One prized instructor was Krishna Nair, the formidable police inspector who also had the title of 'senior law instructor' – and he never let us forget that! He was tall, generously built and sported a majestic upward-sweeping moustache. He treated the Indian Penal Code (IPC) with nothing short of scriptural reverence, and Jacob and I, the only probationers, had to endure his daily sermons on it for long hours. After the morning run and physical training, Jacob and I, utterly exhausted, perfected the art of sleeping with half-open eyes. Mr Nair insisted that every nation possessed its own IPC: in the UK, they had the 'British IPC'; the USA had its 'US IPC'; even the USSR, as it was known back then, had a 'Russian IPC', but an 'IPC' they all had! He meant 'penal code', but 'IPC' was a non-negotiable in his lexicon.

We tackled dusty local statutes like the Hackney-Carriage Act, 1879, the Dramatic Performances Act, 1876, and the Lime Shell Act. One day, our IGP – the post of DGP had not been established then – the very formidable V.N. Rajan, surprised us with a quiz on the Hackney-Carriage Act. When asked if we had studied it, I blurted out, 'Yes, Sir!' – a tactical blunder, for he then demanded I list out the contents of its section 4. I froze. Jacob fumbled. Furious, Mr Rajan threatened to extend our training – until he asked Mr Nair about section 4, and our instructor blanked out too! We were spared by Nair's glorious ignorance, as the IGP gave him a dressing down while we tried to fade into the woodwork!

District training followed. Jacob went to Calicut (now Kozhikode) and I went to Kottayam. The district superintendent of police (SP), R.P.C. Nair, and the district collector, J. Lalithambika, proved good mentors and gracious hosts, often inviting me for meals on weekends and offering guidance whenever I sought it. The district judge was another matter – he remained reserved and aloof. When I requested a courtesy visit to his house (as we had been trained to do at the National Police Academy), he agreed, but the meeting proved painfully awkward. Mid-tea, he asked why I had come. I explained that it was merely a courtesy visit. Later I learned that he suspected I was eyeing his comely, eligible daughter, something that still amuses me.

Training in 'Forensic Science'

My first introduction to a post-mortem examination was on a murder victim – grisly work. Medical assistants handled the body with eerie nonchalance, chatting as if they were on a tea break. Rumour had it that they warmed up with a few pegs of arrack. They smoked beedis and rattled on in Malayalam, which I had yet to learn, while they cut and sawed the cadaver. I also conducted my first police inquest – an apparent suicide by hanging. When noting the cause of death, I was searching for the right words – and the helpful head constable, Balan Nair, earnestly suggested, 'Broken neck.' So much for my training in forensic science!

Near the end of my training at Kottayam, J. Lalithambika asked if I knew one Sayan Chatterji. I did – he was the fellow I'd met at the Dehradun railway station en route to Mussoorie! He had attempted the UPSC exam again, cracked the IAS, got the Kerala cadre and landed in Kottayam – of all places – for district training. Even more remarkable, we soon found out that we'd both attended the same school, Frank Anthony Public School in Delhi, that we were in the same class, same section as well, but I'd left in sixth standard and had no memory of him. Later, when I was posted as the assistant superintendent of police (ASP) in Thodupuzha, he was the sub-collector in the adjoining sub-district of Muvattupuzha. Life truly delights in staging coincidences! And now we meet occasionally for a cup of tea at the India International Centre (IIC) in Delhi. Coincidences or decree?

Kasaragod: The Beginning

My first independent charge was as the ASP in Kasaragod – then the largest, most crime-prone subdivision in Kerala, nearly a hundred kilometres from the district headquarters of Cannanore (now Kannur). Mangalore (now Mangalapuram), forty-eight kilometres away, was closer. Life proved challenging: language problems (I couldn't speak Malayalam, Kannada, Tulu or Konkani), a heavy workload and minimal police experience. I managed a few words of Konkani but otherwise floundered linguistically and hugely detested the laborious report writing – including the GCR or the general conviction register, which I stopped maintaining on realising it served no real purpose except as props for my DIG to issue memos and inspection reports, to which most station house officers (SHOs) and circle inspectors simply responded with 'Sir, noted' (one enterprising SHO even had the audacity to have a rubber stamp for this and got rid of it when I took him to task). I felt that reducing crime by proper patrolling and mounting surveillance on known criminals, ensuring proper investigation through supervision (including well-written case diaries by the investigating officers) and maintaining law and order were far more importantly than scriptory work – and I didn't care what others, including seniors, thought. The fact is that my efforts did reduce property crime and helped maintain law and order very well in my subdivision, notwithstanding the stream of memos from my DIG! I still believe that voluminous after-the-event reports are no substitute for effective policing in the field.

Filarial mosquitoes swarmed everywhere in Kasaragod town, so I followed the government doctor's advice: a thirty-day course of Banocide Forte tablets along with vitamin B complex. To escape the mosquito menace, I rented a nalukettu (a traditional single-storey home, with rooms around a courtyard) near Vidya Nagar Government College on the national highway – perched on a hill and isolated. It included an 'office room' (just a shed) and, surprisingly, a cow and a cowshed to make up for erratic milk supply! ASPs were not allotted offices then, just ₹80 as 'sweeping allowance' (if PWD certified that the sweeping area was of the prescribed size) and a Jeep. My sole possession – a steel trunk from my father – always remained in the Jeep parked in the courtyard.

I retained a teenage cook, Babu, the son of a local chef in Badariya's Restaurant (famous for its chicken curry and biryani). Apart from cooking, Babu handled everything – from ironing my uniforms and other clothes to cleaning the house with spirited efficiency. His cooking filled my quarters with delicious aromas of coconut oil and spices, but his culinary expertise was limited to chicken curry, rice, dal and tea. So I ate chicken curry, dal and rice seven days a week.

Among my few contacts in Kasaragod was the charming Govindrajan Rao, the Poirot-moustached customs superintendent who wore khaki shorts and a solar topee. As gold and imported whisky smuggling was rampant, Mr Rao and I led several raids. Kind and well read, he often lent me books from his collection, dropping them off during his morning walks past my house.

Otherwise, my entertainment revolved around the daily crossword in *The Hindu* and my trusty 13-band Sony transistor, bringing me Vividh Bharati and Forces Request on medium wave (MW), and Binaca Geetmala, BBC and Voice of America on shortwave (SW). My favourites were the weekly Forces Request programme of English songs at night and the Hindustani classical show bringing its listeners Bollywood songs based on classical ragas. For films, Mangalore was my occasional Sunday escape via a 'BH' – Benefit of Holidays. The solitary Kasaragod theatre screened only Malayalam and Kannada films, and its uncomfortable seats harboured battalions of bloodthirsty bedbugs that could bite even through denim jeans.

Another notable figure near Kasaragod in that phase of my career was Swami Kesavananda Bharati, head of Edneer Mutt – yes, the Swamiji of the landmark 1973 Supreme Court case on the Constitution's 'basic structure'. Older than me by a few years, Swamiji was warm and sociable and loved table tennis. I joined him often – not for spiritual uplift but for good-natured matches! When the Students' Federation of India (SFI) announced a strike at the Mutt's school, my DIG – a Swamiji devotee (and a connoisseur of his excellent vegetarian lunch, I suspect!) – dispatched me with full force to manage the protesting primary-school students. Finding it rather absurd to control schoolchildren so young through a section of the Armed Reserve Police but keeping quiet (remembering an IGP's observation that my 'impertinence was exceeded only by [my] ignorance'), I posted the police contingent at a distance with directions not to allow outsiders to enter the school premises. I then took refuge from the sweltering summer heat in a classroom, perched on the teacher's desk, and entertained children with my tales from Mumbai that I narrated in a hotchpotch of broken Malayalam, Hindi and English. I even taught them origami – one breezy afternoon, paper wheels zipped across the playground with children shrieking delightedly behind them. This kept most students in their classrooms and not outside, shouting slogans. Unorthodox policing? Perhaps. Effective? Absolutely!

To Thodupuzha, Where My Life Partner Awaited Me

After a year in Kasaragod, I was posted to Thodupuzha (in Idukki district) to establish a new subdivision from scratch. Here there was no office, no residence – just a Jeep, four staff members and my loyal cook, Babu. I moved into a charming one-bedroom, Mangalore-tiled house with a large, walled compound. My district SP was the lively M.G.A. Ramen, and the collector was the gracious K.M. Chandrasekhar (later Cabinet Secretary). Cricket matches, including games with the Tata Finlay cricket team in Munnar, added cheer to my workdays.

My stint at Thodupuzha included rough patches as well. During one police station visit, a few SFI students stormed in, injuring my men and toppling a part of the compound wall. I ordered a memorable cane charge and the students scattered like rabbits, rubbing their backsides. An inquiry followed, but thanks to K.M. Chandrasekhar's tact, we escaped censure. A year later, during a late-night road check, an overloaded Jeep of political workers refused to pay fines. Their 'leader' argued endlessly that they would not pay the fine as it was a 'party vehicle', so I locked them up in the police station's lock-up for court production the next morning. Just as I was falling asleep, my SP, Mr Ramen, called. He informed me in a serious tone that I had jailed the Leader of Opposition, T.K. Ramakrishnan! Stunned, I prepped paperwork in the early hours, sent mandatory wireless messages to the Speaker, the Chief Secretary, the Home Secretary and the IGP and when the court opened personally escorted them to the court, where the elderly magistrate fined them. They shouted slogans as they exited the court. And here's a twist of fate: Mr Ramakrishnan's party won the elections, and he became the home minister. Rumours flew that my due promotion would now be shelved. Instead, Ramakrishnan graciously phoned to tell me that he was ordering my promotion and posting me as SP in Idukki – a politician's magnanimity I'll never forget.

It was in Thodupuzha that I married Devayani Pradhan, a young lawyer from the Bombay High Court and daughter of a retired army colonel. She had to give up her practice due to my rural postings, language barriers and perhaps my own unease with her appearing in lower courts, given the unsavoury characters that were usually present there. Arriving in that tiny town must have felt like a cruel twist for someone so modern and accomplished, but she handled it with quiet grace. She turned our bare quarters into a home and became the anchor of my life. With no furniture or crockery and just a single Janata kerosene stove to cook on, she never once complained – not then, not during my long absences, never. She remains the most beautiful soul I know, my closest friend and confidant, and the reason my life has turned out so well.

Upon my promotion, I moved to Painavu, the district headquarters, sharing a barrack-like building, the Collectorate – once a drafting shed of the Hindustan Construction Company Ltd (HCC), which built the Idukki Dam – which housed both the District Police Office and the district collector, the efficient Dr P.K. Sivanandan. His wife, Sulochana, then an assistant PWD engineer, was invaluable, for our police buildings finally got renovated on time. Together, we managed a peaceful eviction in the Mankulam forest, earning academic kudos from all quarters. Sivanandan later wrote a paper on our successful methodology.

Idukki had one more dramatic chapter. Torrential rains filled the dams in Kulamavu and Periyar. Rumours of an impending burst at the century-old Mullaperiyar Dam triggered mass panic. But it was 'seepage', the engineer clarified, and not 'leakage' as the media had put it – a good sign according to the engineer. And so the dam was safe. Loudspeakers calmed the exodus, though land-grabbers lurking in the wings weren't thrilled.

I cannot forget the endangered Nilgiri tahr – once on the brink of extinction, now thriving in the highlands near Rajamalai, thanks to the conservation efforts of the Wildlife and Forest authorities. The Kerala Police played a major supporting role in these efforts and I am proud to have been a part of it. The Nilgiri tahr is a muscular, dark-coated herbivore that roams the Western Ghats, best admired when the neelakurinji blooms, painting the Eravikulam National Park violet-blue. If you missed this phenomenon in 2006 or 2018, wait until 2030 – or maybe even 2033 – as these flowers bloom only once in twelve years!

After Idukki, I took over as SP, Thiruvananthapuram Rural, a volatile coastal belt rife with communal tensions. One incident in Poovar escalated so badly that we had to open fire – two lives were lost, prompting a judicial inquiry. It was a harrowing time. Courtroom logic rarely considers the chaos on the ground – being attacked by a drunken mob armed with cleavers and ropes with fishhooks and trying to save a head constable who had been thrown into a well is nothing short of a life-and-death situation. Law and order can't always be maintained with civility; sometimes force is necessary, irrespective of the consequences.

At the Capital

Exactly a year later, I was posted as commissioner of police (CP), Trivandrum – a role made tougher due to severe staff shortages. Fortunately, I had the steady support of my DIG, Sattar Kunju (later DGP of Kerala), and the wise district collector, V.V. Vijayan. I served as CP from 1981 to 1983, a turbulent time that saw two governments and President's Rule in 1982. Labour unrest was at its peak – strikes, hartals, rampant 'kai kooli' demands by labourers in Connemara Market and protests overwhelmed the city. Policing a growing capital with stagnant resources was a challenge. We only had two ageing Willys Jeeps, a few motorcycles and two large buses until Home Minister Oommen Chandy sanctioned four new minivans. Things worsened when the Commissionerate, the Armed Reserve Camp and the City Police Mounted Squad were displaced to accommodate the new Assembly building, leaving me scrambling for space. The Commissionerate shifted to a building in Thycaud, which, I was told, once long ago housed a dispensary for snakebites.

In late December 1982, just as I was about to hand over my duties, a tip-off interrupted my farewell dinner at Hotel Lucia. I rushed to the control room and scribbled a bandobast scheme using carbon paper in the General Diary itself – we had no PCs or word processors back then. The next day there was arson at Chalai Bazaar in what appeared to be a communal riot (which was later exposed as staged). With my Armed Reserve diverted to Alleppey, where there was a genuine communal riot in progress, I was compelled to requisition the army, and two of its columns from the Pangode Brigade stepped in, restoring calm through route marches and a show of strength. My tenure was extended so that the situation could be brought under control and the culprits prosecuted.

It was during my term as CP, Trivandrum that our elder daughter, Aditi, was born in Mumbai. Two years later, in 1983, our second daughter, Chitra, was born at SAT Hospital, Trivandrum. Both have grown up to become accomplished women and have made us, my wife and I, so proud. I believe Kerala shaped their cheerful outlook and enhanced their ability to adjust, learn new languages and make lasting friendships.

Later, I served as assistant inspector general (AIG) at the Kerala State Police Headquarters – a desk job, yet far from being dull. I oversaw crime, law and order files, police construction and VIP duties, including Pope John Paul II's 1986 visit to Kottayam. Jacob Punnoose, as the other AIG, managed the confidential section, transfers and postings. Despite the workload, camaraderie and mentorship – especially from T.P. Gopinath, P.R. Chandran, T.V. Madhusoodan and DGPs T.A.S. Iyer, Vijayan and M.K. Joseph – made my role deeply fulfilling.

Jokes in Uniform

At the Police Headquarters, I encountered amusing old case files. One involved a communal riot where the IGP had scribbled, 'The Sub Inspector (SI) had no business to pull the chestnuts out of the fire!' Though just a comment, it triggered an amusing bureaucratic chain: his Private Secretary sent it to the district SP for remarks, who sent it to the sub divisional police officer (a deputy SP in this case), who passed it on to the concerned circle inspector, and it finally landed on the poor SI's desk. The SI dutifully insisted he'd pulled no chestnuts from any fire. The circle inspector, who perhaps didn't like him, disagreed, painting a vivid picture of the SI running around like a headless chicken pulling chestnuts from the fire. But the SDPO settled it. He concluded his report with this sentence: 'Sir, I can confirm that the SI did not pull chestnuts from any fire as there was no fire, and chestnuts are not grown in this part of the country!' The IGP must have had a good laugh, for he had penned in the margin of the report: 'Ha! Close this file at once!'

In another instance, there was a scene 'mahazar' (description of the scene of the crime) in the Case Diary relating to a rape and murder. In it, the investigating officer (IO) had written, 'Just a few spots of semen seen on the lungi', to which the IGP responded: 'What did he expect, torrents?'

Here's another gem. A DGP once commented on a Chief Secretary: 'First time I've seen an athletic mind in an academic body!' Candid wit wasn't rare back then; humour was part of administrative charm and being politically correct wasn't in fashion. It seems we have now lost all that humour and wit in our official interactions, written and oral, in our attempt to be politically correct whether the situation warrants it or not. This ailment bedevils all levels of the bureaucracy and even the debates and discussions in Parliament and our State Assembly, where cracking a joke at another's expense (particularly at a member of the ruling party) is viewed as a grave crime warranting walkouts, street protests and even suspension from the House! I urge the younger generations to reflect on this. They need to read a book I'd read while I was in Kasaragod – *How to Be an Alien* by George Mikes. It is a humorous, satirical take on societal norms, using irreverence without a trace of rancour or bitterness. I also urge them to read the novels by P.G. Wodehouse and James Michener and Malayalam writers like VKN (as Vadakke Koottala Narayanankutty Nair is popularly known), E.V. Krishna Pillai and 'Beypore Sultan' Vaikom Mohammed Basheer to name a few whose subtle humour did not descend into vulgar slapstick or name-calling and whose biting satire still rings true today. It will hopefully reignite in the younger generation the crucial ability to view life a bit more realistically and broadly, but with wit, humour and a sense of the absurd, which too has its uses, for life without humour is like pickles without the tang of tamarind and the sting of chilli powder – or as the saying in Malayalam goes 'ചുക്ക ഇല്ലാതെ കഷായം ഇല്ല'. I am one who firmly believes, as proven by personal experience, that humour, satire and wit truly help in navigating the ups and downs of life without getting hurt or despondent.

A Roving Cop

In 1986 I went on a deputation to the Cabinet Secretariat, not knowing I'd be away from my cadre for a decade. It was a good change from traditional policing, and I learnt a lot while there. A major challenge came during the Gulf War of 1990 – while I was posted at our embassy in Baghdad, Iraq. I was put in charge of managing the evacuation of Indians from Kuwait via Amman, Jordan, to India after Saddam Hussein invaded Kuwait. As forces allied with the US launched Operation Desert Storm against Iraq, families of all diplomatic officers and staff, including the ambassador and his wife, were evacuated to India. So was my wife, on official government orders, as she had protested her evacuation and wanted to remain with me. Better sense prevailed as my children had already been evacuated, and she took the last flight out of Baghdad. After this I was ordered to remain in Baghdad with just one assistant (who also served as my wireless operator and my only line of communication with my Delhi HQ as all phones and other means of communication were dismantled by the air raids). It was an eerie feeling, being alone and without communication with family and friends in a foreign land devastated by war for the next eighteen months. Despite the extreme hardships and dangers due to incessant bombing by US-led forces, no electric or tap water supply and food shortages, what has stayed with me is the Iraqi grit, courage and resilience under severe sanctions and destruction of Iraq's infrastructure, and their fondness for India. Saddam Hussein reportedly called India 'the land of my sister'. But it was Mahatma Gandhi whose calm defiance of the colonial powers through his non-violent 'Satyagraha' that truly resonated with them; my local plumber referred to him as 'the baldy Gandhi', admiring his open defiance against the British with limited means but enormous moral courage and public support. I stayed in Iraq until 1992 and then moved to Sydney. There I gained new insights into how a modern country operated, and into administration and policing in a developed nation.

Returning to the cadre in 1996 marked a new chapter in my career. Back in uniform, I served in key roles: IGP (Headquarters) at Kerala State Police HQ, additional DGP (Intelligence), additional DGP (Operations, Law and Order) and additional DGP (Crimes), and eventually DGP of Kerala Home Guards and Civil Defence, and commandant general, Kerala Fire Force. Each post brought challenges and opportunities to work alongside exceptional officers, civil servants and public figures, including politicians, writers, actors, businesspeople and other interesting individuals from all walks of life, many of whom became lifelong friends.

In 2008 I went on a deputation again, this time to the Border Security Force (BSF) as its special director general (SDG). I was to oversee our border with Bangladesh, monitor anti-Maoist operations across Chhattisgarh, Orissa and Jharkhand, and supervise the BSF headquarters in New Delhi. For a while I also looked after our border with Pakistan as an additional charge. These roles were intense, involved incessant touring of border areas and districts infested with Maoists, hardships of trekking for miles on foot and even rafts in the riverine areas, facing filarial mosquitoes which could be as deadly as bullets from insurgents, but all this deepened my understanding of India's security matrix and I learnt a lot about how India lives in its villages.

Back Home

In 2010 I was promoted and posted as director general of the elite National Security Guard (NSG), also known as the Black Cats because of their black uniform and their mascot, the black panther, known for its stealth, strength and speed of attack. The NSG's emblem is the 'Sudarshan Chakra' – Lord Krishna's weapon of choice – symbolising the NSG's role as a counterterrorist force (as against an anti-terrorist force, which is a police role) that neutralises its enemy (it takes no prisoners) and returns to base as silently as it operates. My tenure involved managing security for major events such as the 2010 Commonwealth Games and the 2011 Cricket World Cup, and for securing high-risk dignitaries, including US President Barack Obama, Chinese Premier Wen Jiabao, L.K. Advani, J. Jayalalithaa and Narendra Modi (who was then chief minister of Gujarat). There were some Special Ops too, but those cannot be disclosed for obvious reasons. I also led delegations to interact with Special Forces of Israel (the Yamam and Sayeret Matkal), France (Groupe d'Intervention de la Gendarmerie Nationale or the GIGN in short), Germany (Grenzschutzgruppe-9 or GSG-9 on which the NSG is designed), the USA (Delta Force) and Russia (the Spetsnaz).

The NSG commandos cross-train with many of these forces abroad as they in turn train with the NSG in India. They also train with the special forces of the Indian Armed Forces such as the Air Force's Garuds, the Navy's MARCOS and the Army's Para Special Forces. In fact, the NSG is a unique special force under the Ministry of Home Affairs that has 50 per cent officers and commandos from the army and 50 per cent drawn from the Central Armed Police Forces and the State Police. It also has an elite Women Commando Wing and the National Bomb Blast Centre. In all, my experience in the NSG was a good rounding off of my tenures in nearly all wings of the state and Central police forces as well as in the Central and state intelligence departments. I retired on superannuation in 2012, after a satisfying tenure in the NSG and service in the IPS. I consider myself extremely fortunate to have been given this opportunity to serve my country and its people.

Kerala has left a lasting imprint on both my professional and my personal life. My only regret is encountering some vicious people full of hate and negativity – some strangers, others sadly fellow officers whom I will not honour by naming them, who were frustrated professionally or simply jealous of the success of others. Their sole driving force seemed to be chronic, toxic envy. They channelled this through anonymous rumours and petitions, engineered press reports and baseless character attacks in articles and books. I am not the only officer to have faced such accusations from these pathetic people. I also do not claim that they were incompetent. Many of them enjoyed similar or better postings than mine. But I often wonder what satisfaction they derived from their negative mindset and malicious activities. All this hardly affected me or my career – I was confident of my professional abilities and contributions. I can also confidently say that I have maintained the highest levels of integrity and honesty. I have always maintained my dignity, self-respect and composure, never once stooping low by uttering a word against them, for doing so would give them satisfaction, which I certainly don't want to contribute to. I did, however, bring these matters to the notice of my superiors in the department, and in one instance to the government, in confidential notes, and requesting them to inquire into allegations made against me and to take whatever action they seemed fit. I never heard anything from them or the government, so I don't know what they did with my notes, but I gather they found the allegations baseless, motivated by envy and nothing more. But such corrosive traits, like undetected cancers, do more harm to those who harbour them. I can only feel sorry for them as envy, like baldness, is yet an incurable disease – while the latter bares only a benign baldpate, the former reveals a malignant, dark and cold heart.

Thankfully, I don't dwell on this too much. Life is too short to dwell on negative matters! Kerala, with its charm and warm-hearted people, gave me and my family immense joy and lasting bonds. We also grew fond of its cultural heritage, its music, its dance forms, its martial arts and its divine cuisine. We return often to Kerala to rekindle friendships and relive cherished memories.

And so unfolds this curious tale of a physicist-turned-policeman – an odyssey filled with surprises, serendipitous bonds and public service's unpredictable twists. Looking back, I'm reminded of Steve Jobs' wisdom: 'You can't connect the dots looking forward. You can only connect them looking backwards, so … you have to trust in something: gut, destiny, life, karma, whatever.' This quiet sense of trust I've harboured within has made all the difference, never failing me. I am at peace with myself and grateful to the Almighty and my country for giving me so many opportunities.

From the Wild to the Shrine

Surendra Kumar

YOU HUMANS WOULD PROBABLY mock the idea of an elephant writing its own story. Although our species has not yet developed skills with words and letters, we are undeniably excellent at communication. We possess the ability to transmit messages to our family members across vast expanses such as rivers, jungles and mountains. But despite our long association with humans, communicating with them has always been an elephantine problem.

Let me briefly introduce myself. I am Ramachandran. People lovingly call me 'Raman'. They also bestowed upon me the title of 'Ekachatradhipathi', meaning 'the sole emperor'. But behind all these glorious, high-sounding words, there are layers of unsettling, harsh realities that I want to bring forth to humanity.

My Calfhood

People say that I was born as Moti Prasad in the far-off city of Jehanabad in Bihar. But this is far from the truth. I was born in 1964 as a wild elephant calf in the hills of North Cachar, Assam. Some of you humans who play with the wildlife protection laws claim that I am a captive elephant, born to captive parents. No, I was born wild, and the wild is where I belonged. I lived my early life roaming in the jungle with my extended family (which you people call a 'herd').

Life in the forest was full of fun and frolic. As a baby in the herd, I enjoyed everybody's care and attention. Whenever, out of curiosity, I strayed away a bit, I was always lovingly brought back and protected by moving elephantine walls deployed around me. Foraging was our only real occupation. We used to trudge miles and miles through dense forests, open grasslands, rivers and lakes.

Sometimes, we amused ourselves by smearing mud on our bodies and lying endlessly in a large pool of water. We lived, struggled, enjoyed and mourned – all together. Togetherness and intimacy were central to our existence.

All our forest wanderings taught me to be wary of only one species: human beings. Whenever we encountered them, we gave up our right-of-way and let them pass.

The Trap and the Camp

One night, when the moon was still shining in the clear sky and we were leisurely foraging in an open grassland surrounded by towering trees, things changed forever. There was a huge, loud sound, as if lightning had struck the ground. We had grown accustomed to these light flashes and the accompanying thunderous sounds, but that day, the sky wasn't overcast, and so there was no possibility of thunder or rain. Besides, no light preceded the sound. This was something else.

Before we could make anything out of it, the deafening sound filled the night sky again. We were utterly terrified. We frantically sprinted for our lives, trumpeting across the seemingly endless darkness. While running, I fell into a ditch from which there was no escape. I could hear my mom's wailing in the distance, and that was the last I heard of her. This distressing sound was going to haunt me throughout my life, as it later turned out. I was barely four years old when I was captured. I had begun to provide for my own food, although I still relied on my family for my overall safety. Two small tusks already adorned my head. Little did I know that it was these very tusks that sealed my fate. Without them, the humans might have lost interest in me, and I could have stayed in the jungle with my family.

The next morning, the sun rose in the sky as usual, but something irrevocably altered my life forever: a group of humans, part of a gang of hunters, descended into the ditch.

I was miserably confined in a space that was cramped, leaving no room for any movement. They were talking to each other excitedly, after which they dug a trench to reach and capture me. They overpowered me, shackling me tightly. This new iron ornament was to stay with me throughout my life. I had lost my freedom and was destined to remain enslaved for my entire life.

Life in the makeshift camp that I was taken to isn't something I would ever want to willingly recall. A small hut in a forest clearing was occupied by two human beings: one ferocious-looking, robust, bearded man and the other, a half-naked, dark-skinned man with all his bones protruding, looking as if he had been starving for years. Slowly, I learned that the first person was the master and the second was his servant, Pichati, whose whole life revolved around what the master desired. The master frequently scolded and abused Pichati, and he occasionally thrashed him, particularly after consuming a potent drink in the evening.

In the jungle camp, both my front legs were shackled and my left hind leg was tethered to a tree. Occasionally, I found some sustenance spread out before me, but the physical trauma and the psychological distress of losing my family, especially Mom, were too heartbreaking to allow me to nibble anything and feed myself meaningfully. Moreover, Pichati always came and lashed me with a stick whenever I showed any resentment and tried to restore my freedom. While lashing out, he muttered some words that initially didn't make any sense to me. When he repeated the exact words, time and again, demonstrating the expected action on my part, I slowly started responding to them. Whenever my response met his expectations, he would express happiness and encourage me by offering a banana or two while caressing and patting my trunk. But Pichati never understood that I barely needed the food, water or the occasional banana he offered – I required only liberty.

Adieu Jungle

One morning, a group of visitors arrived at the camp. They came towards me and took a close look. I intuitively felt that my life was going to change yet again. One of the individuals was wearing a uniform similar to those I used to see back in the forest. We often ignored their presence in the woods, thinking they were friendly intruders. Sometimes, I saw them trying to rescue other denizens of the forest whenever they needed emergency attention.

The uniformed person's presence instilled hope in me, hope that my freedom would be restored. But I wasn't that lucky. He wasn't like the ones who used to rescue animals in the forest. He was the other kind, who had sold his soul – and eventually got me sold, too. He put me on a strange, round-legged animal that humans called a 'truck'. The truck roared like no other animal I had ever come across and seemed to walk among others of its kind, smaller, larger and similar in size. It rolled on for days and nights, while I kept on standing and balancing my body. The food I was given was barely adequate to keep me alive. Throughout these days, Pichati appeared to be enjoying himself immensely, as he continued to amuse himself with delicious food and beverages in the truck's cabin. After three days of the roller-coaster ride, I finally arrived in the Bihar plains, which were to remain my abode for nearly two decades.

My Golden Days

On reaching Bihar, I was taken to a palatial house surrounded by high compound walls. Although the zamindari system had been abolished by then, zamindars still existed. This house belonged to one such elderly gentleman, Babu Ram Prasad, who had a charming and benign appearance. He had three sons and adopted me as the fourth one. The youngest son, Bhola Prasad, might have been a bit older than me. It was here that I received the name 'Moti Prasad' and thus became the newest entrant to the renowned Prasad clan.

They constructed a separate hut for me and excavated a pond in one corner of the vast complex. They also specifically engaged a person, Badri, to look after me. Initially, I was chained, but the shackles were soon removed. In lieu of the excellent treatment given to me, it wasn't hard for me to obey Badri. All I had to do there was to eat sumptuously, frolic and cool off in the pond, and amble around the compound along with Badri.

Badri wasn't allowed to mount and ride me. This privilege was reserved only for the members of the Prasad clan. This one time, on being away from the eyes of the zamindar, he tried to ride me. I took it as an affront, showing my resentment by trying to force him to dismount by shaking my body and walking in a haphazard manner.

Grudgingly and meekly, he got off me and started walking beside me. I had started believing that I was indeed one of the privileged Prasads!

Life went on comfortably. However, despite meeting all my physical needs, I couldn't really fulfil all my biological and social needs since I didn't have an elephant for company. Isn't it unfortunate that I had to live a celibate life? Celibacy may be a desirable virtue in the human world, but not in ours. Preventing a genetically superior being like me from having progeny was detrimental to the elephant race as a whole.

The Patriarch Takes the Final Bow

Over time, the zamindar grew old. He seldom came out of his house and remained confined to his armchair on the veranda, murmuring the names of gods, closing his eyes and rotating the rosary at the same time. Sometimes he would stop chanting and look at me with concern. His two elder sons had taken up jobs in far-off cities, and they came there only once in a while. Bhola, with whom I had grown up and played during all these years, left for his studies abroad. My life was more or less confined to the company of Badri and his deputy, Sahdeo. Still, life wasn't all that bad.

And one day, Babu Ram Prasad passed away in his sleep. It was shocking to me. I had grown sturdy and healthy only because of his benevolence, kindness and care. The two elder sons arrived, and the final rites were organised with fanfare. There were hundreds of people in the funeral procession. Badri and I also followed.

When Babu Ram Prasad was alive, some visitors from Kerala, a distant land, had watched me with interest. My prominent height, spectacular build and magnificent tusks were the main attributes that had caught their eye. But each time, the stern Babu Ram Prasad had rejected their advances, reminding them that I was his son. And what wretched father would sell his own son?

But now that he was no more, those people from the distant land were contacted, and I embarked on yet another torturous journey in a truck. When I looked back at the haveli, there was nobody to wave at me. My eyes welled up, but no one noticed.

Badri and Sahdeo accompanied me throughout my journey. At every checkpoint, uniformed individuals came and inspected me. They raised feigned objections to my transit until their pockets swelled to their desired levels. I had already lost hope in them after what I had experienced on my last day in the jungle camp in Assam. I wanted to keep moving towards the next unknown destination, as there was nothing left in Bihar for me to look back at anyway.

A Divine Abode and Devilish Mahouts

When I arrived in Kerala, I was taken to an ancient temple, with Bhagavathi as the main deity and several other upadevatas (minor deities). People thronged the temple day and night, dumping all kinds of weird desires and wishes upon the deities. Most of the devotees would come to see me and marvel at their good fortune for having encountered me. Some of them would fold their hands in deference, taking me to be the incarnation of Lord Ganesha. The temple priest rechristened me 'Ramachandran', after their most revered god. However, people affectionately called me 'Raman'. My more enthusiastic and devoted fans affectionately called me 'Ekachatradhipathi', acknowledging my magnificent features and hence seeing me as 'the sole emperor'.

But my daily life wasn't all that rosy. The food I received paled in comparison to what the Prasads used to offer me. The temple staff constantly shackled me. The vast compound of the temple wasn't of any use to me, as I was never allowed to roam about. I wasn't eager to chew the leaves and branches thrown to me, and often I showed my disgust to the mahouts by throwing tantrums. This sort of behaviour was met with iron-rod beatings. I would bleed and wail, but they always failed to see my suffering. Perhaps they wanted me to suffer and perish.

Becoming a 'Serial Killer'

Their persistent misbehaviour renewed my subdued animosity towards the human race. One fine afternoon, during a temple festival, I lost control and brutally murdered both my caretakers. This was a momentous occasion in my life: I had undergone a metamorphosis from a gentle giant in the Prasads' haveli to a brutal killer. I committed my first sin in the proximity of a deity and anticipated the punishment.

The temple staff recruited new mahouts. These mahouts' ability to control a wayward and defiant elephant must have led to their selection. I also resolved to repay them in the same currency. To start with, they tied up all four of my legs and kept me without food and water for a couple of days. At night, when the temple priest retired to his quarters, they would drink toddy and come to me with renewed energy, wielding the dreaded iron rods. One night, in their inebriation, or maybe even with deliberate intentions, they struck my forehead and damaged my eyes. I lost sight in one eye, while I could see only partially from the other. This unbearable agony and trauma made me more resolute in my animosity towards human beings.

During festivities, a golden nettipattam was placed over my forehead and an idol was strapped around my neck. I was accompanied by a panchavadyam, an orchestra involving five traditional instruments: ilathalam, thimila, maddalam, idakka and kombu. Colourful umbrellas would also be displayed. Devotees would go inside the temple and perform the pradakshina three times around it.

The mahouts forced me to perform strange rituals, such as lifting my trunk or kneeling. You may think that these were voluntary actions on my part, in obeisance to the deity. No, they weren't. The mahout would poke sharp iron nails into my body to force me to perform them.

The same worshippers would come to the temple every day. I often wondered what was wrong with them. Were they submitting new requests after their previous ones had been fulfilled by God, or were their earlier requests still pending? Whatever the case may be, their faith in the deity was unwavering and tenacious, and they expected the deity to listen to them at some appropriate and sacred time.

But Bhagavathi Amma never heeded my cries and wails, never saw my wounds and never relieved me of my suffering, although I was in her service almost twenty-four hours a day.

Festivals were great fun for people and an excellent time for my captors to make money, but they were a real ordeal for me. I was made to run from one place to another without proper rest, water or food – mostly chained, beleaguered, hungry and thirsty. The noisy panchavadyam, the explosion of crackers and the cacophony of the multitude all amplified my psychological woes.

Even when I went into musth – a natural physiological state for elephants – I was treated as if I had gone crazy. With the help of certain people who called themselves vets, the temple staff suppressed these symptoms by injecting me with drugs. One of the vets was truly blind – not physically but in another sense. He could never see my wounds or my musth and always gave me fitness certificates, forcing me to attend all these festivals. He was so unreasonable that my blindness was of no consequence to him. The fitness certificates flowed unabated from his pen, yielding this wretched vet a fortune. I nurtured a genuine desire to kill him, but he never came close enough to give me a chance. Perhaps he had guessed my intentions.

Temples weren't the only places of woe for me. Gradually, mosques and churches also started to follow suit, and the demand for my time and that of fellow brethren like me increased.

Very often, my physical and psychological distress surpassed my limits of tolerance, and I ran amok several times, killing scores of people. I am surprised that my fan following continued to swell despite my extremely violent behaviour. I found it difficult to understand why these fans chanted 'Raman, Raman' during my public appearances.

But my last killing wasn't premeditated. I was standing comfortably in a narrow lane. I had been taken there to attend a housewarming ceremony and bless some nouveau riche who had earned lots of money in some foreign land. The music was light and soothing. But then suddenly many firecrackers were lit, and some of them hit me, too. I panicked and ran down the narrow lane, dashing against the walls in my blindness. Amid the chaos, I realised that I had trampled upon two people. But I hadn't meant to do that. After all, what would a blind human do if some firecrackers suddenly hit them? They too would definitely panic and run in any random direction.

This episode did not bother my owner or the general public. Strangely enough, they saw me killing someone once in a while as some sort of a natural right.

But one top official, somewhere in far-off Thiruvananthapuram, knew better. He studied my profile carefully and retired me from public life in the best interests of the people. This decision was in my best interest, too. But the powers-that-be wanted otherwise. They argued in the name of culture and tradition – and, of course, public demand – and tried to reintroduce me to the hellish experience of working in temples.

A Tethered Freedom

This time, I was lucky. The lifelong ban prevailed, and now I live a life of anonymity, away from the glare of light and deafening noises. In a sense, I have retrieved my freedom. There is no torment any more, but, of course, I am still away from my original home, where I belong – the wilderness.

Although life isn't great in this little corner of the temple, under an ancient banyan tree, what else can one do or undo? I understand that joining my family in the wilderness will remain a distant dream, but I have plenty of time to ponder and enjoy my days and nights vicariously.

As I reflect on my remaining days, feeling both desolate and serene, I earnestly wish that humans show greater compassion towards other living beings. I genuinely hope that in the times to come these intelligent and crafty beings will eventually cultivate true emotional intelligence, thereby protecting all species from unimaginable injustice, pain and suffering.

Wayanad: A Settler's Tale

Gopalan Balagopal

My wife and I chose Wayanad as the place to settle after having lived away from Kerala for thirty-eight years. It has now been about twenty years since we made Wayanad our home after my retirement at the end of 2009. The district of Wayanad was carved out of the mountainous areas of Kannur and Kozhikode in 1980. The 2011 Census found that there were just over 8,00,000 residents in Wayanad (out of which 18 per cent were tribals), making it Kerala's smallest district in terms of population.

I hope to share my extraordinary post-retirement experience of living in this beautiful part of the Western Ghats. I also seek to recount some experiences that will reaffirm our faith in the future.

First Impressions

The primary pull factor for us to settle in Wayanad was that our daughter and her family had decided to settle down in Bengaluru, which is less than a seven-hour drive from Wayanad. It's a decision we haven't regretted. The beauty of the hills and valleys, the misty mornings and the birdsong that surrounds us give us great joy. On moving out of my front gate, in just about five minutes, I can enter a forested path for a morning walk. And fortunately, elephants have not yet made their way to our backyard.

We found other friends who, like us, are settlers from outside. A couple who spent their working lives oscillating between the UK and Seychelles built their dream home in Wayanad. It is accessible only by four-wheel-drive Jeeps, involving forty minutes of bumping over boulders and stones. The vista of mountains and clouds drifting by their beautiful home is priceless, but you need to make that eighty-minute round trip even if you want a matchbox or a sachet of milk. And yet, they live in bliss, even being visited by elephants!

Another group of friends from Delhi bought a hilltop in Wayanad, where each family created a home suited to their needs. They have a 'long house' that serves as a common facility, featuring a lounge, a brick-lined pizza oven and a few guest rooms. Cleaning services are provided by women who come daily from the valley below and cook meals for those in need.

In this part-'commune' lives a renowned photographer, married to a food stylist, who periodically travels to metros for photoshoots. A lifelong bachelor, who is a professional hot air balloon operator in the Masai Mara, returns to his signature bachelor pad in Wayanad during the off-season. Like the others, they too have elephants visiting and raiding their vegetable patches.

On the banks of a lovely stream has settled another couple, trained at the National Institute of Design, who had previously stayed in Goa. They conducted a careful study of temperature and rainfall records in many parts of South India to find the most salubrious spot to settle down, ultimately choosing Wayanad.

Anganwadi Stories

My first engagement in Wayanad stemmed from my work on children's issues for fifteen years with UNICEF, before my retirement. I went out to observe some Anganwadi centres in the district. To my surprise, I found no more than five or six children at each site, even though fifteen or twenty kids were registered. I had cut my teeth in West Bengal during the early days of the panchayats and thought I should ask the local panchayat about the dismal state of kids' attendance. However, none of the panchayat members had any clue.

I stumbled upon a book titled *The Integrated Child Development Service: A Flagship Adrift* by K.R. Venugopal, who retired as Secretary to the prime minister. He was a director in the Ministry of Social Welfare when the Integrated Child Development Services (ICDS) programme was created. This book, published in 2012, drew on his experience of conducting a social audit of the ICDS in a district within the undivided Andhra Pradesh after his retirement. Inspired by his insights, I prepared a proposal for a social audit of the ICDS programme in Wayanad and shared it with S.M. Vijayanand, a doyen of the innovations that have come into being in the social sector in Kerala. He connected me with Jitendran, the outstanding director of Social Welfare at the time, and the department chose Abey George from the Tata Institute of Social Sciences (TISS) to coordinate the social audit in Wayanad.

Abey was an inspired choice for leading this work. He identified young tribal women to act as 'village social auditors'. They learned about the objectives of the ICDS programme and spread out across various ICDS centres to observe, speak with children and mothers and take measurements to record children's nutritional status. Abey also brought in student groups from TISS, Indian Institute of Management (IIM) Kozhikode and others for data collection. I recall an all-women team from the Rajagiri College of Social Sciences who, for a week, stayed at a Forest Department dormitory deep in the woods, diligently collecting information on children's diets and childcare practices.

As information emerged from various sources, it became clear that the records of malnutrition available from the Anganwadi registers were far from reality. This is a common problem with administrative data collection, which often discourages honest and accurate recording when the responsibility of data collection and implementation lies with the same individuals. The physical conditions of the majority of Anganwadi centres were poor; many buildings leaked during rains, and some even lacked water sources or toilets.

However, many Anganwadi workers were deeply committed to the children and, in some cases, spent money out of their own pockets to keep the programme going. It was evident that the functioning of the Anganwadis was not a priority for the panchayats – they did not go beyond allocating funds for the feeding programme.

The mood shifted when the expenditure on the feeding programme was found to be disproportionately high compared to the number of women or children availing the services. Initially, rumours spread that this 'audit' was the first step towards privatisation. Fortunately, Abey deftly countered this move before it escalated. There was also an abhorrent attempt to humiliate some of the students and stop their work by spreading canards about their morals. However, the young people were made of sterner stuff and brushed off these attempts to derail their work.

The results of the audit were initially presented at the Gram Sabhas. It was evident that only a few attendees understood what the Anganwadis were attempting to do. Many felt that the Anganwadi facilities could not compete with English-medium nursery schools.

Things started changing when the results were presented at a meeting of all the panchayat presidents in the district, organised at the IIM Kozhikode campus by the student teams involved in the assessment. All the panchayat presidents showed keen interest in the descriptions, videos and photos illustrating the findings. Many reaffirmed the programme's importance. The ICDS district officer later told me that interest from the panchayats in the ICDS had improved after the meeting, leading to the repair of leaking roofs and absent water supplies and thus resulting in overall improvements for the programme in the district.

Floods of 2018–2019

When the rains of 2018 brought unprecedented damage to Wayanad, I witnessed the most amazing response from the district. In the West Bengal districts that I had served earlier, floods were an annual occurrence, accompanied by subsequent ritual evacuations and relief distributions. However, what I saw in Wayanad was an outpouring of support for the flood victims from civil society, doctors, engineers as well as associations from other parts of Kerala and some neighbouring states. The coordination among all these entities, the local and district governments as well as the use of WhatsApp messages to report damage and coordinate rescue efforts was flawless. 'We for Wayanad' was the slogan that united everyone.

Drivers of off-road tourism vehicles gathered around distribution points to take clothing, food rations and blankets to shelters. A large clothing store that had suffered significant losses when its underground storage godowns went underwater matched my contributions in kind.

I spoke with C.K. Vishnudas – who had founded the Hume Centre for Ecology and Wildlife Biology in Wayanad (in honour of India's pioneering ornithologist, Alan Octavian Hume) – about the necessity of documenting the landslides, floods, land subsidence and mudslides occurring around us before these were forgotten. We aimed to accomplish this with the help of local communities and to involve young people and students in the process.

Fortunately, amid the non-stop rains, my friend C. Balagopal, a former civil servant, pioneering industrialist and startup promoter, arrived in Kalpetta. He immediately agreed to support our idea of documenting the damage by providing us with resources. Kamal Pal, India's pioneer in Geographic Information System (GIS) maps, provided us with an app that could be downloaded onto phones that were being carried by student teams to all damage locations. By switching on this app and walking around the perimeter of a landslide zone or flooded area, an accurate map could be uploaded to the cloud along with photographs of damage caused to roads and buildings. Data on the loss of crops, livestock and lives for future retrieval could also be uploaded and maintained.

This data was reviewed by a small team of experts, including geologists, soil scientists, engineers and others, who followed up with 'ground-truthing' visits to selected locations. Archival rainfall data – much of which came from various plantations in Wayanad with records spanning decades – alongside satellite imagery from the Cochin University of Science and Technology (CUSAT) were also incorporated. The final report, rich with maps and satellite pictures in both Malayalam and English, was widely circulated along with panchayat-specific vulnerability maps to all the panchayats in the district.

Later, it was also distributed to panchayats in other districts to aid them in preparing their disaster management plans. The data revealed significant variations in rainfall across Wayanad. Until then, the Indian Meteorological Department (IMD) had collected rainfall data from just one location in Wayanad – Ambalavayal – where the Regional Agricultural Research Station is situated.

The First District-Level Weather Forecasting System

This recognition of the micro-level weather fluctuations in Wayanad led to the development of a district-level weather forecasting intervention there. The Hume Centre designed this intervention as a citizen science partnership with farmers. About 150 farmers across different areas of the district were equipped with standardised equipment for measuring rainfall and temperature. Every morning, these farmers sent WhatsApp messages with their readings to a focal point in Kalpetta (located inside the Hume Centre's campus). Inputs, including satellite imagery from a climatologist at CUSAT, were overlaid onto the local data to generate a four-day prediction of rainfall and temperature. Daily reports on actual precipitation and temperature helped compare forecasts to actual experiences and refine future predictions, covering 5x5 kilometre grids all over Wayanad. 'Climate cadets' were identified in schools, taking responsibility for providing daily reports from their respective locations.

This initiative works closely with the District Disaster Management Authority. The actual rainfall data, when matched against the vulnerability maps, enable warnings to be sent to areas likely to experience landslides or floods. With this system in place and swift action taken to evacuate people, we avoided the loss of any lives for six years following the 2018–2019 floods. However, we tragically lost an estimated 400 lives in 2024 due to a system malfunction caused by an avoidable human error.

The proof of this intervention's utility arises from farmers' feedback, collected during meetings that are held in various parts of Wayanad. During one such meeting, farmers requested a week-long forecast, emphasising that the uncertainty of rainfall was their most daunting challenge. This necessitated additional expenditure for unmanned instruments in remote locations to collect data from mountaintops and forest areas and these were installed in 2025.

The State Disaster Management Authority and the IMD have shown interest in what is being developed in Wayanad, and six other districts in Kerala are replicating the Wayanad model.

School Outreach

There are other inspiring vignettes from the work that the Hume Centre and its partners are doing in Wayanad. The Covid-19 period was hard on children, who were cooped up at home and deprived of contact with their peers. The centre thus organised outreach through YouTube and telephones. One of the initiatives they implemented was called 'Chuttuvattathil' (in our surroundings), which encouraged kids to explore their local surroundings, identify insects, birds, plants and flowers, and send pictures to a coordinator, who would respond via WhatsApp and post explanatory videos on YouTube.

Many of Wayanad's schools, especially those in rural areas, lack key facilities. While most schools have computers, thanks to infrastructure strengthening through the Sarva Shiksha Abhiyan, only a few have science labs. Therefore, children do not have the opportunity to learn physics, chemistry or biology through hands-on experiments.

Responding to this gap, the Hume Centre established basic laboratory facilities at its premises in Kalpetta, available free of cost to any school wishing to bring its teachers and children for practical learning.

Mentoring students to participate in science talent searches was another initiative yielding unexpectedly positive results. Over the last three years, children from Wayanad – including some from tribal communities – have progressed to the national level from district- and state-level science talent searches. A project conducted by students on the lives of ants also secured a national award. This achievement has sparked excitement and interest in Wayanad, leading to hundreds of children and teachers stepping forward to participate. One of the funding agencies supporting the Hume Centre even provided it with a molecular laboratory as a corporate social responsibility contribution. This lab is now freely available to all the schools, students and teachers.

Fostering an Inclusive Approach in Early Education

A significant challenge for schools in Wayanad is the disadvantages faced by children in Adivasi communities, particularly those belonging to the most vulnerable Paniya and Kattunaicker tribes. These disadvantages begin with language barriers: Adivasi children attending preschools struggle when teachers communicate in Malayalam, which is unfamiliar to them as they speak their own indigenous languages at home. Unable to connect with their peers at this initial stage, many withdraw, creating barriers to their equal participation with non-tribal children.

During the Covid-19 period, Adivasi settlements faced additional hardships as educational outreach through TV programmes or smartphones failed to reach them. The Hume Centre endeavoured to bridge this gap by supplementing government schemes that provide TVs to schools. They also tried to arrange for local mentor teachers who could meet the tribal children in their hamlets, offering in-person support. This initiative has evolved into continuing programmes in five hamlets, aiming to create a model to address the disadvantages faced by tribal children. A notable feature of these activities is the inclusion of children, including non-Adivasi ones, from nearby schools. This allows both tribal and non-tribal children to participate together, mingle and learn from one another. Activities such as forest walks and bird observation are regularly conducted under this initiative.

The support provided by professional artists, musicians and theatre practitioners – including a professional singer from the Adivasi community – to enrich the learning experience through these art forms is heartening. I spent a day with children in a forest location in Begur, Wayanad, where the Forest Department provided accommodation for a four-day residential camp. The children presented various themes (that they had chosen themselves) using music, theatrics and narratives. They presented Kattunaicker songs and danced with great energy and enthusiasm while sharing stories about life in the forests, highlighting the importance of preserving this heritage. The Hume Centre has recently acquired land with the help of a generous donor and is in the process of designing its own campus. The first construction on the land was a Kurichiya tribal koottupura – a beautiful mud, bamboo and thatch structure sitting gracefully on the thickly wooded hillside, overlooking a broad mittam (courtyard). Wayanad's first Bird Festival was held in this location in the middle of November 2025.

Human–Animal Interface

With the constant expansion of human habitation, cultivation and tourism infrastructure in proximity to forests, the risk of zoonotic diseases reaching domestic animals and the human population is a major concern in Wayanad. The Hume Centre undertook the first mapping of the district to identify the prevalence and nature of both human–animal conflicts and zoonotic diseases. Its methodology mirrored the one that was developed for conducting annual bird counts, where volunteers would come three times a year to count birds across five-kilometre grids covering the district. For the zoonotic disease prevalence study, volunteers visited households within the same grids to gather information regarding various types of human–animal interactions, including those involving monkeys, rats, stray and domesticated dogs, bats, wild boars and elephants. The number, nature and consequences of these interactions were recorded, leading to the creation of a heat map of the district which illustrated various human–animal interfaces.

Contrary to popular perception and the narratives highlighted by media outlets, the study underlined that the problems caused by tigers and elephants were merely a fraction of those posed by stray dogs and rats. The Health Department found this pioneering study particularly valuable. What the Hume Centre did next is genuinely inspirational. They decided to share this knowledge with grassroots communities through the panchayats, employing two frameworks. The first is the concept of 'One Health', which highlights the importance of focusing on the health of animals, insects, birds and other life forms (in both domestic and natural environments) as well as the overall ecosystem's health in order to safeguard human well-being. The other framework integrates the current development plans of the Pozhuthana panchayat in Wayanad with a large tribal population. The centre started by educating elected representatives in Pozhuthana. I was present in this 'classroom', where a vibrant twenty-eight-year-old tribal woman who serves as the panchayat president led the effort. In the next stage, the centre took this understanding to the Gram Sabhas of the Pozhuthana panchayat to review the current annual plan in the light of the 'One Health' framework. They are now in the process of developing a 'wellness index' to measure how prepared they are to implement this 'One Health' initiative throughout the district.

Carbon and Coffee

In the early 2010s a group of individuals in the town of Meenangadi, Wayanad, embarked on a voluntary effort to restore a denuded forest area of about 36 acres surrounding an ancient Shiva temple. They approached the M.S. Swaminathan Research Foundation's Agrobiodiversity Centre (in Wayanad) to acquire indigenous tree saplings. The Meenangadi panchayat supported this initiative through the Mahatma Gandhi National Rural Employment Guarantee Scheme. In the wake of this initiative, it also declared its intention to become India's first carbon-neutral panchayat. Professor Thomas Isaac, then the finance minister of Kerala, was part of the Indian delegation to the 2015 Climate Summit in Paris. Convinced of the need for action to minimise carbon emissions, he visited Meenangadi and connected its panchayat to IIT Delhi, the Delft University of Technology (TU Delft) in the Netherlands and Thanal, a Trivandrum-based NGO. These connections assisted the Meenangadi panchayat in assessing the carbon footprint associated with various activities within the town – including power consumption and carbon emissions from the thermal plant in Mysore supplying electricity to Meenangadi, vehicular emissions from the national highway cutting through Meenangadi and emissions from waste disposal. These assessments informed the development of a mitigation plan.

Professor Isaac continued to propose additional ideas, including a 'tree bank' initiative designed to encourage farmers not to cut down trees and instead plant and nurture new ones. Under this initiative, farmers could plant saplings of certain approved species on their lands and formally register the saplings with the local cooperative bank. The bank received a corpus of ₹10 lakh for this purpose, and the interest earned was used to make annual payments of ₹50 per tree to tree-owning farmers. After several years, once the trees matured, farmers could harvest them, repay the bank and retain the remaining profit. Although technical issues have hindered the advancement of this scheme, it remains an innovative idea, worthy of revisiting, to protect the environment.

A collaboration with TU Delft led to the recognition that shade-grown Wayanad coffee plays a critical role in mitigating temperature rise and climate change. Dr P.V. Aravind, who studied engineering in Kannur before pursuing higher studies in the Netherlands, was an assistant professor at TU Delft when his connection with Meenangadi began. Now a professor at the University of Groningen, he leads a team tasked by the Netherlands government with advising on transitioning energy dependence from fossil fuels to wind energy and hydrogen over the next decade.

Aravind's connection to Wayanad has resulted in a 'triple helix' collaboration between the Dutch government, private sector entities and academia to support carbon neutrality efforts in Wayanad. A platform of Indian and expatriate experts is being established to bring cutting-edge science in biological and engineering fields. This will help in increasing profits earned by certified coffee farmers, boosting farm productivity through value addition and mitigating climate change impacts in this biodiverse environment.

In contrast to neighbouring Kodagu (formerly known as Coorg), where most Arabica coffee is cultivated in large corporate estates, the majority of Wayanad's coffee farmers (approximately 68,000) own less than a hectare of land. Many Wayanad farmers operate at a small scale, cultivating crops like pepper (now increasingly rare), jackfruit and spices alongside their coffee. The price they receive for these crops amounts to just 7–9 per cent of the price the consumer pays. Currently, there is no correlation between the quality of coffee produced in Wayanad and its market price.

Opportunities exist to market single-origin robusta as speciality coffee, which can potentially increase farmers' incomes dramatically. The government of Kerala has established Kerala Coffee Ltd to manage this initiative. A beautiful twenty-acre piece of land has been acquired for establishing South Asia's first 'coffee park' to provide support to Wayanad's coffee farmers to produce high-quality coffee and market it for higher prices. This intervention also brings to Wayanad essential scientific knowledge to mitigate the adverse consequences of climate change, considering this district is one of the most vulnerable parts of the Western Ghats' mountain ecosystem.

In these times of growing anxiety about the geopolitical and environmental challenges surrounding us, I hope these vignettes from Wayanad will serve as a small antidote.

My Kerala: Memories of an Expatriate Son

Shivshankar Menon

My first memory of Kerala is of being woken up in a dark railway carriage – perhaps on the Madras Mail – as it slowed for the great bend in the Bharatapuzha and being pushed out of the moving train's window, above the twin bars, along with the baggage, onto the platform of Ottapalam railway station. This was before Ottapalam had grown large enough for trains to stop there and when I was small enough to fit through the window along with the baggage. Going home to Kottakkal, my father's home, where he had studied in school, was another kind of adventure for a young boy. We got to ride in a Second World War–vintage Studebaker or DeSoto taxi and were told by a driver called 'Baby' what I now know were mythological tales of the wonders the cars had performed during the war in Burma.

Fascinating Roots

For a boy like me, Kerala was a wonderland. Like many Malayalee families, for several generations, ours earned its living elsewhere but came home for important samskaras like births, marriages, deaths and – much more significant to a child – school holidays. The Ottapalam or Kottakkal that we returned to each summer seemed a world apart from what we had previously experienced. We bathed in the kolam (tank) attached to the old family home, swimming with the water snakes and other inhabitants in peaceful coexistence; walked in the warm monsoon rains among the paddy fields; fished in the river; and tried, unsuccessfully, to climb coconut trees. We watched, fascinated, petrified and trembling, as the Velichappadu (temple medium or oracle) came by in the dark night, announced long before by the ominous beat of the drums, which heightened the suspense and tension. And, for once, we children were allowed to stay up for as long as we wished, to watch the Kathakali performances at Cheruthuruthi across the river. It is the sense of freedom and security, of all being well with the world, that I still remember. If there were rules or difficulties, they have been wiped clean from memory, leaving me with a better appreciation of what Mahabali must have felt upon his banishment.

But change comes even to a child's idyll. I still remember the excitement when electricity first came to Ottapalam in 1962, for two hours in the evening and when the roads, other than the highway, were first macadamised.

Kerala is also associated with darker memories. It was soon after we got electricity that I remember sitting on the Palat House padi (veranda) and hearing on a small radio Jawaharlal Nehru's emotional voice speaking of the war with China and how badly it was going. When my father passed away young while abroad, we brought him back to Kerala to be cremated and scattered his ashes on the land and waters that he loved so deeply, that had made him who he was.

These childhood memories of Kerala imprinted a strong sense of belonging and pride in my homeland, which has endured a lifetime of wandering. At fourteen, I tried to learn Malayalam to find my roots – a task that remains unfinished and will probably never end – and then got sidetracked to learning Sanskrit since my grandmother, my tutor, said that I couldn't learn one without the other. Swami Vivekananda said, after walking through India to Kanyakumari, that the one place where he could hold a conversation in Sanskrit was in Kerala, with Nair women. It is this combination of tradition with change, often revolutionary change, that Kerala has represented for me.

A Vicarious Pleasure

An expatriate Keralite takes pride, albeit vicariously, in Kerala's achievements in human development, health, literacy and education, and joy in the result, which is a diaspora that is flourishing and omnipresent. Wherever you go in the world, you are likely to meet a Keralite or their descendants. Sometimes, however, we take our particularities abroad. In Vienna in the late 1970s, a population of about 500 Keralites would hold four separate Onam celebrations until I, as a Keralite in charge of the Indian Embassy, insisted that I would only attend if they held one jointly. I am told – and sincerely hope – that such divisions are now rare.

If I were to think of what Kerala has meant to me, I would say that the idealised Kerala – of harmony, religious tolerance, fierce independence and rationalism – has been a source of inspiration throughout my life. Whether it reflects reality or whether we live up to it is beside the point. It is in the motivation to do better and to be good that my Kerala has had its greatest influence.

Naturally, there is no going back to the idealised past, to the Kerala of a child's memory. But there is also no gainsaying the deep impact and imprint that Kerala leaves even on its expatriate offspring. As that tribe grows with the continuing diaspora, long may it prosper and long may the ideal of Kerala endure.

Acknowledgements

WE OWE A DEEP debt of gratitude to all who joined us, encouraged us and supported us throughout this venture. First and foremost, our heartfelt thanks go to the contributors. Each one of them is a senior citizen actively engaged in various fields of their interest. Despite their own commitments, they recognised the value of sharing their wisdom and experiences with others – especially those in the civil services, aspirants preparing for these roles and the general public, many of whom may not be fully aware of the intricate realities of administration, social development, history and, most importantly, the lived experiences of individuals who have served across multiple states, diverse services and under a range of circumstances.

We extend our sincere appreciation to our publisher, Bloomsbury India, whose support was invaluable. Our special thanks to Krishan Chopra, who was then with the organisation, for bestowing upon us the title of the book and guiding us through its contents. We are equally grateful to Jaishree Ram Mohan, whose unwavering presence and encouragement accompanied us at every stage of the book's creation. Rhea Gupta's meticulous copy-editing greatly enhanced the manuscript, for which we are most appreciative. We also thank Mekhala Moorthy, who was instrumental during the first reading of the book.

We are especially indebted to Dr T.V. Somanathan, Cabinet Secretary, and Dr Shashi Tharoor, member of Parliament and acclaimed writer. Both are extremely busy individuals, yet they graciously found the time to write a foreword and a special message respectively, lending immense value to this work.

During the initial stages, we benefited from the editorial insights of P.K. Surendran, former head of bureau, *The Times of India*, Thiruvananthapuram, and we thank him sincerely for his invaluable support.

Last, but by no means least, we express our gratitude to G. Praveen, secretary to the director, Centre for Development Studies, who facilitated the compilation of this book and assisted with all necessary correspondence. Our heartfelt thanks are also due to Professor C. Veeramani, director, for kindly permitting us to use the institute's facilities for our meetings.

To all who have walked with us on this journey – your encouragement, guidance and support have made this endeavour possible. Thank you for being an integral part of this achievement.

About the Editors and the Contributors

Editors

K.M. Chandrasekhar retired from the Indian Administrative Service in 2011 as Union Cabinet Secretary. Subsequently, he was appointed vice chairman of the Kerala State Planning Board with the rank of a Cabinet minister. He has been an independent director on the boards of several companies and has written extensively in newspapers and periodicals. He was the president of the Sree Chitra Tirunal Institute for Medical Sciences and Technology from 2014 to 2019 and the president of the Centre for Development Studies, Trivandrum, from 2015 to 2021. Currently, he is a distinguished fellow of the Gulati Institute of Finance and Taxation and a professor of practice at the PSG College of Technology, Coimbatore. His memoir *As Good as My Word* was published by HarperCollins in 2022.

T.P. Sreenivasan served in the Indian Foreign Service from 1967 to 2004, with postings in Tokyo, Thimphu, Moscow, New Delhi, New York, Yangon, Suva, Nairobi, Washington and Vienna. He was a senior fellow at the Brookings Institution in Washington, a member of the National Security Advisory Board, the vice chairman of the Kerala State Higher Education Council and a visiting professor at the Central University in Kasaragod. He is a mentor and adjunct professor of eminence at Somaiya Vidyavihar University, the chairman (and former director) of the Academic Council of the NSS Academy for Civil Services and the director general of the Kerala International Centre. He has published eleven books on diplomacy and education and regularly writes in Indian and foreign journals.

Contributors

K.J. Alphons (Alphons Kannanthanam) is a politician and former Indian Administrative Service (IAS) officer from the 1979 batch and the Kerala cadre. He first gained national acclaim as the district collector of Kottayam, where he spearheaded the historic campaign that declared Kottayam the first 100 per cent literate town in India in 1989. Later, as commissioner of the Delhi Development Authority, he earned the moniker 'Demolition Man' for his fearless drive against illegal encroachments in the capital.

Resigning from the IAS in 2006, he entered active politics, initially serving as a member of the Kerala Legislative Assembly. He later joined the Bharatiya Janata Party and served as a member of Parliament in the Rajya Sabha. In 2017, he was inducted into the Union Council of Ministers as the minister of state (independent charge) for Tourism and for Electronics and Information Technology. He is also a widely read author, best known for his motivational bestseller *Making a Difference* (1996). His most recent publication is *The Winning Formula: 52 Ways to Change Your Life* (Bloomsbury, 2024).

Gopalan Balagopal is a retired Indian Administrative Service officer from the 1974 batch and the West Bengal cadre, and a former diplomat who transitioned from the Indian civil service to international leadership with UNICEF. His administrative career in India included roles like district collector and Special Secretary, while his tenure at UNICEF involved key positions in Bangladesh, New York and Geneva. Most notably, he served as the UNICEF country representative in North Korea from 2006 to 2009, overseeing critical humanitarian healthcare and nutrition efforts.

Post-retirement, Balagopal remains deeply engaged in policy and development. He currently leads the Climate Smart Coffee initiative in Wayanad under the Kerala Development and Innovation Strategic Council, promoting sustainable, carbon-neutral farming. He also continues to consult globally on civil registration and vital statistics systems and advocates for constitutional values and electoral integrity as a member of the Constitutional Conduct Group.

T. Balakrishnan is a former member of the Indian Administrative Service and was part of the Kerala cadre. He is based in Trivandrum and has lived and worked in Kerala, Tamil Nadu, Delhi and the US. His areas of interest include history, travel, international relations and the economy of Kerala and India.

E.K. Bharat Bhushan is a retired Indian Administrative Service officer from the Kerala cadre, of the 1979 batch. He is known for his strict administrative integrity and proven ability in turning around loss-making public sector companies. A Harvard alumnus with a master's degree in public administration, he served as Chief Secretary of Kerala from 2013 to 2015, where he focused on innovative restructuring of government, efficient governance and fast-tracking of development projects.

His career gained national attention when, as director general of Civil Aviation, he acted resolutely to restore the credibility of the sector caught in the headwinds of the fake pilot scandal and the Mangalore crash. He is known to have introduced wide-ranging reforms in the working of the aviation watchdog, setting up modern protocols in line with international norms, aimed at proper maintenance of aircraft and airports. He also held senior positions in the Union Ministries of Commerce, Tourism and Information Technology. In Kerala, he has worked as Principal Secretary in the departments of Forests and Tourism, among others, and as district collector of Malappuram district. He achieved notable success in improving the functioning of certain large public sector companies and was known for his 'no-nonsense' approach.

Vijay Chandran, an Indian Administrative Service officer from the 1973 batch and the Kerala cadre, was born in Kerala and completed his education there. He spent nearly all his working years in Kerala, beginning as a college lecturer and retiring as Principal Secretary to the state government. After retirement he worked as a consultant to the World Bank for some time and lived for more than twenty years in the UK and in Europe with his wife Geetha, who was working there as a Montessori consultant. There, he pursued his passion for Indian spirituality, giving occasional lectures, teaching Sanskrit to beginners and translating into English Swami Chidananda Puri's Malayalam explanation of Adi Shankaracharya's Sanskrit commentary on the Bhagavad Gita. He has published the first three volumes and is currently engaged with the fourth.

Dr Bransdon Corrie belongs to the 1980 batch of the Indian Forest Service. He has held various positions in the Kerala Forest Department (KFD). He served a tenure in the northeastern regional office of the Ministry of Environment and Forests at Shillong. He headed the KFD in the latter part of his career. He pursued his education in Chennai, Bengaluru and Shillong. For his master's, he focused on forest hill ecosystems. For his PhD, he conducted a technical audit of social forestry in Meghalaya. He has a degree in law and a diploma in computerised office management. He has undergone a training programme on environmental impact assessment in the UK and was granted the Fulbright Indo-American Environmental Leadership Award, through which he studied the management of natural capital by various agencies in the US. Dr Corrie is a thought leader with progressive ideas and out-of-the-box thinking. He adopts a systems approach in his work. His focus has been on using advances in forestry, adopting new technologies and utilising management tools to achieve improved functioning. The many initiatives undertaken under his leadership in KFD bear witness to this. He believes that government departments can amaze with their performance if personnel adopt a code of ethics and are provided with an enabling environment of fairness, performance ratings are objective, working is professionalised and system improvements are institutionalised.

Dr K. Ellangovan embarked on his professional journey with a Master of Science in Orthopaedics. In 1992 he entered the Indian Administrative Service and was allotted to the Kerala cadre.

With over three impactful decades within the IAS, he has served in key positions in the Government of Kerala and the Government of India. Before superannuating as Additional Chief Secretary in 2022, he held the post of Additional Chief Secretary in the Industries and Commerce Department and the Non-Resident Keralites Affairs Department; he served as Principal Secretary in the Health and Family Welfare, General Education and Transport departments. He was also chairman and managing director of the Kerala State Electricity Board.

On the academic front, Dr Ellangovan went on to join a PhD programme at IIT Madras, which he completed in 2013. His thesis on performance dimensions in public hospitals received the Best Thesis Award from IIT Madras in 2013.

He is the author of *Creating Value in Health Care*, which discusses enabling factors that lead to better clinical and physician outcomes in a hospital. The book is well received in academic and medical circles both in India and abroad.

Presently, K. Ellangovan is working as the managing director of INKEL Limited, a company involved in designing and building healthcare infrastructure for the Government of Kerala. He is also the chief executive of the Kerala Infrastructure Fund and the Kerala Innovation Fund.

L.C. Goyal joined the Indian Administrative Service in 1979 and was allotted the Kerala cadre. Over a span of forty-three years, he held critical and sensitive positions in public service in both the Government of Kerala and the Government of India. These include collector, Kozhikode; Kerala Finance Secretary and Joint Secretary (Internal Security), Ministry of Home Affairs; Additional Secretary, Health, Government of India; Special Secretary in the Cabinet Secretariat; Secretary, Rural Development, Government of India; and Union Home Secretary. Post-retirement, he was the main driving force behind the making of the Bharat Mandapam in Pragati Maidan, where the G20 Summit was held from 9 to 10 September 2023. He is widely recognised for bringing about structural, strategic and systemic changes and reforms in whatever responsibility he was tasked with.

M.P. Joseph is a distinguished former civil servant belonging to the 1978 batch of the Indian Administrative Service and was part of the Kerala cadre. With a foundation in physics and advanced studies in human resource development from the University of Manchester, he held pivotal administrative roles in Kerala, including district collector of Ernakulam and a unique concurrent tenure as the mayor of Cochin Corporation. He is also noted for having the longest tenure as the state's labour commissioner.

His career is defined by significant international service with the International Labour Organization. He served as chief technical adviser for the International Programme on the Elimination of Child Labour in India and later in Cambodia. His humanitarian efforts in Cambodia were recognised with the prestigious Sahametrei Sena Medal by the Royal Government of Cambodia. Post-retirement, he has served as an adviser to the Government of Kerala (Labour Reforms) and authored the memoir *My Driver Tulong* (2017). Joseph also stood as a United Democratic Front candidate in the 2021 Assembly elections from the Trikaripur constituency in Kasaragod district. He lost the elections but continues to be active in Kerala politics. His book *Trikaripur Chora Puranda Kathakal Parayumbol* captures his experiences during the elections.

Amitabh Kant is a retired Indian Administrative Service officer from the 1980 batch and the Kerala cadre. He is widely regarded as a key architect of India's modern economic and brand identity. A Chevening Scholar with a master's degree in international relations from Jawaharlal Nehru University, he is celebrated for his transformative leadership in governance and policy.

Kant served as the longest-tenured CEO of NITI Aayog from 2016 to 2022, where he drove critical national initiatives like the Aspirational Districts Programme and the National Monetisation Pipeline. As Secretary, Department for Promotion of Industry and Internal Trade, he spearheaded the Make in India and Startup India campaigns. Earlier, he revolutionised Indian tourism by conceptualising the Incredible India campaign and establishing Kerala as 'God's Own Country'.

Most recently, as India's G20 Sherpa, he played a pivotal role in achieving the historic New Delhi Leaders' Declaration. He is also a prolific author, with books like *Branding India* (2009) and *How India Scaled MT G20* (2025) cementing his legacy as a reformist thought leader.

Surendra Kumar is a former Indian Forest Service officer who worked in Kerala for decades and handled matters relating to forests and wildlife. Presently, he works for the United Nations Development Programme and engages in occasional story writing in Hindi and English.

K.B. Valsala Kumari is a distinguished former civil servant, boasting a stellar academic and leadership track record that began at St Joseph's Convent Girls' High School, Kollam. She graduated from St Teresa's College, Ernakulam, and went on to earn a Master of Arts from Miranda House, Delhi University. Later, she completed her PhD from Rutgers, The State University of New Jersey. A natural leader from her student days, she held the unique distinction of serving as the college union president at both St Teresa's College and Miranda House.

In 1998, her academic excellence was further recognised when she was one of only two candidates from India selected as a Hubert Humphrey Fellow to study in the USA. Her professional career was dedicated to the Government of Kerala, where she served in various departments, eventually retiring as Principal Secretary, Revenue and Disaster Management.

Rajan K. Medhekar, a distinguished Indian Police Service officer from the 1975 batch and the Kerala cadre, served for thirty-seven years in roles critical to national and state security, law enforcement, crime investigation and intelligence. His postings spanned the Government of India and the Kerala government, including tenures with the Cabinet Secretariat and the Border Security Force. He culminated his career as director general of the National Security Guard, India's premier counterterrorism and anti-hijack force. He is a recipient of the Indian Police Medal for Meritorious Service and the President's Police Medal for Distinguished Service.

Post-retirement, he has served as a security consultant to governments and private enterprises. He headed the International Institute of Security and Safety Management, New Delhi – an ISO 9001:2015-certified institution for training in security, safety and loss prevention – as its director general. He serves on the board of advisers of the Centre for National Security Studies at Ramaiah University of Applied Sciences, Bengaluru.

His interests include photography, travel, writing and golf. He was active in cricket and tennis and maintains a keen interest in computer science, artificial intelligence and software development.

Shivshankar Menon is currently a visiting professor at Ashoka University, Haryana, and the chair of the Ashoka Centre for China Studies.

He was the national security adviser to the prime minister of India from January 2010 to May 2014 and the Foreign Secretary of India from October 2006 to July 2009 and has served as the Indian ambassador or high commissioner to China, Pakistan, Sri Lanka and Israel.

He is the author of *Choices: Inside the Making of Indian Foreign Policy* (2016) and *India and Asian Geopolitics: The Past, Present* (2021).

K. Mohandas joined the Indian Administrative Service in 1974 and was part of the Kerala cadre. He started his career as sub-collector, Trivandrum, in 1976; he went on to become district collector, Kottayam, and later Secretary to the state government in various departments, with fairly long spells in Industries, Local Administration and Higher Education. He served the Union Government as Additional Secretary in the Revenue Department and Secretary in the Ministry of Overseas Indian Affairs. He retired as Secretary for Shipping in 2012. Subsequently, he served as the chairman of the Eleventh Kerala Pay Revision Commission. He has authored the book *The Right to Good Governance: A Guide for the Young Indians* (2024).

T. Nandakumar joined the Indian Administrative Service in 1972 and was allotted the Bihar cadre and subsequently moved to the Jharkhand cadre when the new state was formed. He has served in various capacities in Bihar and Jharkhand. He served as chairman of the Spices Board in Kochi for five years and worked with the United Nations Conference on Trade and Development for three years. He was Food Secretary and later Agriculture Secretary, Government of India. He served as a member of the National Disaster Management Authority and as chairman of the National Dairy Development Board. He was also a member and the chairman of the Board of Governors at the Institute of Rural Management Anand. Currently, he is a senior fellow at the World Resources Institute and an adviser for the International Food Policy Research Institute, the Somaiya group of educational institutions and the Bharti Institute of Public Policy. He writes on matters related to food, nutrition, agriculture and sustainability for major newspapers in English and Malayalam.

R. Narayanan is a retired Indian Administrative Service officer from the 1962 batch and the Kerala cadre. He was the collector of Alappuzha and a Joint Secretary in the Planning Department. He was deputed to Cambridge for a course on development administration, and he served the Central government as part of the Cabinet Secretariat and then went on to serve as the development commissioner in the newly inducted state of Sikkim for nine years. He worked as Finance Secretary for four years, after which he became the chairman of the Kerala State Electricity Board. He was also Additional Secretary in the Ministry of Defence and then chairman of the Food Corporation of India, and he retired as Secretary in the Department of Youth Affairs and Sports. After retirement, he became devaswom commissioner of the Travancore Devaswom Board, chairman of the Kerala Financial Corporation and chairman of the Eighth Pay Revision Commission.

P. Joy Oommen is a former member of the Indian Administrative Service who has served in Madhya Pradesh, Tamil Nadu, Karnataka, Chhattisgarh and Kerala. He holds postgraduate degrees in economics from Kerala University and in development economics from the University of East Anglia, UK.

He was Chief Secretary of Chhattisgarh (2008–2012) and also served as chairman of the Naya Raipur Development Authority, which planned and developed the new capital of Chhattisgarh. His other assignments include joint chief controller of Imports and Exports, Chennai; chief executive officer and Member Secretary, Central Silk Board, Bengaluru; chairman, Chhattisgarh Electricity Board; collector, Dewas district; and Finance Secretary, Madhya Pradesh. After retirement, he served the Government of Kerala as chairman and managing director of the Kerala Financial Corporation (2013–2016).

Vinod Rai is presently a distinguished visiting research fellow at the Institute of South Asian Studies in the National University of Singapore. He is also a trustee on the global board of trustees of the International Financial Reporting Standards Foundation, London. Starting his career in the Indian Administrative Service in 1972, Rai rose to become the eleventh comptroller and auditor general of India in 2008. He demitted office in May 2013. In 2016, Rai was appointed the first chairman of the newly created Banks Board Bureau, Government of India. In 2017, the Supreme Court of India appointed him as the chairman of the Committee of Administrators to oversee reforms in the Board of Control for Cricket in India.

He is the author of *Not Just an Accountant* (2014) and *Not Just a Nightwatchman* (2022) and has co-edited *Seven Decades of Independent India* (2018), *Transforming the Steel Frame* (2023) and *India and the Future of G20* (2023). Vinod Rai was awarded the Padma Bhushan by the President of India in 2016 in recognition of his services to the nation.

N. Ramachandran joined the Indian Police Service in 1978 and was part of the Assam–Meghalaya cadre. Following his retirement, he founded the

Indian Police Foundation (IPF), a multidisciplinary think tank dedicated to police reform and raising professional and ethical standards in Indian policing. Since its inauguration by India's home minister on 21 October 2015, the IPF has grown into one of the leading institutions in the country for law-enforcement research and policy.

Ramachandran has extensive experience across district, state and national policing. He served as Assam's state intelligence chief from 1997 to 2000, revamping the intelligence and counterterrorism apparatus. From February to August 2011, he served as director general of police (DGP), Civil Defence and Home Guards, in Assam and subsequently as the DGP and police chief of Meghalaya. Earlier, from 1988 to 1997 and from 2001 to 2005, he held senior positions in the elite Special Protection Group, overseeing the security of eight successive Indian prime ministers.

From 2005 to 2011, he served as chairman of the Cochin Port Trust, where he led several transformative infrastructure projects, including the Vallarpadam Terminal (India's first international container transshipment terminal), the Kochi LNG Terminal and other major connectivity projects. He is widely credited with implementing significant labour reforms at the port. His experiences at the Cochin Port are chronicled in his book *Notes from Willingdon Island* (Konark Publishers, 2025).

Madanamohan Rameshkumar is a retired Indian Administrative Service officer from the 1975 batch and the Maharashtra cadre. He was educated in Kerala and has a postgraduate degree in Botany. He also has a Master of Science in Social Planning from the London School of Economics. After his retirement in 2010, he worked as an administrative judge in the Maharashtra Administrative Tribunal till 2015. He has two children, who are both doctors, and his wife is a former teacher who retired in 2016.

Dr B. Sandhya is a distinguished retired officer of the Indian Police Service, from the 1988 batch and the Kerala cadre, and a celebrated literary figure. She retired as the director general of Kerala Fire and Rescue Services in 2023, having previously held critical leadership roles, including additional director general of police (South Zone), additional director general of police (Modernisation) and director of the Kerala Police Academy.

Dr Sandhya is renowned for spearheading the Janamaithri Suraksha Project, a pioneering community policing initiative in Kerala. She also introduced the Pink Patrol and Women's Helpline in Kerala to enhance safety for women. She holds a PhD from BITS Pilani and received training in human resources from the University of Wollongong, Australia.

Beyond policing, she is a prolific writer with published works in poetry and children's literature, earning accolades such as the Edasseri Award. Post-retirement, she continues her public service as a member of the Kerala Real Estate Regulatory Authority.

Alkesh Kumar Sharma is an Indian Administrative Service officer from the 1990 batch and the Kerala cadre. He is serving as a member of the Public Enterprises Selection Board, Government of India. He was Secretary in the Ministry of Electronics and Information Technology and Secretary (Coordination) in the Cabinet Secretariat. He also worked in Kochi Metro Rail Ltd and National Industrial Corridor Development Corporation Ltd. He was part of Kerala's Industries and Tourism departments and held positions in the Ministry of Road Transport and Highways, Government of India, with a focus on sustainable urban and industrial infrastructure development. He worked with the United Nations Development Programme as national project director of Urban Development and Poverty Alleviation. Some of his notable contributions include the promotion of Kerala tourism; the introduction of FASTag, an e-tolling system on Indian highways; and the planning, designing and execution of Yashobhoomi, a convention and exhibition facility in Delhi. He is also contributing to the progress of ongoing projects such as the India Semiconductor Mission, the Digital Personal Data Protection Act, the IndiaAI Mission and India Stack (India's digital public infrastructure system).

S. Subbiah, a former Indian Administrative Service officer who was part of the Kerala cadre, has a unique educational background, combining a degree in veterinary science (Bachelor of Veterinary Science) and a degree in business administration (Master of Business Administration). His professional focus encompasses public administration, rural development and resource management, complemented by a personal commitment to farming.

He is distinguished by his track record in institution building, having successfully established several key government bodies in the state. His contributions include the creation of the Kerala Veterinary and Animal Sciences University in Pookode, the Government Medical College in Palakkad, the Centre for Research and Development for Social Transformation in Kozhikode and the Community College for Engineering Training in Vadakkencherry. Beyond his administrative achievements, he has actively contributed to academic and policy discourse by presenting papers at national and international conferences and authoring articles for books.

Joy Vazhayil is a former bureaucrat who served as Secretary to the Government of India and Chief Secretary to the Government of Kerala. He has nearly four decades of administrative, managerial and professional experience. Currently, he is the chairperson of the Kerala Public Enterprises (Selection and Recruitment) Board and an honorary professor at the Indian Institute of Technology in Palakkad. He is a Malayalam poet and has published fourteen works of poetry. Besides two novels in Malayalam, he has published three works in English and various research papers in international journals. His academic interests include public policy, literature, science, philosophy and education.

S.M. Vijayanand is a former Indian Administrative Service officer from the 1981 batch and the Kerala cadre, widely celebrated as a pioneer of democratic decentralisation in India. He served as the Chief Secretary of Kerala and held significant roles at the Centre, including Secretary in the Ministry of Panchayati Raj and the Ministry of Rural Development.

Vijayanand played a seminal role as the architect of Kerala's historic People's Plan Campaign, which was instrumental in devolving powers to local self-governments and institutionalising the Panchayati Raj system. A gold medallist in English literature from the University of Kerala, he is renowned for combining administrative expertise with deep intellectual rigour. Since his retirement in 2017, he has continued his public service as the chairman of Kerala's Sixth State Finance Commission and chairman of the Centre for Management Development. He remains an active voice in civil society, advocating for governance reforms and grassroots democracy.